Ronald Brunlees McKerrow:
A Selection of His Essays

compiled by

John Phillip Immroth

The Great Bibliographers Series, No. 1

The Scarecrow Press, Inc.
Metuchen, N.J.   1974

Library of Congress Cataloging in Publication Data

McKerrow, Ronald Brunlees, 1872-1940.
    Ronald Brunlees McKerrow: a selection of his essays.

    (The Great bibliographers series, no. 1)
    Includes bibliographical references.
    CONTENTS: Greg, W. W. Introduction: Ronald
Brunlees McKerrow, 1872-1940--Some notes on the letters
i, j, u and v in sixteenth century printing.--The
supposed calling-in of Drayton's Harmony of the church,
1591. [etc.]
    1. Bibliography--Addresses, essays, lectures.
I. Title. II. Series.
Z1005.M33   016.082   73-19882
ISBN 0-8108-0690-8

PREFACE

To the modern student of bibliography Ronald B. Mc-Kerrow is best remembered as the father of twentieth century descriptive bibliography. His best known work is An Introduction to Bibliography for Literary Students, still a standard textbook in both this country and the United Kingdom even though it was written in 1927. The methods of bibliographical description presented in this book served as the basis for practice and expansion of descriptions used by Sir Walter W. Greg in his monumental Bibliography of English Printed Drama before the Restoration. McKerrow's methods also served as the basis for the detailed Principles of Bibliographical Description (1949) by Fredson Bowers. Definitely, McKerrow's Introduction is one of his major contributions; it is not only an introduction to bibliographical description but also a basic source on the techniques of hand printing in the sixteenth century.

Besides the Introduction other major accomplishments of McKerrow include his definitive edition of the works of Thomas Nashe in five volumes (1904-1910) which still serves as an example of how the works of an Elizabethan author should be edited; and his Prolegomena for the Oxford Shakespeare (1939), of which The Times Literary Supplement wrote at his death: "he left so clear an account of his purpose, his principles and his methods that the way lies plain, and nothing need be lacking unless if were McKerrow's peculiar nicety of judgment and mastery of detail in places where the science of bibliography reveals itself as what he preferred to consider it, an art."[1] In addition, McKerrow was responsible for three basic reference works in bibliographical study: A Dictionary of Printers and Booksellers, 1557-1640 (1910), Printers' and Publishers' Devices in England and Scotland, 1485-1640 (1913), and Title-page Borders used in England and Scotland, 1485-1640 (1932). The student of bibliography should acquaint himself with all three of these works and carefully study the introduction to each. From 1925 until his death McKerrow also served as the editor of Review of English Studies and for a few years as the editor of The Library. His major contributions, besides bibliographical descriptions, may be seen to include essays on printing, printers, booksellers, editing, and Shakespeare studies.

All of these interests and areas of expertise may be found in articles and reviews. It is the purpose of this present volume to bring together in one place a selection of these more fugitive writings of Ronald B. McKerrow. As the bibliography at the end of this book demonstrates fully, only a small selection of the great banquet of articles and reviews could be chosen. Four articles dealing with techniques of sixteenth century printing were included. These deal with the use of i and j, and u and v, red printing, the use of the galley and the composition of reprints. Three longer articles present examples of McKerrow's concept of the Elizabethan printer; and one of these is concerned with the Elizabethan bookseller and stationer as well. Four letters to the Times Literary Supplement on bibliographical terminology have been selected both for their discerning definitions and as examples of McKerrow's clarity in a very short article. Three reviews are presented as examples of McKerrow's high degree of objectivity and analysis. One article on Shakespeare's text is given as supplemental reading to McKerrow's Prolegomena. Also, McKerrow's last published writing, "Form and Matter in the Publication of Research," is included.

As an introduction to this selection of McKerrow's shorter works the memoir written by Sir Walter W. Greg has been chosen as finer than anything this compiler might write. The order of the articles is chronological. The bibliography at the end of this collection has been updated. It is to be hoped that the reader of these essays will react as G. B. Harrison did in a memorial article in RES: "It might fairly be said of McKerrow that he brought bibliography down from heaven to inhabit among men. In this field particularly he showed himself an admirable teacher; he remembered things that had once puzzled him, and set himself to explain them to others, and for all the fascination that the subject held for him he never thought of bibliography as a mistress, but as a handmaid, invaluable, and indeed essential to literary study."[2] And, as the previously quoted entry in the Times Literary Supplement states, "No one did more than he to forward the remarkable progress of English scholarship during the present century, but all his work was addressed to students and experts in his own studies, and the results only reached the public through others.   His complete mastery of bibliography, in the larger sense of the word, from the making of paper to the selling of the finished book, was of incalculable service to the proper understanding of other literature besides that of Elizabethan England, in which he was chiefly interested. "3

The compiler wishes to acknowledge encouragement given him by colleagues and students at the University of Pittsburgh.   Especially, I wish to thank Dr. Norman Horrocks, the general editor of this series, for his countless suggestions and assistance, and Miss Nancy Davenport for her bibliographical assistance.

J. P. I.

Notes

1.   The Times Literary Supplement, Jan. 27, 1940.

2.   G. B. Harrison, "Ronald Brunlees McKerrow, " The
       Review of English Studies, Vol. XVI, no. 63, July
       1940, p. 261.

3.   The Times Literary Supplement, op. cit.

TABLE OF CONTENTS

CHAPTER 1: INTRODUCTION

RONALD BRUNLEES McKERROW
1872-1940*

by W. W. Greg

Ronald Brunlees McKerrow was born at Putney on 12 December 1872. He was the grandson of William Mc-Kerrow, D. D., of Manchester, who in 1877 was Moderator of the Presbyterian Church of England. His father, Alexander McKerrow, took to engineering, and married the elder daughter of Sir James Brunlees, who in 1882-3 became President of the Institute of Civil Engineers. Ronald's mother died in 1878, and from the age of six he lived at his grandfather's house, Argyle Lodge, overlooking Wimbledon Common, where he was brought up by Lady Brunlees and her unmarried daughter. He had a boy's interest in natural history, and once told me that he used to find a rare moth on the palings of my own home a few hundred yards away. We went, I believe, though at different times, to the same kindergarten on Putney Hill; later he was sent to a private school, Temple Grove, at East Sheen. In the autumn of 1887 he entered the house of the Rev. J. A. Cruikshank at Harrow. Here he began on the classical side, but after reaching the upper school changed over to the modern, where he got into the sixth form and came under the famous Edward Bowen. Of him he had some characteristic stories to tell--I never knew how literally McKerrow's stories were to be taken--but I have no reason to suppose that Bowen's influence went very deep; at any rate it did not turn him into an historian. He was in the rifle corps and shot for the school at Bisley his last summer term. His career there, however, was uneventful and short, for he left at the end of 1890 and spent some months abroad learning languages.

*Proceedings of the British Academy, Vol. 26, 1940, pp. 488-515. Reprinted by permission of The British Academy.

From October 1891 to July 1893 he studied at King's
College, London. It was the natural wish of his family that
he should take up engineering, and he went through the
regular course and even entered the family business of
Brunlees & McKerrow. Both at Harrow and at King's he
had taken prizes, not only in chemistry and physics, but
significantly in English, English Verse, and even in Divinity.
It amused him to recall that those who showed the best
knowledge of this subject had the least definite religious
beliefs.

He had, however, little taste for engineering as a
career, and after he came of age and into some money of
his own he decided to abandon it and go up to Cambridge.
This he did, entering Trinity College in October 1894. He
began by reading Political Economy for the Moral Sciences
Tripos, but when at the end of his first year he won the
Chancellor's Medal with a poem on Joan of Arc (a set subject, of course) his tutor, St. John Parry, persuaded him
to take Modern Languages instead, on the ground that they
afforded a better opening for his talents. The advice was
probably welcome, for McKerrow's chief interest was certainly in literature, while it is easy to believe that the
rather severely theoretical tendency of economic teaching
under Marshall may have been alien and even repugnant to
his own bent of mind. He turned therefore to English and
French and after two years' study took a Second Class in
the Medieval and Modern Languages Tripos in June 1897.

After spending his first year in "digs" he had the
good fortune, as Chancellor's Medalist, to be assigned
rooms in the Great Court of Trinity. It was a comfortable
set on the ground floor with the homely dignity of the most
august academic foundation in the world, but the living-room
was rather dark, the window overlooking the fellows' bowling
green at the back being small, while those on the court
were overshadowed by great creepers. The decoration, as
I remember it, was Morris, for his taste in those days
was Pre-Raphaelite. His favourite poet was Swinburne,
whose sonorous verse he was fond of reading aloud. He
was also, unexpectedly, a student of Blake. The college
cat took up its residence with him, and he used to dry it
with blotting-paper when it came in out of the rain.

I had first known McKerrow on the rifle-range at
Harrow; now in our second year at Trinity we renewed
acquaintance walking back from Gollancz's famous lectures

on west-midland alliterative poetry.   Between us we compiled verbal indexes to Pearl and Gawain.   In time we came
to do much of our work together in his rooms at night.   At
least, he did the work and I tagged behind: it was not only
that he was two or three years older, but he had a quicker
brain and a readier power of assimilation.   Discussion often
lasted into the small hours, and was continued on walks together and during one vacation that we spent reading at
Tintagel.   Not the least absorbing were projects for editing
Elizabethan drama and the textual methods to be used, for
these, however crudely, already occupied our minds.   It
was the companionship of those days that fashioned the whole
of my later life.   Between us we started a short-lived English Society that met to read and discuss papers either
written by us students or for which we shamelessly bad-
gered our teachers.   The minutes are still extant at the
end of the volume later used for those of the Malone Society.   Both Skeat and Gollancz read papers; so did A. W.
Verrall and A. J. Wyatt.   McKerrow's contribution was an
investigation into the Elizabethan experiments in classical
metre, which later appeared in The Modern Language
Quarterly in 1901-2.   As printed and no doubt rewritten
it is a mature and balanced study of a particularly be-
wildering subject.

      One evening he seemed unusually preoccupied and
silent.   I rose to go, but he begged me to stay a little
longer.   At last midnight struck, and he pulled himself together and poured out drinks.   Then he told me that some
time before a fortune-teller had warned him that he would
not live beyond that day.   I asked him whether he had be-
lieved it.   "Well, no; but I have not risked bicycling for
a fortnight."   I suggested that a road accident was not the
only way out of life.   His reply was characteristic: "One
would feel such a fool to kill oneself in fulfilment of a
prophecy!"

      Shortly after taking his degree he was offered, and
accepted, the newly created post of Professor of English in
the Government School of Foreign Languages at Tokyo, and
spent the next three years in Japan.   Not content with
teaching, he devoted himself to learning Japanese, and he
always maintained that the endeavour to master a language
so different in structure helped greatly to the understanding
of our own.   He also had a small printing press and made
himself practically familiar with the craft.   In order to
enter as far as possible into the life of the country he took

a house and lived in company with one of his students, Mr.
Katayama.   Teaching English to orientals impressed on him
the importance of phonetics, and he wrote a text-book on the
subject with reference to English, which was published in
Katayama's Japanese translation.   With him he also travelled
in vacation, visiting many of the remoter parts of the islands
and pushing as far afield as Korea and the Kuriles.   He used
to tell how, arrived at an out-of the-way village on the coast,
he stood at the window of the guest-house waiting for the hot
bath he had ordered, and idly watched men setting up a huge
cauldron on the rocks of the shore, filling it with sea-water,
and kindling a fire beneath.   Gradually it dawned on him that
this was his bath, which he proceeded to take before the ad-
miring gaze of the populace.   Having gone out to Japan by the
Canadian-Pacific, he returned via Suez and spent a holiday on
the Riviera before reaching England.

      Towards the end of 1900 he settled in London, living
first with his father and aunt at Richmond, later in lodgings
in a more central district.   This was, I think, the formative
period of his life, a time of wide activity during which he
made literary and social contacts.   He had many interests and
associations of which I knew nothing, but one that we shared
was enthusiasm--if one may use that word of McKerrow's always restrained appreciation--for the Vedrenne-Barker productions at the Court and later at the Savoy.   We saw most
of them together from the pit, with Frank Sidgwick often making a third.   Another memory of those days are the lunches
at the Vienna Cafe near the Museum, where scholars congre-
gated from all over Europe, and where Moore Smith and John
Masefield were often to be found.   Sometimes one would drop
in on Furnivall in his tweed cap at an ABC near by.

      In 1903 McKerrow joined the Bibliographical Society,
to which he was later to give such devoted service.   I have
an idea that his earliest work was done for Gollancz, who
with characteristic energy was at this time running several
series of Shakespearian reprints, and that it was in connexion
with these that he worked for a while in the office of Chatto
& Windus.   For "The King's Library" (A. Moring) he edited
Dekker's Gull's Hornbook in 1904:   the editing is unpretentious,
but discrimination is shown in the choice of matter reprinted
in the appendix.   A more fruitful and lasting connexion was
with A. H. Bullen, the wide ambit of whose breezy enthusi-
asms no one interested in Elizabethan literature could in those
days easily escape.   It must have been soon after McKerrow's
return from Japan that they met, and Bullen must almost at

once have suggested an edition of the works of Thomas
Nashe, for McKerrow was collecting biographical material
as early as 1902. The three volumes of text appeared in
1904-5, the notes in a fourth in 1908, the fifth, with the introduction and index, followed in 1910 (published by Sidgwick & Jackson after Bullen had retired). Thus it represented eight or nine years' labour and will deserve fuller
mention later. It was at once recognized as a model of its
kind, and established its author in the front rank of English
scholars. He submitted it as his thesis when he took the
degree of Litt. D. at Cambridge the year following its completion.

For Bullen's "Variorum" Beaumont and Fletcher Mc-
Kerrow edited two plays in 1905, The Spanish Curate and
Wit without Money, and duly identified the manuscript whence
the former was printed in the folio of 1647 as a prompt-
copy. During 1906 Bullen edited the venerable but mori-
bund Gentleman's Magazine, imparting to it a brief spell of
vigour, and in this McKerrow acted as his assistant, doing
in fact much of the work, for Bullen was already living
mostly at Stratford-on-Avon, where he was printing his edition of the local poet at the Shakespeare Head Press.

The same year, 1906, McKerrow joined in founding
the Malone Society, which grew out of a suggestion of A.
W. Pollard for reprinting Elizabethan plays. In this, one
of our early dreams came to fruition. He himself prepared
or helped in the preparation of five plays between 1907 and
1911, including the recently discovered Comedy of Patient
and Meek Grissill by John Phillip. Some years before a
similar series of reprints had been launched by W. Bang at
Louvain, and to this he contributed three volumes, the first,
Barnabe Barnes's Devil's Charter, being notable for his
pioneer work on the variation of formes. For many years
he kept up a close correspondence with Bang and his suc-
cessor De Vocht. Their Materialien offered greater scope
for editorial prowess than the austere form of the Malone
reprints, and this no doubt appealed to him, for when in
1911 he started a tentative series of his own, though the
outward guise was suggestive of the latter, he furnished the
texts with more generous apparatus. Only two volumes appeared, one containing B. R. 's Greene's News both from
Heaven and Hell and R. B. 's Green's Funerals, the other
the Epigrams of John Weever. They may be regarded as
parerga of the Nashe and bear witness to the same wide
reading. Although he allowed that the News was "by no

means lacking in merit," I hardly think he did justice to
Rich's racy scurrility. It is worth noting that he acknowl-
edges a debt to Charles Crawford, that curiously gifted rail-
wayman, another correspondent with whom he remained in
touch.

Other work was done for the Bibliographical Society,
of which in 1912 he became joint secretary with A. W. Pollard. Already in 1910 he had edited for the Society A Dictionary of Printers and Booksellers, 1557-1640, designed to
link up Gordon Duff's Century of the English Book Trade with
Plomer's similar Dictionary, 1641-1667. Though indispensable, it is a disappointing production, for McKerrow was
not sufficiently alive to the unsatisfactory nature of the material placed in his hands. The introduction contains a useful summary of the organization and control of the book trade
of the period, but this has been superseded. He also contributed the fascicule on Grafton to the Society's Handlists of
English Printers. A more important work was his illustrated
monograph on Printers' and Publishers' Devices in England
and Scotland, 1485-1640, the outcome of several years' patient labour, which appeared in 1913. It describes, figures,
and traces the history of 428 devices, and with its careful
indices is an invaluable help to the student of English printing. The same year he "put together" for the Society's
Transactions a long paper entitled Notes on Bibliographical
Evidence for Literary Students of English Works of the Sixteenth and Seventeenth Centuries, which was reissued in the
form of a hundred-page pamphlet in 1914, and formed the
basis of one of his most important works, An Introduction to
Bibliography for Literary Students. Closely connected with
the work of the Bibliographical Society was The Library,
which had long been edited by A. W. Pollard. To this Mc-
Kerrow contributed several articles, including a particularly
important investigation into the early use of those troublesome letters i, j and u, v.

When in 1908 the firm of Sidgwick & Jackson was
formed to take over the business of A. H. Bullen he became
a director, and though at first he had little active part in the
management, he did much to help in the capacity of reader
and adviser. It may be worth putting on record that he assisted Granville-Barker in preparing his adaptations of those
pungent Anatol dialogues of Schnitzler that give such vivid
glimpses of pre-war Vienna. He also prepared, as one of
the firm's Christmas-card booklets, a translation of the four-
teenth-century French version of The Story of Asseneth (Jos-

eph's Egyptian wife) from the <u>Speculum Historiale</u> of Vincent of Beauvais.

In 1913, with the support of Walter Morley Fletcher and others, I did my best to persuade McKerrow to fill the post of librarian at Trinity College, Cambridge, that I was myself vacating; but he could not make up his mind to leave London. I found it difficult at the time to understand his refusal, but I have no doubt that from his own point of view he was wise.

He was now settled in a flat at Brook Green, Hammersmith, in more comfort than lodgings could offer, and to his literary activities he added an interest in science. He had always been, and continued to be, specially concerned with chemistry and medicine. He bought a good microscope and subscribed to a "lending-library" for slides, besides preparing many himself. I got the impression, however, that he was as much interested in optical and mechanical contrivances as in the sections of diseased liver and the like that he examined. His energies also found an outlet in social work; he used to visit the East End, and was for a time secretary of the Fulham After-School Care Committee.

We used to meet on holidays as well as in London. We tramped in Cornwall, man-hunted in the Lakes, scrambled in the Alps, walked and sight-saw in Italy. I recall with particular delight the Egginerhorn arête at Saas in sun and swirling mist, and the sweltering road from Gubbio to Urbino through the heart of the Apennines.

Then came the war. McKerrow was over-age for military service, but he joined the R.N.V.R. and was attached to a searchlight unit in London. When many of the younger teachers were swept away he returned once more to King's College as lecturer in English, and continued teaching there till 1919. He also lectured on bibliography, and later, when A. W. Pollard became professor, resumed a short technical course on the subject. Further, the affairs of the publishing house came to demand his attention. Jackson had joined the army and was killed in 1917, after which McKerrow became a managing director; and when later Sidgwick was called up he had to shoulder the whole burden of the business. On the raising of the age-limit he, too, became liable for service, but since he was now forty-five and in a low medical class he remained to look after the firm.

It was during the war, in 1915, that he married Amy, daughter of William Bonnet.[1] At first they remained at the Brook Green flat, but moved in 1917 to a small house at Great Missenden, where in February 1919 twin sons were born. Here he lived for twelve years, till in 1929 he built himself a more commodious home on a parcel of ground known as Picket Piece (or the pointed field) near Wendover, where the rest of his life was spent.

The years that followed the war were a period of varied activity. He continued to share the management of the firm of Sidgwick & Jackson, while the joint secretaryship of the Bibliographical Society involved a considerable amount of work. But other interests were not neglected during what was for many a time of intellectual ferment. He had in 1916 contributed a chapter on "Booksellers, Printers, and the Stationers' Trade" to Shakespeare's England. In 1921 he wrote for the English Association a pamphlet on the teaching of English language and literature. This may have been partly suggested by his experience at King's but it contained revolutionary proposals for recasting the whole system. These few pages reveal, I think, a bolder sweep of imagination than anything else he wrote, but they do not seem to have attracted much attention and one cannot help wondering how many of the English schools of our universities could furnish such a course as he contemplates. The following year he contributed to the Association's Essays and Studies a highly original paper on "English Grammar and Grammars" which is also of some biographical interest as reflecting his early experience in Japan. Between 1923 and 1932 he was one of a group of friends who helped me in producing a series of English Literary Autographs, 1550-1650.

In 1925 he founded The Review of English Studies, the editing of which remained one of his chief concerns to the end of his life. It naturally took a foremost place among the technical literary journals of the day, and through the help he was always ready to give and the direction he was able to afford to the younger research students, its editor came to exercise a welcome influence on the course of English scholarship. The last thing he published was an editorial article on "Form and Matter in the Publication of Research" that appeared in January 1940. It crystallizes fifteen years' experience of the shortcomings of contributors with all and more than all his wonted vigour: "I have sometimes wondered whether the fate of 'English Studies' will not eventually be to be smothered in a kind of woolly and impenetrable fog of wordiness that few or none will be bothered to penetrate." The advice to beginners is sound, but it is not only at beginners that its shafts are levelled.

In 1927 appeared what is probably his best-known work, the Introduction to Bibliography. It is a book quite original in conception and surprisingly comprehensive, of which I shall have more to say.

The same year he received the degree honoris causa of Doctor of Philosophy and Letters (Ph. D.) in the University of Louvain. He had kept up his interest in the series of Materialien founded by Bang and continued by De Vocht, and was also concerned, I believe, in the restoration of the University Library after the disastrous fire during the German occupation of Belgium. Now, at De Vocht's suggestion, he was one of those invited to represent English scholarship at the ceremonies in connexion with the fifth centenary of the founding of the University.

In 1928 he was appointed Sandars Reader in Bibliography at Cambridge, where he delivered four lectures on the printing of Elizabethan literature, his general thesis being that it was much more accurate than is usually represented. These were never published, but in accordance with the terms of the foundation a typewritten copy was deposited in the University Library. They also provided materials for a paper read before the Bibliographical Society in 1931 and printed in The Library under the title of "The Elizabethan Printer and Dramatic Manuscripts." In this he developed the important theory that the confused texts of many plays (apart from the recognized "bad quartos") are due to their having been printed from the "foul papers" or rough drafts of the author, the fair copy being used as the prompt-book and remaining in the hands of the actors. With this paper may be grouped two articles in R. E. S. : "A Suggestion Regarding Shakespeare's Manuscripts" (1935), on the inference to be drawn from the forms of speakers' names in early texts, and "A Note on the 'Bad Quartos' of 2 and 3 Henry VI and the Folio Text" (1937), arguing that certain passages in which the quartos agree closely with the folio are not, as usually supposed, fragments of good text embedded in the bad, but on the contrary, fragments of bad text surviving in the good. Together these three papers form his most important contribution to what I should have annoyed him by calling the bibliographical criticism of dramatic texts.

Meanwhile work for the Bibliographical Society was always claiming his attention. Besides routine administration a good deal of labour went to the supervision of publications. Much of the unofficial business of the Society was done by the co-secretaries over lunch at a small restaurant near the Museum, where Molly (who managed it without apparently possessing a surname) knew us as "The Rare Folios." Here the project was hatched by which in 1920 The Library was amalgamated with the Transactions and became the official organ of the Society. In 1932 appeared the illustrated monograph on Title-page Borders used in England and Scotland, 1485-1640, which McKerrow prepared in collaboration with F. S. Ferguson. It forms a companion volume to the Devices of twenty years before and is hardly less important for the history of printing. It lists 306 borders, besides fragments, every occurrence of which is recorded. A supplement was printed in The Library in December 1936. The Devices also needed supplementing. McKerrow had long intended to revise the book and bring it up to date, and had, I believe, made provisional arrangements for a new edition. Unfortunately the pressure of other work and failing health prevented him from carrying out the project. In 1934 A. W. Pollard retired from the secretaryship of the Bibliographical Society and the whole burden fell on McKerrow. For three years he edited The Library in addition to R. E. S. until relieved by the appointment of F. C. Francis as editor and joint secretary in 1937.

In 1929 McKerrow was awarded the Society's gold medal and in 1932 was elected a Fellow of the British Academy. The following year he delivered the Academy's Annual Shakespeare Lecture on "The Treatment of Shakespeare's Text by his Earlier Editors, 1709-1768." In this he demonstrated how great a debt the current text owes to the critics of the eighteenth century from Rowe to Capell and defined more clearly than before the characteristic contribution of each.

In 1933 McKerrow, who had hitherto belonged to the Reform Club, became a member of the Athenaeum, to the great pleasure of a small circle of friends. For a while four of us, Pollard and Dover Wilson completing the square, used to meet there once a week for lunch. Before long, however, Wilson drifted off to the North, while Pollard began to find the journey into town more and more irksome. But until his final illness McKerrow and I kept up our habit of weekly luncheons and talks. These were largely technical, for he was becoming more and more engrossed in the details of editorial practice, and it was here that we concluded the discussions we had begun on the Grantchester grind more than forty years before.

All this was in preparation for the last and greatest task he was to undertake. After the completion of the Nashe he had for a while entertained the idea of an "old spelling" Shakespeare, but the project had to be abandoned. Twenty years later, in 1929, the Delegates of the Clarendon Press invited him to prepare an edition of Shakespeare on modern critical lines, and he at once accepted the commission. It was an obvious need and he was the ideal person to supply it. How much, on his side, he was gratified by the invitation to realize a long-cherished dream can be read between the lines of the preface to the Prolegomena, the only portion of the work he lived to see published. The task of preparation was his main concern for the last ten years of his life. After long cogitation and experiment the principles of construction were laid down to the last detail, and a substantial portion of the work was actually prepared for press. The plays were to be arranged chronologically, and I am informed by the officials of the Oxford press that of the first two volumes, containing nine plays, the text and part of the notes are in proof and the introductions in draft, while the text of the third, containing another five plays, is also in an advanced state of preparation. Thus we may hope to see fourteen plays substantially in the form in which McKerrow intended them to appear, and I understand that it is the wish of the Delegates to complete the edition on the lines he laid down. Meanwhile all that we actually have is the slender volume of Prolegomena published in May 1939. Unlike the three substantial volumes of Prolegomena to the 1821 "Variorum," this does no more than define the principles and methods upon which he worked; but embodying as it does his mature and considered opinions upon the craft of editing, it merits careful study and will claim attention at the end of the present notice.

So far McKerrow's health had not given cause for alarm, although he was not conspicuously robust. Had he been able to relax and lead an easy life all might have been well, but that neither nature nor circumstances allowed. Heart trouble showed itself at the end of 1937 and he was seriously ill till May the following year, when he recovered sufficiently to resume a more or less normal life and take up work again. But Sidgwick's sudden death in August 1939,

followed by the outbreak of another war, subjected him to
further strain, and his health failed rapidly. After a visit
to London on 21 November he was confined to bed, and he
died on Saturday, 20 January 1940, at the age of sixty-
seven.

Though he was known to be ill, his death came as a
shock to many friends who held him in personal regard and
appreciated his position in English scholarship. I think all
who came in contact with him were impressed by the integ-
rity that was the keynote of his character, what someone
has called "his honour, truth, and humanity." His natural
modesty made light of his high standing and no man was
ever less inclined to adopt a superior pose. If strangers or
students found him a little unapproachable at first, this was
due to a vein of shyness and diffidence and not to any wish
to stand aloof. At the same time he was not one whom it
was easy to know well, for he was encased in shell within
shell of reserve. In forty-five years of close friendship and
association I do not think I ever got to know him thoroughly.
It is possible and likely that others were more successful,
but though on the intellectual plane intercourse with him was
always easy, I fancy that those who penetrated the more intimate recesses of his personality must have been remarkably
few.

In reviewing McKerrow's contribution to English studies three works stand out as of special and permanent importance. The edition of Nashe was the largest that he
brought to completion: it established his reputation as a
scholar and has come to be accepted as a standard by many
whose interests lie in the same field. Also the wide range
and representative character of Nashe's writings, the full-
ness of the annotation, and the excellence of the index com-
bine to make the edition one of the most useful books of reference that the student of Elizabethan literature can have.
The work is mature and scrupulous in every part; the notes
show how wide his reading was, not only in English but in
the continental writings of the renaissance both Latin and
vernacular; while in its own strictly controlled style the introduction is no less than brilliant. So severe, however, is
the restraint that the quality of the writing is easily overlooked. Only once is the curb relaxed--over Bale's Acts of
the English Votaries: "One may indeed wonder what can
have led [Nashe] to peruse and even to quote from such an
abominable legend of lies as this 'exposure of the monastic

system' [as it is called in the D.N.B.], than which hardly
anything more malignant has disgraced even the literature
of theological controversy." I may remark that this was a
purely critical judgement and was not inspired by any tender-
ness towards the Roman church. From first to last the
work bears the impress of the writer's cool and analytical
mind working counter to all hasty and popular conclusions.
Nothing, for example, could be more characteristic than his
treatment of the well-known passage in the Preface to Mena-
phon that has been supposed to prove Kyd's authorship of an
early Hamlet, in regard to which he evinced an incredulity
that despite all controversy he maintained to the end. This
was not due to obstinacy or disregard of others' arguments,
for in a private letter he wrote as late as 1936: "I am very
glad to see that you agree exactly with me about this 'Hamlet' business. I had begun to wonder whether I was being
pig-headedly sceptical." Many, too, will recall his demonstration (in The Gentleman's Magazine for February 1906)
regarding a cancel in Greene's Quip for an Upstart Courtier,
which was brilliantly confirmed by the discovery of a copy in
the original state in the Britwell sale in 1919.

Nevertheless it was neither the comprehensive sanity
of the introduction nor the copious learning of the notes that
gave the book its peculiar distinction and made it a landmark
in Elizabethan studies. It must have been, I think, in the
autumn of 1907 that one of the greatest of American scholars, whose death we have also lately had to lament, John
Matthews Manly, remarked to me on an evening at Cambridge that in his Nashe, McKerrow had set a new standard
of English editing. That was at a time when only the text
had appeared. He may have been thinking partly of the accuracy of the reprints and the record of variants: but after
all these were not unknown features in the work of earlier
editors. What, I fancy he had more particularly in mind,
was the care bestowed on the bibliographical foundations of
the text and upon editorial method. Editors have usually
been curiously disinclined to explain or defend their own procedure. McKerrow devoted much attention to determining
his methods and was punctilious in defining them. In this
we may perhaps trace the influence of his early scientific
training. He also saw the rock-bed of editing was the choice
of the text to be taken as the basis of a reprint. For this
he invented the term "copy-text," which was passed into critical use, though I regret to see that the Supplement to the
Oxford English Dictionary fails to recognize it. Some editors have been content to reprint blindly from the earliest

edition of a work, or what they took for it; others have chosen
the last edition printed in the author's lifetime, at whiles
with disastrous results. McKerrow insisted on "the general
principle of making the last edition that seems to have been
corrected by the author the foundation of the text." Moreover, he recognized that an editor is offered two alternatives: either to print from the earliest edition, incorporat-
ing corrections from the latest revised by the author, or else
to print from the latter, correcting typographical errors by
the former. He added: "I have chosen the latter as being
on the whole the more consistent." He can only have meant
that it gave a slightly more consistent text: in any case, after a good deal of consideration, he came in the end to in-
cline to the opposite course.

Since in an appraisal of his work it is largely the
principles of his editing that must interest us, I may be allowed to quote one passage that illustrates both the difficulties of the subject and a certain critical bent of the author's
mind (ii. 197):

> fortunately it is not now considered to be the duty
> of an editor to pick and choose among the variant
> readings of his author's works those which he him-
> self would prefer in writings of his own, but mere-
> ly to present those works as he believes the au-
> thor to have intended them to appear. Whether,
> from a literary point of view, the first or the sec-
> ond edition of The Unfortunate Traveller is the bet-
> ter, is perhaps open to question. But with this I
> have no concern whatever, at any rate here, for
> if an editor has reason to suppose that a certain
> text embodies later corrections than any other,
> and at the same time has no ground for disbeliev-
> ing that these corrections, or some of them at
> least, are the work of the author, he has no
> choice but to make that text the basis of his re-
> print.

I think the words I have italicized [underlined] will surprise
many who have given thought to the subject, but we shall see
that in his latest work McKerrow adhered to the opinion
that, once the fact of correction has been established, all
changes in the corrected edition must be accepted without
further inquiry into their origin.

Although in his edition of Nashe he was still a learner

in the unexplored paths of bibliography and did not, for instance, always clearly distinguish between variants, issues,
and editions, he was already acutely conscious of the importance of the subject in literary investigation, and an article
in The Library for November 1903 on variations in The Return of Pasquill shows that he was able to analyse a bibliographical problem with precision, even though he refrained
from venturing on an explanation. No doubt there are points
at which, had he been doing the work to-day, his treatment
would have been somewhat different. He hoped that a new
edition of Nashe would ultimately appear. "He would indeed
be foolish who should dream that any work of his in this kind
could be final: he would, I think, be no well-willer to English scholarship who should even hope that it might be so,"
he wrote in the preface to the final volume. To speak of
an edition as definitive is always silly, but I can hardly imagine a future edition of Nashe being anything but a revision
of the one that McKerrow completed at the age of thirty-
seven.

The bibliographical insight that distinguished the Nashe
bore fruit in the years that followed. McKerrow, of course,
was not the first to apply bibliographical methods to the elucidation of literary problems, nor was he alone in recogniz-
ing the value of such technical training for the textual student. Already A. W. Pollard combined in his own person
the expert book-man and the experienced editor and was the
accepted leader of a small band who shared his twin interests. He it was who preached the doctrine that the literary
student should never lose sight of the actual pieces of paper
or parchment on which an author's words are preserved.
But it was McKerrow who had not only the wit to perceive
the need for definite bibliographical instruction but the necessary knowledge and energy to provide it.

McKerrow never subscribed allegiance to any sect or
school or tolerated a label of any kind, and he sometimes
spoke with impatience of what has been called the "bibliographical" method in textual criticism, for no better reason,
so he averred, than that some who have practised it have also been bibliographers. Of course he knew that there were
critics for whom "bibliography" covered the whole process
of the material transmission of texts: his impatience seems
to have been due in part to himself taking a narrower view
of its extension, in part to a very reasonable distrust of the
sometimes daring and even fantastic theories that have been
put forward in its name. But if there is a bibliographical

school of textual criticism, McKerrow must certainly share
responsibility for its existence, for his teaching helped materially to encourage it and give it a sure foundation.

I digress for a moment in order to define the ideas
underlying what is rightly or wrongly called the bibliographical approach to textual criticism and make plain the position at the time McKerrow began his teaching.   Textual criticism admits of two lines of approach: the internal and literary, which concerns itself primarily with the variants of
reading and their aptness to express the supposed intention
of the author; and the external or bibliographic, which makes
its chief aim the tracing of documentary transmission and
considers the readings only in relation to the source whence
they derive.   To the old-fashioned literary critic textual variants were merely counters in a guessing game, he applied
himself strictly to estimating their intrinsic merit: to-day
the bibliographer is first of all concerned with their derivation and the endeavour to determine the authority of the
source.   I do not wish to imply that one approach is essentially vicious, the other by nature scientific, or even that
one is superior to the other: for the moment I am merely
drawing a distinction and stating what appears to be an historical fact, at any rate so far as English literature is concerned.

There is, as McKerrow recognized (Treatment of
Shakespeare's Text, pp. 20-1; Prolegomena, p. 36), a broad
and at the same time rather deep distinction between the
textual study of manuscripts and that of printed books, and
the bibliographical impact has affected the two rather differently.   In the manuscript field the investigation of documentary sources led three-quarters of a century ago to the establishment of what is known as the genealogical method,
which seeks from the ancestry of extant documents to ap-
praise the authority of their readings.   The critical outlook
that led to this revolutionary change was essentially a bibliographical one, being concerned with the relationship between the material vehicles of transmission, though this was
not explicitly recognized at the time.

It was not till more than a generation later, when
bibliographical criticism was emerging into self-conscious-
ness, that it began systematically to affect the textual study
of printed books.   This is at first sight curious, since bibliography was popularly supposed to be particularly concerned
with this field.   But perhaps because the textual problems

presented by a printed work appeared to be generally simpler than those of manuscripts, it was not immediately recognized that they were after all closely related. However, in the end bibliography, ever intent upon its material pieces of parchment or paper, asked essentially the same question as before, only now it took the form: What was the nature of the copy that the printer had before him when setting up the text? This seemingly innocent question has proved a curiously powerful solvent to traditional modes of thought.

Of course, all question of labels apart, [2] there is no doubt to which "school" McKerrow belonged, for the whole significance of his teaching lies in the importance he attached to the derivation of the text. And if he had not been hampered by a rather narrow view of the scope of bibliography he might have felt less reluctant to avail himself of certain methods of investigation than his later writings show him to have been.

In An Introduction to Bibliography for Literary Students an earlier essay grew into a substantial volume of 350 pages and more. By the title I suppose he meant that it was to introduce literary students to an essential but neglected part of their equipment, for in no other sense is the work introductory, being in fact a remarkably thorough and comprehensive treatment of the bibliography of printed books in so far as their material form has a bearing on the transmission of the text and so becomes the concern of the critic. With manuscripts he did not attempt to deal, tacitly assuming that bibliography was specially concerned with printing. The book became at once a stand-by of every serious student of English literature of the three centuries following the introduction of printing, and although only thirteen years have passed since its appearance, many to-day must wonder how they ever got on without it.

Three ingredients go to its make-up. First it contains a most lucid summary of the technical processes of book production based on recognized authorities; secondly it gathers together an immense amount of relevant bibliographical and antiquarian information from a great variety of sources unfamiliar to the ordinary student; lastly to this it adds much drawn from his own experience and research, and shows the bearing of the whole upon literary and textual problems. His original contribution is by no means the least valuable part of the work, for his powers of observation and interpretation were remarkable. A trifling, but to me always surprising example is his detection of the peculiar use of long ∫ in Capell's <u>Prolusions</u> of 1760.

Even so the book hardly gives a full idea of the richness and curiosity of his knowledge or of his power and ingenuity in applying it to the problems that came before him. His help was at the disposal of any serious student who wished to consult him, and he delighted to give it. For forty years I was in the habit of taking every bibliographical difficulty to him, and I do not think I ever failed to get some enlightenment. Occasionally, though it was not in his nature to be "squashing," consulting him might be a chastening experience. During the last months of his life a bibliographical study of my own was passing through the press, and since it was for the Bibliographical Society, the proofs went to him as a matter of course. I had been puzzled by a minute abnormality in a single copy of the first edition of <u>King Lear</u>, which appeared to involve a mechanical impossibility. While correcting the proofs a possible explanation occurred to me. I was rather pleased with myself, for it was, I believe, an altogether novel idea and threw light on an obscure point of procedure in Elizabethan printing. Next morning I had a letter from McKerrow in a postscript to which he casually remarked: Isn't this offset business the explanation of your puzzle?--the very one I had been so proud to discover! In this kind of trained imagination, in the detective ability to infer from any peculiarity the manner of its origin, he was supreme. In another more speculative kind of imagination he may have been deficient.

McKerrow's greatest undertaking, and the one by which we may still hope that he will be remembered in the history of English scholarship, was the Oxford Shakespeare, of which he lived to publish only the <u>Prolegomena</u>. But when we deplore his untimely death we may at least be thankful that to the end there was no failing of intellectual grasp and vigour. His last article in <u>R. E. S.</u> is as incisive as anything he wrote, and the <u>Prolegomena</u> has an importance out of all proportion to its slender bulk. In considering his latest work we are spared the sad necessity of making allowance for the encroachments of age.

"When in 1929 I began work upon this edition of the plays of Shakespeare in old spelling, I was far from realizing how little systematic consideration seemed ever to have been given to editorial methods as applied to English writings in general and to those of Shakespeare in particular." With

him the natural result was "A Study of Editorial Method" in
which, with his usual precise care, he laid down both the
general principles and the detailed procedure to be followed
in his own work.   They are alike the fruit of long experience and consideration, and much experiment went to the
elaboration of detail.   In the field to which they are applicable, that is the period in which English literature depends
mainly on printed sources, McKerrow's study is, I believe,
the fullest and, if the term may be allowed, the most authoritative in existence, and its influence on future editors can
hardly help being at once salutary and profound.   "In the
whole history of Shakespearian scholarship there is nothing
comparable to these pages.... [The] problems are discussed
with a grasp only possible to one who has worked at the text
of the plays for many years and who came to his task already a master of his craft."   So wrote a reviewer who is
himself one of our ablest Elizabethan scholars.   Inquiry is
all the more necessary as to what, if any, reserves should
be made in respect of its teaching.   This is no place for detailed examination, but a few remarks will be in place in so
far as they bear upon the character and workings of the author's mind.

     The book falls into two very unequal parts: there is
first a short account of what we may take to be the principles which McKerrow conceived to govern the construction of
a critical text; then follows a necessarily much longer discussion of the methods and conventions proper to the presentation both of text and apparatus.   These methods are beautiful in their comprehensive economy.   They are not, indeed,
universally applicable, and some may think them over-ingeni-
ous; but I have had too much experience of the soundness of
McKerrow's judgement in such matters to feel disposed to
criticize.   General principles are on a different footing.
They are infinitely more important and of much wider application, and we are able to check them in practice according
as they affect the choice and treatment of the copy-text.
Here I think one may without pedantry or impertinence suggest that a somewhat different approach to certain fundamental questions is possible.

     Reduced to its elements what we may call McKerrow's
editorial theory is as follows.   The first and obvious re-
quirement is that the text "should approach as closely as the
extant material allows to a fair copy, made by the author
himself, of his plays in the form he intended finally to give
them" (p. 6), or, which is not perhaps quite the same thing,

"our aim is ... to produce a text ... as near as possible
to what the author wrote" (p. 14). For this purpose we
must select as our basis or copy-text the "most authoritative" edition, this being "that one of the early texts which,
on a consideration of their genetic relationship, appears
likely to have deviated to the smallest extent in all respects
of wording, spelling, and punctuation from the author's
manuscript" (pp. 7-8). Next he draws the distinction between "substantive" editions, those not derived from any other extant edition, and "derived" editions, namely those derived, whether immediately or not, from other extant editions; and he remarks that "It is evident that the 'most authoritative text' of which we are in search must be a 'substantive' one" (p. 8). Further, having selected our copy-
text we must "reprint this as exactly as possible save for
manifest and indubitable errors" (p. 7). The only exception
is if we are able to satisfy ourselves that some later "derived" edition has been corrected by the author or from an
authoritative source, in which case, while still in general
following our copy-text, "we must accept all the alterations
of that [corrected] edition, saving any which seem obvious
blunders or misprints" (or presumably printers' modernizations) and not pick and choose among them (p. 18).

There is nothing very novel in these principles except the clearness with which they are enunciated, and they
impress the reader as eminently reasonable and sound; indeed, in general application sound they undoubtedly are.
Nevertheless, the circumstances are often so complex that
it is difficult to lay down any rigid rules, and it seems open
to question whether McKerrow allowed sufficiently for the
extent to which editorial procedure most conform to variable
conditions.

Thus even in the minor matter of correction by the
author difficulty arises from the fact that analysis may show
that while certain changes are due to him others have a different origin. In such a case must we still "accept all the
alterations"? McKerrow, it will be remembered, had dealt
with a case of correction in Nashe, when he printed The
Unfortunate Traveller from the second edition "Newly corrected and augmented" by the author. But while there is no
reason to doubt that Nashe was responsible for most of the
alterations, McKerrow himself showed that others must have
been made by the printer for purely typographical reasons
and others again by someone who misunderstood the author's
meaning. Is there any reason why a critical text should ad-

mit such alterations any more than "obvious blunders and misprints"?

So with the treatment of the copy-text whenever an editor has to choose between two or more "substantive" editions, for the same considerations that show one edition to be on the whole more authoritative may equally show its inferiority in some particular respect. Thus there is no doubt that the folio text of Richard III, which McKerrow recognized as superior to that of the quartos and rightly chose as the basis of his own, has been more or less censored in the matter of oaths in deference to the statute against profanity. In this it may have followed the manuscript from which it is mainly derived, but it cannot be thought to represent the author's intention. But adherence to rule would necessitate the absence of the oaths from McKerrow's text. Thus in certain cases the principle of following the copy-text exactly may conflict with the more important principle of presenting the text in as close an approximation to the author's intention as the evidence permits.

But the most curious refusal to make use of critical analysis is in the choice between "substantive" texts to serve as copy. One would suppose that the most pertinent ground of choice would be the nature and source of the several texts, whether they were derived from reports, transcripts, promptbooks, author's drafts, and so on. This, indeed, is what McKerrow's words imply when he says that the authority of the texts should be decided "on a consideration of their genetic relationship" (pp. 7-8). He also explicitly admits the possibility and legitimacy of inquiry into "The general character of the copy from which the substantive text ... was set up" (pp. 8-9). Yet he appears to have been so deeply impressed by the uncertainties into which such speculations may lead (detailed on pp. 9-10) that when he comes to discuss the problem of choice he refuses to entertain any such considerations and maintains that "the editor must select the text which appeals most to his critical judgement and this ... will as a rule be the one which appears to be the most careful copy of its original and the most free from obvious errors" (p. 14). I have quoted what seems to me the weakest passage in the book, not as typical of his work--for in this respect I believe his practice to have been bolder than his theory--but because I think it illustrates a certain bent of his mind, a shrinking from critical adventure and a groping after some more or less mechanical rule.

No doubt his reluctance to permit the intrusion of individual judgement into the detailed construction of the text was reinforced by, if it did not originate in, a realization of the extent to which Shakespeare had suffered from the eclectic methods of previous editors. It may be that native Scottish caution made him doubt how far a surrender to imagination might not carry him if he once allowed it a footing in his editorial practice. Yet in a slightly different connexion McKerrow emphasized the need of being guided by "an informed and disciplined imagination," while adding, "I am far from claiming to have any such qualifications myself" (p. viii). This was misplaced modesty. He was in fact eminently qualified both by wide reading and by shrewd judgement to tackle just such questions of text and interpretation as confront an editor of Shakespeare. I regret that out of critical diffidence he should have circumscribed his liberty of action.

But even granting contributory causes, there can be little doubt, I think, that the want of elasticity I have noted in his methods does in a way reflect the workings of a particularly concrete mind. He distrusted and was inclined to discount anything that appeared to him to fail of such a degree of certainty as the nature of the subject allowed, while admitting that this was often only a degree of probability-- for he held that "in the domain of literary research the words 'proof' and 'prove' ... can seldom be appropriate." He instinctively fought shy of speculation, and his dislike of far-reaching theories was characteristic. This showed itself no less in his attitude towards science. He had a much better knowledge than most literary men of the general scientific theories that were orthodox in his youth, and he kept up his interest in them to the end. On the other hand, the recent developments of physics were to him a closed book that apparently excited no curiosity. Although he was, of course, far too shrewd ever to express such an opinion, I fancy he never rid his mind of a suspicion that the theory of relativity, for instance, involved some quite elementary fallacy. He seemed by nature incapable of imagining that there might be fields in which the habits of thought based on our ordinary experience are--to use his own phrase-- inappropriate, that physical space may be quite different from that of the metaphysicians, and gravitation not a force but a geometry! We have all felt the difficulty, but McKerrow had no impulse to overcome it. Once, when someone mentioned the Michelson-Morley experiment, I heard him murmur unhappily, "I suppose it is true."

But in spite of all, the few pages in which he discussed the grounds of his practice as an editor remain the most important he ever penned and should prove the most helpful guide that has yet been vouchsafed to English critics whose concern is with printed texts. With the intricacies of manuscript transmission he never had occasion to deal, and characteristically he refused to interest himself in a subject in which he felt no certain footing. In his own field he was a great critic, and one of the sanest; had he ventured more he would have been greater still.

Notes

1. I am much indebted to Mrs. McKerrow for assistance in preparing this memoir.

2. Despite McKerrow's objection, and for the sake of an argument, I have retained the term "bibliographical" criticism which seems to me legitimate and helpful, but if anyone prefers "material" I should not quarrel with it.

CHAPTER 2

SOME NOTES ON THE LETTERS
i, j, u AND v IN SIXTEENTH
CENTURY PRINTING*

We can regard with equanimity the statement in Watt's
Bibliotheca Britannica[1] that Louis Elzevier, "who printed at
Leyden from 1595 to 1616, ... was the first who made the
distinction of u from v and i from j; which was shortly after followed by the introduction of U and J among the capi-
tals, by Lazarus Zetner of Strasburg, in 1619"; for the work
of Watt, excellent as it was in its own day, has in many
points long ago been superseded. When, however, we find
this statement cited in the New English Dictionary,[2] apparently as the latest and most authoritative dictum on the
subject, we may naturally feel some surprise, even though
the citation is accompanied by evidence which shows that it
cannot be accepted as a true presentation of the case. And
yet if we were asked to what work of more recent date we
would refer an enquirer who had noticed that the use of these
letters in the early part of the sixteenth century was very
different from what it is now, and who wished to know how
the change came about, we might be hard put to it for an
answer. There are notes on the subject here and there;
Herbert has several in his edition of Ames's Typographical
Antiquities; but, so far as I have been able to learn, the
last attempt to deal with the question at all fully was early
in the eighteenth century, in a "Dissertation sur le tems
auquel les imprimeurs ont introduit l'J & l'V consonnes,"
which is to be found in the Continuation des Mémoires de
Littérature et d'Histoire of P. Desmolets, vol. vii.[3] This
article, though a good piece of work within the limits which
it prescribes, naturally says nothing about what is of most

*The Library, 3d Series, Vol. I, no. 3, July 1910, pp. 239-
59. Greg says of this article, "a particularly important investigation into the early use of those troublesome letters i,
j and u, v." Reprinted by permission of the Council of The
Bibliographical Society.

interest to us, namely, the history of these letters in England.

To deal with the subject exhaustively would, of course,
require much time and the systematic examination of a large
number of books; for, with the exception of Herbert, few
bibliographers--at least of those who have dealt with sixteenth century printing--seem to have been interested in the
letters and characters themselves, or to have noticed peculiarities in their use.   An exhaustive treatment is, however,
far from my intention.   I wish merely to bring together a
few more or less disconnected notes bearing upon the matter.   They will at least show that Watt was grievously in
error.

It is well known that until the sixteenth century i and
j were, as a general rule, regarded as merely two forms
of the same letter, the like being the case with u and v.
Such differentiation as there was in their use was merely a
matter of calligraphy; either letter of the pair could stand
equally well for a vowel sound or for a consonant.   Indeed
the complete separation of the letters is of quite recent date,
for until the last century was well advanced, the i- and j-
words were arranged together in dictionaries, as were also
those beginning with u and v.   The particular point which I
wish to discuss is the change which took place between about
1520 and 1630, [4] by which j and v from being merely graph-
ic variants of i and u came to represent different sounds,
the change, in short, by which it came about that the Latin
words which in 1500 were commonly written "inijcere" and
"vua" had by 1650 taken the forms "injicere" and "uva."
The fortunes of the two pairs of letters in question were not
identical, but were sufficiently similar to allow of their being treated together.   The slight gain in clearness which
might result from taking each pair separately seems to be
outweighed by the tediousness of narrating a great part of
their story--a dull one at best--twice over.

The practice of the earliest printers, which they presumably took over from the scribes of their time and country, with regard to the letters under discussion was as follows:

(1) There was an upper-case letter approximating in
shape in Gothic founts rather to the modern J than to I, but
serving indifferently for either.

(2) An upper-case letter approximating in shape in Gothic founts to U, and serving for U and V.

(3) A lower-case i, serving for both i and j.

(4) A lower-case j, used for the second of two i's in words like "perij," and in Roman numerals as "viij."

(5) A lower-case u, serving for both u and v, but only used medially or finally.

(6) A lower-case v, serving for both u and v, but only used initially.

There were no doubt exceptions to the general rule: it has been stated that certain of the German printers used j for the consonantal sound of i from the earliest times,[5] and the two letters were distinguished in Spanish printing:[6] but the practice of the great majority of the German, Dutch, and English printers until the end of the sixteenth century was in general as stated--in the case of black-letter printing almost invariably.

In books printed in the roman character there is, however, from its first introduction, some fluctuation in usage. Not indeed in the majuscules, for the roman I and V served precisely the same double purpose as the black-letter J and U, but in the lower-case letters, where u seems to have trespassed to some extent on the province of its companion v. Thus in the first book printed in Italy, the Lactantius of 1465, we find u instead of v initially in such words as "uita," "uero," and "unus," where in Germany printers would have spelled "vita," "vero," "vnus." Indeed, neither j nor v seems to be employed in the book at all.[7] This practice of using u initially seems to have been followed by the majority of the Italian printers; Jenson, for example, in his roman type seems not to employ v at all, save in the roman numerals. In his black-letter work he, however, followed the German practice, though with some irregularity, probably due to the compositors' knowledge of both systems. The Italian use of u soon spread outside that country, and in the sixteenth century was very commonly followed by those printers who printed chiefly in roman type, especially at Basel and Paris, while in North Germany, Holland, and England, the older system of using v as the initial letter was generally adhered to, both in roman type and in black letter.

So far, the letters of each pair have been regarded as differing merely in form; the use is purely a matter of appearance: but even in Roman times it had been noticed that the letter u or v, whichever form it took, represented two different sounds, the same thing being true of i, though of course in neither case was the pair of sounds the same as it was at the period with which we are now dealing. Probably in all ages attempts have been made by enthusiasts to cause the written language to represent with greater accuracy the spoken sounds, but the only early one which seems to have met with even temporary success is that of the Emperor Claudius, who proposed to use the digamma in such words as "servus" and "vulgus."[8]

It is indeed not until well on in the sixteenth century that we find any serious and sustained effort to discriminate in writing between the two sounds represented by each pair of the letters under discussion. So far as I have been able to ascertain, the first printed books in which the differentiation is observed were the works of the Italian poet Giangiorgio Trissino (1478-1550), who attempted to introduce a reformed method of spelling of which this innovation is a part. Trissino's Epistola de la vita che dee tenere una Donna vedova, printed by Lodovico de gli Arrighi Vicentino and Lautitio Perugino at Rome in 1524, has the modern use of u and v throughout, both in lower-case and majuscules, besides certain other new letters with which we need not concern ourselves, but does not distinguish i and j. The like is true of two other small works of Trissino, issued by the same printers in the same year, but an undated pamphlet apparently first printed to accompany these books, namely the Epistola de le Lettere Nuovamente aggiunte ne la Lingua Italiana, further distinguishes the consonantal sound of j.[9] The j is, however, used much less frequently than in the author's later work. Trissino had also devised a kind of sloping line to serve as a majuscule J, but there seems to be no example of its use.

The Epistola was reprinted by Tolomeo Janiculo da Bressa in 1529. A preface informs us that much criticism had already been directed against the new letters, and the writer complains that excellent as the system is, the critics "con la invidiosa nebula de la loro eloquenzia hanno quasi adombrato la incredibile utilita di essa."[10]

From 1524 to 1548 at least Janiculo printed a number of works in the new spelling. Most, however, if not

all, were either by or connected with Trissino, and it is not
clear that the innovation had much success.   The attitude of
the majority towards it is exemplified by the republication
in 1583 of Trissino's translation of Dante's De Vulgari Elo-
quentia, "di nuovo ristampato, e dalle lettere al nostro idi-
oma strane purgato. "11

   At about the time when Trissino was attempting
to introduce his new letters in Italy, were beginning in
France those spelling controversies which occupied so much
of the attention of the learned world throughout the century.
Curiously enough, however, in the earlier writings on the
subject, though the double value of the letters under discussion was of course recognized, the idea of making use of v
and j to represent the consonants does not seem to have
been suggested.   For example, the work of J. du Bois,
written under the name of "Jacobi Sylvii Ambiani in Linguam
Gallicam Isagoge, " 1531, distinguishes the consonantal
sounds as i- and u-, as in "i-e, " "Au-ril, " "receu-oir, "
but Du Bois does not seem to intend the hyphen to be used
in ordinary script; it is no more than a diacritic for scientific purposes.   Similarly the leader of one of the most important schools of spelling reform, Louis Meigret, in his
Traité touchant ... l'escriture Françoise, 1545, 12 recog-
nizes that i and u each represents two distinct sounds, and
would have them differentiated.   He approves Claudius' idea
of writing "une ʃ renversée" for the consonantal sound of
u, but the obvious idea of using a v does not occur to him.
In this work he keeps to the old practice as regards both u
and i.

   In a later book, however, Le tretté de la Grammere
Francoȩze, 1550, 13 though he still follows the old practice
of using v always initially and u always medially, we find a
change as regards i.   He now writes i for the vowel and j
for the consonant according to the modern practice, having
"je, " "ajouter, " etc.   Either he or his printer, however,
found it somewhat difficult always to remember the new letter, and we often find an i used instead.   Exactly the same
rule, u and v according to the old fashion, i and j according to the new, is to be found in another work published in
the same year, the Dialogue de l'Ortografe e Prononciation
Françoese of Jacques Peletier du Mans, where we have
"je, " "majesté, " "déjà, " etc., but in this work the use is
somewhat more consistent.

   In most of the works of the spelling reformers the

changes proposed had been too numerous and elaborate, and
had given to the print too great an air of oddity and extrava-
gance for them to have much chance of success; but this cannot be said of the next work which we need notice, the
Grammatica of Pierre de la Ramée, or Ramus, first published in 1559. Though its author was later to propose
most thorough-going reforms in the spelling of French, in
this Latin grammar there were no departures from the current orthography save as regards the i and u, and the intrinsic importance of the work was sufficient easily to out-
weigh any slight strangeness which there might be in the use
of these letters. It is not surprising that the authority of
the writer and that of the printing-house of Wechel at Paris
and Frankfurt, from which this and many of Ramus's other
works issued, should together lead to the ultimate triumph
of the new method.

Of the first edition of the Grammatica I have been
unable to see a copy, but so far as regards the matters
with which we are now dealing, it is said to be identical
with the third, published in 1560 by Andreas Wechel at Paris. In this we have not only the modern use of i and j, u
and v throughout, but a majuscule J and U[14] of approxi-
mately modern form. Indeed the only departure from the
practice of to-day seems to be in the case of the italic v.
Wechel uses the ordinary curled italic v for the consonantal
sound initially, but probably disliking the appearance of the
letter within a word, he substituted a roman v medially.
He had no italic majuscule I, but used a roman letter instead.

The reform, although as we have seen earlier attempts towards it had been made, was at the time and generally afterwards associated with the name of Ramus,[15] the
letters j and v being even called "consonnes Ramistes,"[16]
but Ramus himself does not seem to have claimed to be the
inventor of the new system. Indeed his references to the
matter, which are somewhat vague, point rather to Andreas
Wechel, or some other printer, as the originator of the
modern usage. Ramus does not indeed name him, but in
his French grammar of 1562 he says with reference to the
letter v, "nous avons mis en latin vau suivant l'autorité de
Varron et de nos imprimeurs. La raison en est semblable
en notre langue,"[17] and in his Scholae in liberales artes,
1578, col. 29, 1. 36, he says: "Typographi vero nonnulli
tacito consensu figuram vav consonae hanc v nempe, pro
digamma illo Acolico induxerunt." Both these passages

seem to attribute the change to the printers, but before
1562, at any rate, no printer in northern Europe seems regularly to have adopted the modern usage as regards v, nor
does Wechel himself seem to have followed it in work earlier
than Ramus' own Grammatica. [18]   The problem should be
easily solved by those familiar with foreign printed books of
the middle of the sixteenth century, but it is on the whole of
little importance, for whether or no Ramus was the instiga-
tor of the change, it is certain that it was the weight of his
name and the fact that the new system was from 1560 onwards regularly adhered to in his works which gave it its
whole chance of success.

We need not follow the further progress of the change
in continental printing.   At first it is found chiefly in the
works of Ramus and his followers, and it cannot be said to
have made any great progress until towards the close of the
century.   From about 1620 it seems to have become the usual thing, but books may be found as late as the middle of
the seventeenth century, in which the old practice is followed.

When we turn to the use by English printers of the
letters under discussion we find a perplexing story.   There
seem to have been several attempts to introduce the modern
usage, and before 1600 a good many books had appeared in
which it was followed, but they are the work of a number of
different printers, and seem to have little connection one
with another.   We cannot point to any particular men as active promoters of the new system, and even those printing
houses from which were issued several works in which the
letters in question had their modern values, seem generally
to have returned again to the old practice.   The reform,
though one would think it ought to have attracted some attention, seems to have passed almost unnoticed, and there is,
so far as I have seen, no single contemporary reference in
any printer's preface or elsewhere to the change of style.
We are, in fact, left without other information about it than
can be derived from the books themselves.

Long ago Herbert remarked that J. Banister's History
of Man, printed by John Day in 1578, was the first book
wherein he had seen the v an j "properly used," [19] and I
cannot learn that an earlier English example of the new practice has been found since.   In this work we have on the title-
page "objurges," "Privilegio," "Majestatis," and the modern
usage is similarly followed in some Latin quotations in the

preliminary matter, and in a Latin letter on *I^V, in such
words as "Invidia," "livor," "ut," etc. In the work itself,
however, the old use is retained both in the English and in
such Latin words as occur in it, e.g., "vena caua."

In the History of Man no italic v or j was used, but
in another book printed in the same year, also by John Day,
the Catechismus parvus pueris primum Latiné qui ediscatur,
proponendus in scholis, we have, according to Herbert, 20
the lower-case letters i and j, u and v, employed according
to the modern usage both in roman and italic. It was, however, impossible, for want of the necessary type, to carry
out the same rule in the majuscules in which the Creed,
Commandments, etc., are printed, and a lower case j or u
are consequently substituted for the upper-case letters. In
one respect the printer adhered to the older custom, for he
has "Filijs," "Officijs," etc. A similar system seems to
have been followed in a third book printed by Day, namely,
the Christ Jesus Triumphant of 1579. Herbert21 has a note
upon this work, from which it might be inferred that Day
had now a majuscule J, but his language is somewhat obscure, and I have not been able to see a copy of the book.

The other productions of Day's press both at this
time and later seem all to have followed the older practice
as regards the letters in question, and we next meet with
the modern usage in the work of Henry Middleton. In the
years 1575-9 Andreas Wechel had printed at Frankfurt a
Latin Old Testament in four parts, translated from the Hebrew and annotated by Emmanuel Tremellius and F. Junius.
In this work he had throughout conformed to the same rules
with regard to j and v as he had followed in the Grammatica
of Ramus. 22 This Old Testament was reprinted in England
by Henry Middleton in 1579-80, and a New Testament, also
by Tremellius, was printed to range with it by Vautrollier.
In Middleton's part we find the modern use of lower-case v
and j throughout, both in roman and italic, and we also find
a majuscule J and U in the roman founts in which the text
and notes are printed. There is no italic *U*, a roman U
being used instead. For the italic J the *J* is used. 23 The
New Testament, printed by Vautrollier, follows the old practice, with the exception of a few words in the preliminary
matter. Possibly this was printed by Middleton, whose device appears on the title-page of this part as of the others.
The whole work was reprinted in 1581; again, the Old Testament, by Middleton, follows the modern usage, the New Testament, by Vautrollier, the old one. The same is the case

with the edition of 1585, save that in this the New Testament, as well as the Old, is printed by Middleton. In the
first few pages of this New Testament the printer seems to
have made an attempt to follow the modern style, but it is
soon abandoned, and Vautrollier's text is followed letter for
letter. The fourth English edition of the work, however,
printed by G. Bishop, R. Newbery, and R. Baker, in 1592-
3, follows the new practice throughout.

     Though we cannot give Middleton any particular cred-
it for originality, as he was but following his copy letter for
letter, he seems at any rate to have introduced the majuscule
U and J into this country--unless, indeed, the latter had been
used by Day before--and to that extent may be regarded as a
pioneer. He does not, however, seem to have made as much
use of the new letters as we might have expected and in most
of his later work he reverts to the old system. I have indeed
only come across two later works of his in which the modern
practice is followed, namely, the Epistola de Dialectica P.
Rami of William Temple in 1582, and the Animadversiones in
Dialecticam P. Rami of J. Piscator, 1583. These had, of
course, a special claim on the new method as being concerned
with Ramus, and we find it also followed in the P. Rami Dialec-
ticae Libri Duo, Scholiis G. Tempelli Illustrati, printed at
Cambridge by T. Thomas in 1584. [24]

     The next printers to take up the reform seem to have
been Ninian Newton and Arnold Hatfield, who in 1584 printed
two works for John Wight, namely, Edmund Bunny's Sceptre of
Judah, and the same writer's edition of R. Parsons' Book of
Christian Exercise, together with his own Treatise of Pacifica-
tion. Both these works, so far as the lower-case letters are
concerned, follow the modern practice, but the printers evidently had no J or U. In another edition of the Book of Christian Exercise, printed for Wight by J. Jackson and E. Bollifant
in 1586, i and j, u and v, are, according to Herbert, "properly
used" in the roman, but not in the italic. This edition I have
not seen.

     Probably from this time onwards there was year by
year a small production of books in which the rules of Ramus or
Wechel were conformed to, but the next examples that I have
seen date from three years later. They are the work of Jackson and Bollifant who, as we have seen, had already printed in
this style. The first is Richard Bancroft's Sermon of 9th
February, 1588-9, printed soon after the date of preaching,
by E. B. , presumably Bollifant, for G. Seton. In this work

the modern usage is followed throughout in lower case, but
there is again no J or U. The same may be said of the
second edition of La Primaudaye's French Academy, translated by T. B., which was published in this year by G.
Bishop, without printer's name. The earlier edition (1586),
printed by Bollifant, had followed the old practice throughout.

A third book published in 1589 is J. Lea's Answer
to the Untruths published and printed in Spain in glory of
their supposed victory, printed by J. Jackson for T. Cad-
man. Jackson had still no italic j, and used roman instead, but otherwise in the lower case he followed the modern practice exactly. Apart from the edition of Parsons'
Book of Christian Exercise, 1586, I have not been able to
find the modern system in any other work from Jackson's
press.

In this same year, 1589, were published a group of
Puritan pamphlets, belonging to the Marprelate controversy,
some being printed on the famous secret press, and others
by Waldegrave at Rochelle or Edinburgh. In four of these,
namely, Penry's View of Public Wants, Some in his Colours,
and the Appellation, and Martin Senior's Just Censure of Martin Junior, we find j used as it now is, e.g. "Majestic,"
"subjects," "just," etc., but v and u according to the old usage
--a strange departure from the practice of other printers of the
time, who seem invariably to have treated j and v alike in this
respect. The other tracts of the group conform in all respects
to the old rule, and we may perhaps suppose that this use of j
was the freak of some particular compositor, though there is
some difficulty in reconciling the assumed dates and places of
printing of the four tracts with their having been all set up by
the same man.

From 1589 there seems to be a gap of some years
before a fresh attempt was made by any London printer to
bring about the reform. The only London works which I
have met with between this date and the end of the century
in which the new style is followed are the Latin Bible already mentioned and the third edition of La Primaudaye's
French Academy, 1594. In this the roman v and j, U and
J, are used as at present, but roman j and J are substituted for italic ones. It may be remarked, as an instance
of the little headway which the reform was making at this
time, that in the second part of the French Academy, published together with the third edition of the first part, the

old practice is adhered to, as it is also in the case of the
third part published in 1601.

While, however, the old practice seems to have had
the upper hand in London, a curious modification of the new
was being tried at Oxford. In the year 1587 Joseph Barnes
had there printed an edition of the Sum of Christian Religion
of Z. Ursinus, in which the old system was followed throughout. In reprinting this work, however, in 1589, he introduced a curious variation in the use of v. He still kept it
in all cases as an initial letter, printing "vs," "vntil," etc.,
but medially used either u or v according as the letter represents a vowel or a consonant: thus we have "vniustly,"
"avoid," "even," etc. In the case of i he follows the old
practice.

In the next year he took a further step forward, for
in his Libellus Rogeri Baconi ... de retardandis senectutis
accidentibus, 1590, we find j used according to the modern
fashion in such words as "ejus" and "injicere," though he
still retains the old "alijs," "judicijs," etc. As regards u
and v, the same mixture of systems is followed as in the
Sum of Christian Religion, 1589, and we have "movere,"
"vnus," etc. Barnes did not use his new system in many
English books, nor in by any means all of his Latin ones,
though he did not entirely abandon it. We find it later at
London in the work of Valentine Symmes, who in 1605 followed it in two books, The School of Slovenry, a translation of Dedekind's Grobianus, and the Treatise of Spectres,
translated from P. le Loyer. Symmes prints, for example,
"vse," "abuse," "advise." With regard to i he seems to
follow the old practice, though occasionally a j appears.
Save in the work of Barnes and Symmes I have come across
no other instances of this insistance on the initial v.[25]

The only other work which I need mention lies indeed
somewhat outside the limit of date fixed, but is important as
being--so far at least as I can learn--the first folio volume
in English to employ the new method, namely, Philemon
Holland's translation of Plutarch's Moralia, printed in 1603
by Arnold Hatfield. In this we find the modern practice followed throughout, at first, it is true, with a certain number
of accidental lapses, but towards the end with great consist-
ency. In the final portion of the book we have majuscule I
and J regularly distinguished both in roman and italics. The
roman majuscule U is used in most sizes of type except the
largest, but the printer seems to have had no italic U, nor

had he in the type in which the text is printed in italic j.

    After this date the new practice seems to have spread
more and more, though it was not until about 1630 that it
became the normal one.   A reprint of an earlier work published after that date will generally substitute the modern
usage for the old, though there are still exceptions.   Sometimes the two spellings are mixed, as they are in Heywood's
Pleasant Dialogues and Drammas, 1637, where we find "alive, "
"giue," "grieves," "deuours," and the like, at first used in-
discriminately, though as the book proceeds the modern practice gets the upper hand.   In respect of the majuscules the
old spelling is retained throughout.   Such mixtures are common at the date.

    There are several subsidiary points in the history of
these letters which seem to call for investigation, but this
paper is long enough already, and in any case I fear that I
could do little more than propound queries for others to
solve.   One would like, for example, to know when j and v
first came to be admitted into the alphabet as separate and
distinct letters, and how they came to have the names by
which they are at present known.   As regards the latter point,
the evidence of rimes and puns shows clearly that in the
Elizabethan period the letter V was called "you," and the
fact that J often stands for the pronoun I seems to indicate
that our present name for the vowel symbol served alike for
both letters. [26]   Some interesting remarks bearing upon the
subject are to be found in A. Hume's Orthography and Con-
gruity of the British Tongue, written c. 1620, where, speak-
ing of the letters under discussion he says:

> Heerfoer, for distinctiones of both sound and sym-
> bol, I would commend the symbol and name of i
> and u to the vowel sound; as, indifferent, unthank-
> ful; the symbols of j and v to the latin consonants,
> and their names to be jod and vau; [27] as, vain
> jestes; and the symboles y and w to our English
> soundes, and their names to be ye and we, or yod
> and wau; as, yonder, wel, yallow, wool. [28]

    Elsewhere, in reference to the teaching of the alpha-
bet in schools, he remarks:

> I would wish ... the masters teaching their puples
> to ... name w not double u, nor v single u, as
> now they doe; but the last vau or ve, and the first

wau or we; and j, for difference of the voual i,
written with a long tail, I would wish to be called
jod or je.[29]

From these passages it seems clear that the modern
names for these letters had not yet come into use. Whether
Hume himself had anything to do with their introduction I
cannot say.

Notes

1. Vol. i., p. 336a.

2. In the article on the letter j.

3. The article is said to be by Philibert Papillon, see
    Goujet, Bibliotheque Françoise, 1741, etc., vol. i.,
    p. 43. The Continuation des Mémoires appeared in
    1726-31, but I have only seen what I presume is a
    reprint, in which vol. vii. is dated 1749. In this the
    article, which is not signed, occupies pp. 217-29.

4. According to information kindly given by Mr. Robert
    Steele the modern use of these letters in English
    Proclamations dates from September, 1637, and this
    may be taken as marking their final triumph. --Ed.

5. See N.E.D., art. j. I have not come across these
    printers, but have no reason to doubt the truth of the
    statement.

6. Thus, in books printed by Friedrich Biel at Burgos in
    1485-7 we find mejor, trabajos, viejo, etc. In Span-
    ish the letter j stood, as it does now, for a guttural
    aspirate. It is said to occur as distinct from i in
    Catalan MSS. of the fourteenth century (Grand Ency-
    clopedie, 1887, etc., art. j).

7. Even in Roman numerals we have u, as "lu," "xuii,"
    etc.

8. See Quintillian, Inst. Orat. i. 4. 8, and the commenta-
    tors thereon. The letters of Chilperic, often referred
    to in conjunction with those of Claudius, do not seem
    to have included a v or j (Greg. Turon., Hist Franc.,
    v. 45).

9. In such words as "ajuto." The sound indicated is of
    course the true consonantal sound of i, as in "Halle-
    lujah," not the sound usually associated with j in Eng-
    lish.

10. I do not follow Janiculo's spelling in all its details.

11. It may be said in passing that Trissino's scheme of
    spelling reform was both simple and valuable. It
    distinguished between close and open c and o, and be-
    tween the dz and ts pronunciation of z--things which
    have worried all who have ever tried to learn Italian
    since.

12. There was an earlier edition in 1542, which I have not
    seen.

13. It is interesting to note that this was printed at Paris
    by C. Wechel, whose successor Andreas Wechel was,
    as we shall see, the printer who had most to do with
    bringing about the change in practice.

14. The majuscule U employed by Wechel and other six-
    teenth-century printers resembles in form our u, but
    it is, nevertheless, I think, incorrect to regard it as
    being merely a lower-case u of a larger fount. When
    it is possible to compare a majuscule U with a true
    lower-case u of the same size, the letters will usu-
    ally be found to differ slightly, the majuscule being
    as a rule somewhat broader.

15. See, for example, the Monumentum of Freigius [c.
    1585], p. 24.

16. Nouv. Biog. Générale, art. Ramus.

17. Gramere, p. 24. I do not follow Ramus' reformed
    spelling.

18. The two books by Ramus which Wechel printed at Paris
    shortly before the Grammatica, namely, the Ciceroni-
    anus in 1557, and the Liber de Moribus Veterum Gal-
    lorum, 1559, both conform throughout to the old prac-
    tice as regards the letters under discussion.

19. Ames, Typog. Antiq., ed. Herbert, 664 note.

20. Ames, Typog. Antiq., ed. Herbert, p. 665.

21. op. cit., p. 668.

22. He seems only to have had italic majuscules of U and
    J in one fount, a large one used in the preface to
    the second part of the book.   Elsewhere roman maj-
    uscules are used instead.

23. I am indebted to Mr. W. W. Greg for calling my at-
    tention to Middleton's practice in this Bible.

24. In the Latin-English Dictionary which Thomas compiled
    there is some attempt to discriminate between u and
    v, and sometimes between i and j, at any rate in the
    editions of 1592 and 1596, printed by Legate.   I have
    not seen that which Thomas himself printed.   His
    Grammatice Latine ... liber secundus, 1587, may
    perhaps also follow the modern style, see title in
    Typog. Antiq., ed. Herbert, p. 1418.

25. Certain spellings in the description of the verses In
    Catilinarias proditiones ac proditores domesticos,
    1586, given in the Typographical Antiquities, suggest
    that this work may offer an earlier example of
    Barnes's mixed style as regards u and v; but I have
    not seen a copy of the book, and in such points as
    this the most accurate transcribers are likely to err.

26. See Gascoigne's Council to B. Withipoll (Works, ed.
    Hazlitt, i., 376), where 'three double Vs' rimes with
    'stewes.'   Also Day's Humour out of Breath, 1608,
    G 2 (IV., iii.): "Ass[istance].   How now? who calls?
    Hort[ensio].   Why saucie knaue tis J. Ass. You,
    what you? Hort.   A single V, I came in double, but
    I thanke them, they are gone out, and left me here a
    single-- Ass. Foole, and so I leaue you."

27. The Hebrew names by which Ramus and other spelling
    reformers generally referred to them; cf. Ramus,
    Grammaticae libri quatuor, 1560, pp. 9, 10.

28. Hume's Orthography, etc., ed. Wheatley (E.E.T.S.),
    p. 13.

29. op. cit., p. 16.

CHAPTER 3

THE SUPPOSED CALLING-IN OF
DRAYTON'S "HARMONY OF THE
CHURCH," 1591[*]

In the introduction to his edition of Poems by Michael Drayton, printed for the Roxburghe Club in 1856, pp. xi. - xii., J. P. Collier, having quoted the entry of Drayton's Harmony of the Church in the Stationers' Register on 1st February, 1590/1, proceeds to state that from a memorandum in the records of the Company, "dated in the same year," we learn that the book was seized by order of the authorities. The passage referred to is as follows:

> Whereas all the seised bookes menconed in the Laste accoumpte before this, were sould this yere to master Bysshop: Be yt Remembered that Fortye of them, beinge Harmonies of the churche[1] ratid at ij^S le peece, were had from him by warrante of my lordes grace of Canterburie and Remayne at Lambithe with master Doctor Cosen and for somme other of the said bookes, the said master bisshop hathe paid iij^u as appearethe in the charge of this accoumpte, and the Residue remayne in the hall to thuse of Yarrette James. --(Arber's Transcript, i. 543.)

Collier's statement that the Harmony was suppressed seems to have been accepted without question by all later writers on Drayton, and is repeated in every account of him which is known to me, including those in Dictionary of Na-

[*]The Library, 3d Series, Vol. I, no. 4, October 1910, pp. 348-50. This is an excellent example of McKerrow's devastatingly concise ability to correct commonly held errors. Reprinted by permission of the Council of The Bibliographical Society.

tional Biography, the Cambridge History of English Literature, and Professor Elton's monograph. In most cases as-
tonishment is expressed that a work to all appearance so innocent should have incurred official censure. It would indeed be astonishing, if it were true.

Unfortunately, however, for the theory, the memorandum in the records of the Stationers' Company upon which
it is based is not "dated in the same year" as the entry of
copyright, but occurs in the Company's accounts for the year
10th July, 1589, to 15th July, 1590, and was therefore made
at latest some six months before Drayton's work appeared.
Further, as the books to which it refers had been "men-
coned in the Laste accoumpte before this," they must have
been seized not later than 1588-9.[2] It is evidently quite impossible that Drayton's Harmony can have been among them.

As long ago as 1790 the memorandum, which Collier
thought he had been the first to notice, had been cited by
Herbert in his edition of Ames' Typographical Antiquities,
vol. iii., p. 1417, as referring to a puritan work of somewhat similar title to Drayton's, but of very different contents, namely, An Harmony of the Confessions of the faith
of the Christian and Reformed Churches, which had been published at Cambridge in 1586. That this had been called in
by authority is, as Herbert noted, definitely stated in the
Marprelate Epistle printed in the autumn of 1588, where after mentioning "the Harmonie of the Confessions of all those
Churches" the writer continues: "Which Harmonie, was
translated and printed by that puritan Cambridg printer,
Thomas Thomas. And although the booke came out by pub-
like authoritie, yet by your leaue the Bishops haue called
them in, as things against their state" (Epistle, ed. Arber,
p. 8).

There is then no reason for doubting that it was to
this Harmony of the Confessions, and not to Drayton's work,
that the memorandum in the Stationers' Register refers.

Notes

1. Herbert, Typ. Antiq., iii. p. 1417, prints Harmonies
    of the Churches.

2. Indeed, from certain memoranda in earlier accounts
       (Arber's Transcript, i. 521, 524, 525, 530, 535), it
       seems probable that they were seized in 1586-7.

CHAPTER 4

THE RED PRINTING IN THE 1611 BIBLE*

The article by Mr. Horace Hart on "The Red Printing in the 1611 Bible," in the April number of The Library,
is of great interest to all those bibliographers who care for
an exact knowledge of how the early printers worked, but,
rash as it may seem to differ from so great an authority
on practical printing, I venture to question whether he has
not in certain respects been too much influenced by his fa-
miliarity with modern methods of work. Little seems to
have been written about red printing in the seventeenth century, but there has been a certain amount of discussion of
the methods followed at a somewhat earlier date, and there
is now, I believe, little difference of opinion regarding
them.[1] I wish to suggest that the printer of the 1611 Bible
worked on exactly the same lines as his predecessors.

The usual process of printing in red and black during the sixteenth century seems to have been as follows:[2]

1. The printer set up and proved the whole forme,
red and black together.

2. He then cut out a frisket so as to allow only the
red to print.[3] The soft packing used in the tympan would
drive the paper down sufficiently to allow it to reach the type
through the holes in the frisket.[4]

3. The red having been printed, the forme was
cleaned and the portions that had been printed in red were
taken out, and the spaces left by them were filled with quads.

*The Library, 3d Series, Vol. II, no. 7, July 1911, pp.
323-27. This is a definitive statement on two-color printing
in the sixteenth century based on physical evidence and observation. Reprinted by permission of the Council of The
Bibliographical Society.

The frisket was also removed.

4.   What was left of the forme was then inked with black ink, and the sheets were run through again.

The points of difference in the method described by Mr. Hart are: (1) That, according to him, the black was printed first; (2) that underlays were used to bring up first the black and then the red above type height; (3) that the red portions remained in the forme throughout the whole process.

To take these in their order.   Whether the red or the black was printed first can often be determined by examination, for unless the register is quite perfect it will usually be found that here and there one ink is on the top of the other.   In the case of many sixteenth century books it is quite clear that the black ink is on the top of the red, and that the red, therefore, must have been printed first.[5] I believe that if Mr. Hart will have another look at the 1611 Bible he will find that this is the case there also.   In a copy which I have examined at the British Museum the black seems to be quite clearly on the top, and Dr. Greg tells me that the same is true of a copy which he has examined at Cambridge.

That underlaying was not necessary may be seen by inspection of some of the folio Bibles printed by Barker towards the end of the sixteenth century.[6] These have a woodcut border to the title and, at the end of the preliminary matter, a full-page woodcut of Adam and Eve in the Garden of Eden.   Parts of both these woodcuts, such as the royal emblems and the hair of the putti in the corners of the title-page, and the faces of the lions, etc., in the Garden of Eden, are printed both in red and black.   The slight error in register causes the red lines to appear alongside the black, producing a peculiar brown or bronze-like effect. In this case underlaying was obviously impossible, for the parts printed in red and black are on the same block as those printed in black alone, and, therefore, cannot have been raised above the general level.   Underlaying is a troublesome process, and if the printer could do without it in this case, why not in others?

That the red portions were removed after the first printing seems to me to be deducible from a careful examination of the calendar of almost any red and black Bible of the time--including that of 1611.   When horizontal rules print accidentally both in red and black, it will, I think almost always be found that, on any one page, the red lines are either all above or all below the black ones, showing that the arrangement of the forme has not been disturbed vertically.   In the case of vertical rules printing in both colours, however, we very frequently find that the red line appears sometimes to the right and sometimes to the left of the black one, [7] showing that there has been some lateral disturbance of the forme between the two printings.   Now, surely, this is just what would happen if the red words or letters had been taken out, and the quads, or spaces, inserted to fill up the room of each had not exactly done so; [8] and otherwise it seems difficult to account for.   Further, the red portions seem never to be partially duplicated in black ink, as the black portions are in red.   If they remained in the forme during the whole process it is not easy to understand this, especially as these red portions are generally surrounded by black, and the use of a frisket to prevent them from printing is therefore out of the question.

Notes

1.   At any rate as regards the second half of the sixteenth century.   The process is described in Mr. Robert Steele's Earliest English Music Printing, 1903, pp. 4-5.   There is considerable doubt as to how some of the earliest printing in two or more colours was done; cf. R. M. Burch, Colour Printing, 1910, pp. 4-6.

2.   Leaving out of account the possibility of the forme having sometimes been dissected according to the method commonly employed now-a-days.   It has been stated that this method was also used, but the evidence for it does not seem to be conclusive.   Irregularities in the casting of the type and in the furniture would, one might suppose, have made it difficult to obtain perfect register from two formes.

3.   A number of frisket sheets used in printing certain sixteenth century service-books were found some years ago by Mr. Robert Steele.   I am indebted to Mr. R. A. Peddie for showing me one of them now in the Technical Library of the St. Bride's Foundation. From their condition Mr. Steele infers that the printer

inked the whole forme with red ink, not merely the
immediate neighbourhood of the red words, as one
might have supposed. The method seems wasteful of
ink, besides being very messy, and one would have
expected the ink to creep along the edges of the frisket holes and impress the outline of them on the paper, unless, indeed, ink was used which dried extremely quickly. More might perhaps be learnt from
these frisket sheets if the work in the production of
which they were used could be identified. Of a suggested alternative method--namely, inking through a
similarly cut stencil or mask--I have seen no evidence, but as the inking was done by balls, it might
have been a workable plan, and there would have been
no difficulty in devising an attachment so that such a
stencil could be quickly placed in position for each
inking.

4.   It may be remarked that the underlaying method de-
     scribed by Mr. Hart necessitates the paper being
     driven down at least as much, for otherwise how did
     the rules, etc., which were not underlayed, contrive
     to print?

5.   I have not come across any book in which the black ap-
     pears to have been printed first; but, of course, if a
     forme was to be principally in red, with only a few
     black words here and there, one would expect the usu-
     al order to be reversed.

6.   I may refer to the one dated 1591. This has the inter-
     esting peculiarity that in the heading of August in the
     calendar the month was first stated (in red) to have
     xxx. days. In the black printing a j was printed over
     the full-stop of the xxx.

7.   Even when on any one page all the red lines appear on
     the same side of the black ones, the space between
     them will generally be found to vary considerably.

8.   If, I mean, in filling up the spaces left by two or more
     red words in a line the printer had put rather too
     much in one space and too little in another, so that
     the intervening portions of the line were moved to left
     or right. Of course the total amount inserted would
     have had to be equal to the total length of the words
     removed.

CHAPTER 5

BOOKSELLERS, PRINTERS, AND THE STATIONERS' TRADE*

There were many things in the England of Shakespeare upon which we can look back with satisfaction and even with pride to-day, but among these the condition of printing, and of the book trade in general, is certainly not to be numbered. Not unpromising in its beginnings, the art of printing never developed in England as it did on the Continent: with very few exceptions the books produced here are not to be compared, whether in beauty, in correctness, or in perfection of workmanship, with the ordinary output of the chief foreign presses. More especially during the century 1551-1650 was there a steady decline not only in the mechanical art of the press, but in the enterprise, ability, and social position of the masters and men engaged in all the various branches of book production and distribution. In the earlier part of the period we indeed find a few printers, such as Richard Grafton, John Day, and Reynold Wolfe, who were men of education and even of learning, but how far are even these from ranking with the Etiennes at Paris and Geneva, Paolo and Aldo Manuzio at Venice, the Elzevirs at Leyden, or Christoffel Plantin at Antwerp! Later, the trade came more and more into the hands of an inferior class, until the great majority of those who dealt in books were tradesmen pure and simple regarding their business solely from the point of view of immediate returns.

There were two chief reasons for this inferiority of the English book-trade. In the first place, the press was

---

*Shakespeare's England, Vol. 2, Oxford, 1916, pp. 212-39. This is a lucid and significant discussion of the Elizabethan "publishing industry." Reprinted by permission of The Clarendon Press, Oxford.

in the main a vernacular one, and lacked the consideration
which would have been lent to it by the association of the
learned.   The circulation of elaborate and expensive editions
of the Greek and Latin classics in England alone was insufficient to make their production remunerative, even if England had been more favourably situated than it was as regards manuscript sources, and the demand for such works
was easily and cheaply supplied by importation from abroad.
English printers and publishers not unnaturally preferred to
invest their money and labour in wares more readily saleable, and so far as they printed the classics at all, devoted
their attention mainly to cheap editions for school purposes.
We meet with several complaints on the part of scholars of
the difficulty of getting their works properly printed in this
country, and of the want of enterprise shown by the trade in
general.

The second and indeed chief cause of the general
slackness was the censorship which was exercised by the
Government over all kinds of book production.   This, while
far from efficient as regards the purpose for which it was
instituted, produced its usual effect of diminishing the enterprise and lowering the character of all who came under its
influence.   It was indeed of such importance in its results
upon the trade in general that it will be necessary to give
some account of its beginnings and progress.

In the early years of printing in this country there
appears to have been little, if any, attempt at control on the
part of the authorities, and practically the sole official recognition which the trade received was the appointment from
time to time of a King's Printer.   Even when the State began to concern itself in the matter, its attention was at first
entirely directed to the foreign printers resident in England,
and to the importers of books from abroad, and its action
was designed to protect the native workman.   In 1484 an Act
to regulate the conditions under which foreigners might trade
in England had expressly excluded from its provisions scriveners, binders, and printers, who were allowed to carry on
their business where and how they pleased.   This complete
free trade in books lasted until 1523, when an Act was
passed forbidding aliens who practised any handicraft in England from taking other apprentices than English-born, and
from keeping more than two foreign journeymen.   The Act
makes no special mention of printers, who are, however, of
course included among handicraftsmen.   In 1529 a more
stringent Act was passed which had the effect of preventing

any further establishment of foreign presses in England, but did not interfere with those already existing. The last of these ordinances which we need notice was in 1534, when the importation of <u>bound</u> books was prohibited, and the purchase from foreigners of any books printed abroad, except for the purpose of the wholesale trade, was forbidden. Aliens were, in fact, simply to act as importers, selling their wares to the English booksellers, not direct to the public. Mr. Duff notes that these enactments against aliens were so effective that "whereas in the first forty years after the introduction of printing into England the majority of persons connected with the book trade were foreigners, the second forty years saw this state of things entirely changed, all the important men of business being Englishmen, and the foreigners decreasing in number and status."

The year 1538 saw the commencement of a long series of enactments of a different kind; those, namely, which had for their object the suppression of treasonable or heretical literature. Before, however, we turn to these, it may be well to say something as to the purpose and justification of the Tudor censorship in general. Theoretically the control seems to have been theological, political, and moral; practically, however, it was exercised solely for political purposes, though the books censored were, for the most part, theological. It is generally hard for a later generation to understand the workings of the censorship in an earlier one, or to see why one book is deemed obnoxious, while another far more revolutionary in its teachings is allowed to pass, but it seems clear that the principal anxiety of those who directed the censorship was to prevent the circulation of anything which could bring into question the unity and authority of the Established Church, whatever at the time it might be. Heresy as heresy mattered little, what did matter was the danger of schism; there was nothing of religious bigotry, or even of the desire to save souls; the intention was throughout political, to avoid the danger of civil dissension.

That the censorship was so exercised is its main defence, even, some may think, its justification; for the unity of the English Church was, in the sixteenth century, vital to a degree which we can now scarcely realize. To the mass of the people outside London the Church was the chief visible symbol of the unity of the State: in days when communication was so slow and the dissemination of news so irregular, it must indeed have been practically the only one. Without it, a centralizing Government of the Elizabethan type

would hardly have been possible. The maintenance of that
unity was, then, indispensable; and if we grant this, we cannot greatly blame the Government for objecting, in so important a matter, to a freedom of discussion for which the
times were clearly not ripe.

The various injunctions, proclamations, and decrees
establishing or confirming the censorship are so closely in-
terconnected and in some points so obscure that it is impossible to give an intelligible account of them in a few words,
and those desirous of knowing more about them must be referred to Mr. Duff's introduction to his Century of the English Book Trade and to that by the present writer to A Dictionary of Printers, 1557-1640. The importance of the earlier decrees at any rate is overshadowed by the great change
which was made in the conditions and status of the book-
trade by the incorporation of the Stationers' Company on
May 4, 1557.

Next to the establishment of Caxton's press at West-
minster eighty years earlier, this was the most important
event in the history of English printing. The Company was
indeed not altogether a new thing. It had existed since 1404
in the form originally of a brotherhood of scriveners or
copyists, and seems to have admitted printers to membership almost as soon as the art was introduced into England.
Unfortunately, however, no records of its doings earlier
than 1554 are now extant, and practically nothing is known
of its early history. The incorporation in 1557 made probably little difference in the membership of the society, but
it profoundly altered its position and power of constituting
it to the official authority over the whole of the book trade
in the country, and holding it responsible for the doings of
its members. For the future almost all decrees as to the
printing and sale of books were issued in the form of in-
structions to the master and wardens of the Company, who
were to see to their being carried out.

The charter of incorporation sets forth that the society shall consist in the first instance of a master, two
wardens, and ninety-four freemen, all of whom are named,
being "freemen of the mystery or art of a stationer of our
city of London and suburbs thereof." They are authorized
to hold meetings to elect their master and wardens from
time to time, make such rules as are necessary for the
well-being of the society, own a limited amount of property
in London, and sue and be sued as a corporate body. They

are given the sole rights of printing throughout England, saving that other persons may be permitted to print by royal warrant, and the wardens are empowered to search the premises of any "stamper, printer, binder, or seller of any manner of books within our kingdom of England," and to seize any books printed "contrary to the form of any statute, act, or proclamation made or to be made." They may burn the books thus seized, and imprison the printer of them, or any one resisting them in their search, for three months, and fine him 100s., the fine going half to the Company and half to the Crown.

It is unnecessary to insist on the immense importance of this charter to the trade. Not only did it give the Company supreme power over printing, but the right of search permitted the wardens to exercise quite effective, if somewhat anomalous, control over all stationers, publishers, importers of books, or bookbinders not belonging to the Company, as well as over its own members. From the point of view of the Government it was an excellent piece of policy, for it is easy to see how much more effective a search for contraband literature or secret presses would be if made by the wardens of the Company, familiar as they were with every detail of the business, than if--as was formerly the case--it was entrusted to bishops and justices of the peace, who might fail to recognize printing materials even when they found them.

The charter of the stationers was confirmed by Queen Elizabeth in 1559, and in the same year began the strict censorship, which was maintained--at least in intention-- throughout the reign. Twenty-one years before, it had been ordered that certain classes of books should not be printed without having been previously examined by the King or the Privy Council, but there is little evidence that this rule was strictly enforced. Now in 1559 we find new injunctions on much the same lines, but far more precise. According to these,

> no manner of person shall print any manner of book or paper of what sort, nature, or in what language soever it be, except the same be first licensed by her Majesty by express words in writing, or by six of her Privy Council or be perused and licensed by the Archbishops of Canterbury and York, the Bishop of London, the Chancellors of both Universities, the bishop being ordinary, and

the Archdeacon also of the place where any such
shall be printed, or by two of them, whereof the
Ordinary of the place to be always one.

The names of such as shall allow the book are to be
added at the end--presumably at the end of the manuscript--
"for a testimony of the allowance thereof." Similarly,
pamphlets, plays, and ballads, which appear not to come under the description of "any manner of book or paper," are,
before printing, to be approved by at least three members
of the Court of Ecclesiastical Commission; and, lastly, all
books dealing with religion, polity, or government, whether
printed abroad or at home, are to be submitted to the same
body, which may permit or prohibit them at its discretion.
The only exception to these rules is in favour of books which
have been or are generally used in universities and schools.
The injunction is addressed especially to the Wardens and
Company of the Stationers, who are evidently expected to see
it carried out.

In 1559 and for some years after, a few printers
made use, on their title-pages, of some such formula as
"Set forth and allowed according to the order appointed in
the Queen's Majesty's Injunctions," to indicate that the terms
of the injunctions had been complied with. Later we sometimes find "Seen and allowed" (as on the title-page of the
first edition of Bacon's Essays, 1597), less frequently "Perused and allowed"; at the end of Stubbes's Anatomie of Abus-
es (1583) there is an example of a much fuller form:

> Perused, authorised, and allowed, according to the
> order appointed in the Queen's Majesty's Injunc-
> tions.

We need not delay over a Star Chamber decree of
1566, much on the same lines, but further requiring that all
engaged in the trade should enter into recognizances of reasonable sums of money to observe the law, and we may pass
at once to the still more stringent enactment of 1586. By
this time it was provided that all printers should deliver a
note of the number of their presses and of any which they
should erect hereafter. There was to be no printing save at
London, Cambridge, and Oxford. In view of the excessive
number of printers already in business--some fifty-three in
London, as we know from other sources--the erection of any
new presses was forbidden until the number should be dimin-
ished. On its being decided by the Archbishop of Canterbury

and the Bishop of London that there was room for a new
printer, they were to inform the master and wardens of the
Stationers' Company, and the Company should then elect out
of their number a fit person to have the grant of a license.
Severe punishments were decreed against the use or possession of any secret press and against the printing of anything
which had not been perused and allowed by the Archbishop
of Canterbury and the Bishop of London or one of them.
Lastly, the number of apprentices that might be taken by
any printer is limited.

This was in several respects the most important enactment dealing with the press during the period. From
1586 until after Shakespeare's death there is nothing which
materially alters the position of affairs.

Such, then, were the chief regulations affecting the
book trade in the sixteenth century. They were severe
enough, and should have rendered quite impossible the sale
and circulation literature obnoxious to the authorities. Like
many Elizabethan ordinances they seem, however, to have
been very irregularly observed--indeed, so much is indicated by their being several times renewed. Secret printing seems to have gone on almost continuously until towards
the close of the century, and there must also have been
much smuggling of forbidden books from the Continent. It
is improbable that the demand for contraband literature was
anything like what it was for Lutheran books in Henry VIII's
days, when, according to John Foxe the martyrologist,
"some gave five marks, some more, some less, for a
book; some gave a load of hay for a few chapters of St.
James, or of St. Paul in English," but now there were both
the Catholics and the extreme Puritans to be supplied, and
one can imagine that the trade would be fairly profitable.
Even apart from that secret printing which was in intentional defiance of the law, there seems to have been much slackness in obeying the regulations as to licensing. The authorities named in the injunctions could not of course themselves
peruse all the books which were submitted for license, and
frequently delegated their functions to others: it is not improbable that it was only when books were by suspected authors or upon dangerous subjects that any care was taken
that the orders should be strictly followed. Unfortunately in
the case of a very large number of works we have no evidence whether they were licensed or not.

Little or nothing in the shape of reports or discus-

sions of the working of the censorship has come down to us.
Our knowledge of it is, save for the injunctions and a few
miscellaneous papers dealing with special cases, derived almost entirely from the records of the Stationers' Company.
These records, which happily are almost complete from the
date of the incorporation of the company to the present time,
deal of course with a variety of matters: among them are
lists of apprentices taken by the various members, proceedings of official meetings, fines levied for offences, as well
as the ordinary accounts of the Company, but their chief interest to us at the present day is that they include a series
of entries of books published. This is of the highest bibliographical importance, for it enables us to ascertain the date
of original publication of many works of which the early editions are undated or have disappeared, and incidentally tells
us much about the licensing. The original purpose of these
entries seems to have been as a register of copyright. Any
member of the Company proposing to publish a book was apparently entitled and even required to have it entered to his
name upon payment of a small fee, and, provided that no objection was raised to the entry on the ground of a prior
claim, he then had the sole right of printing or publishing it
for the future. Presumably the register was open to inspection by members of the Company in order that they might
guard their interests in this respect. Transfers of copyright from one publisher to another were often, though by no
means always, recorded in the same list.

The register of copyrights seems, however, to have
served at the same time another purpose, namely, as a cer-
tification that the conditions imposed by the law had been
duly complied with. Whenever a license was required, the
wardens of the Company apparently demanded the production
of the license before permitting the entry of the book in the
register. Thus, although the Company in no way took any
direct part in the censorship, an entry in the register--at
any rate from about 1566 onwards--may be taken to imply,
in the absence of any statement to the contrary, that the
book had been duly submitted to the censors and passed by
them. From 1569 onwards the name of the licenser--in early
times generally the Bishop of London--is frequently given in
the entry.

There is evidence that all books were supposed to be
entered in the register of the Company, with the exception
of certain classes of works which were the monopoly of particular firms, such as Bibles, almanacks, and a few school-

books. Many books, however, were published without this having been done. The reason for the omission is not clear, for the fee demanded was too small to be worth serious consideration when set against the possibility of losing the copyright of a book by non-payment. In some cases it is probable that the printer was not anxious to call undue attention to his work, in others the cause of non-entry may have been simply carelessness, or the conviction that the book was not one which would run to a second edition, and that therefore it would be a waste of time and money to secure the copyright. Whatever the reason, this irregularity in the entries must make us suspect that there was similar irregularity in submitting works for license.

The influence of the censorship upon the book trade was undoubtedly bad, in the main because it tended to stifle free competition among the printing houses. Success must have depended far less upon enterprise or good workmanship than on being in favour with the authorities. A printer who stood well with them would no doubt have a much better chance of getting books that had been submitted by him, or which he was known to be about to print, licensed quickly, than one who was regarded with dislike or suspicion. As we know from more than one complaint, the work of Puritan writers was especially liable to long delays, even when a license was finally granted; and the whole system must inevitably have led to favouritism of the worst kind. On the other hand, it can hardly be maintained that literature suffered at all by it. There is, so far as the writer is aware, not a single instance of a work of literary importance having been lost to us through the refusal to license it; though of course we cannot say what might have been written had freer criticism of current affairs been permitted. But even had there been no formal censorship, there would undoubtedly have been other checks on the publication of anything seriously obnoxious to Queen Elizabeth or her ministers.

The Puritan grievance is loudly voiced by Stubbes in A Motive to good Workes (1593):

> I cannot but lament the corruption of our time, for (alas) now-a-days it is grown to be a hard matter to get a good book licensed without staying, peradventure, a quarter of a year for it; yea, sometimes two or three years before he can have it allowed, and in the end happily rejected too; so that that which many a good man hath ... travailed long

> in ... shall ... never see the light; whilst ...
> other bookes, full of all filthines, scurrility,
> baudry, dissolutenes, cosenage, conycatching and
> the like ... are either quickly licensed, or at
> least easily tollerate.

By the censorship the whole body of the trade was affected alike, but there was another practice of the day which bore especially hardly on the smaller printing-houses. This was the granting by the Queen of monopolies for the printing of certain classes of books. Thus at one time Jugge had the sole right of printing Bibles and Testaments, Tottle of printing law-books, Roberts and Watkins of almanacks and prognostications, Marsh of certain school-books. John Day of the A B C and the Catechism, and so on. A decennial monopoly granted to Day for the printing of Ascham's Scholemaster is indicated at the foot of the title-page by the legend, "Cum Gratia et Privilegio Regiae Maiestatis, per Decennium." Even persons who were not printers at all might be granted privileges of this kind; thus, the musician, William Byrd, had a monopoly of music-books and paper ruled for music, and one Francis Flower, a gentleman, had the sole right of printing Lily's Grammar, a right which he farmed out to a group of printers for £100 a year. The existence of these patents was naturally a great grievance to the poorer members of the Company, for it deprived them of much of the most profitable work, and there was in 1582 a serious attempt at revolt, which at one time threatened to cause a split in the society. Several of the younger members declared their intention of printing whatever seemed to them good, without regard to the patents, and their action resulted in the Star Chamber case of John Day against Roger Ward and William Holmes for illegally printing the A B C and Catechism in contravention of his privilege. The matter was eventually settled by the patentees agreeing to give up a number of their most valuable monopolies for the benefit of needy members of the Company.

The history of the formula, "Cum privilegio ad imprimendum solum"--used by Shakespeare in The Taming of the Shrew, IV. iv. 93, with allusion to marriage rites--is somewhat curious. It has recently been pointed out by Mr. A. W. Pollard that the original intention of the phrase was to make clear that no other privilege had been granted than that of a mere license to print. Hence, in 1538, printers were expressly forbidden to use the words "cum privilegio regali" without adding "ad imprimendum solum." Later,

however, it was taken to mean that the printer had a monopoly of printing the book, and it is evidently in this sense
that Shakespeare understood it.

Up to this point we have treated the book trade as
though it were a homogeneous body all engaged in the same
business. It seems certainly to have been so regarded by
the Government, but, in reality, the distinctions between the
several branches of printer, publisher, bookseller, and
bookbinder, were clearly recognized, although there was a
good deal more overlapping than there is at present. As
regards the two first we shall not be far wrong if we say
that, at any rate towards the close of the sixteenth century,
all printers were also publishers, but many publishers were
not printers; this being indeed what we might expect from
the strict limitation in the number of printers and from the
fact that publishers did not necessarily belong to the Stationers' Company, whereas printers did. There seems to
be no evidence of any master printer who was merely a
printer, that is to say, who did not himself deal to some
extent in copyrights and issue books on his own account. On
the other hand, even as early as 1582, we learn that the
smaller printers were becoming financially dependent upon
the publishers. In that year Christopher Barker, the Queen's
Printer, reporting on the condition of the trade, said that
the provision of type, etc., was so costly that most of the
printers were driven to compound beforehand with the booksellers (i.e. publishers) at such low rates for their work
that they made little, if any, profit. The booksellers now,
he says, keep no printing-house, but merely pay for the
workmanship. In this report we have a clear indication that
the two branches of the trade were tending to become altogether distinct, though it was some time before they actually became so.

Printing and publishing were then recognized as separate trades: can we say the same thing of publishing and
bookselling? On the whole it seems not; but the evidence is
too scanty to enable us to speak with certainty on the point.
It seems clear that the publishers, as well as many printers,
had open stalls either in St. Paul's Churchyard or before
their own houses, at which they sold books; what we do not
know is whether the books which they sold were their own
publications alone or whether they dealt in all books, new
and second-hand. The most probable view seems to be that
the larger publishers dealt chiefly in their own works, but
also did a certain amount of business in foreign books as

well as in English books of the better class, while the
smaller firms, who published little themselves, carried on
a general trade in the cheaper literature. Such general
book-shops are referred to in the prologue to Rowlands's
Tis Merrie when Gossips meete, and in Dekker's Guls
Horne-booke.

A good deal of bookselling was, as we should expect,
done at Oxford and Cambridge, and there were 'stationers'
at several of the larger provincial towns, but the amount of
their trade in books cannot be ascertained with certainty.
The lighter literature probably found a ready sale at the numerous fairs throughout the country, and ballads were sold
by itinerant hawkers. London, however, was during the
whole period the main book-mart for the country, and this
not only because there was, save at the Universities, no
printing outside it, but at least as much on account of the
great influx from the provinces which took place into London
at each of the four law-terms.

Few personal details have been preserved of the
Elizabethan printers and publishers; not one of them seems
to have been of remarkable attainments. Save for one or
two of the University printers and a London compositor who
was also a pamphleteer and dramatist--Henry Chettle--we
find among them no scholars, no authors, and hardly even
a compiler of importance. They were merchants pure and
simple. One or two of them such as Waldegrave the Puritan have some small place in religious history, but the most
noteworthy are known for their commercial achievements
alone. For the most part they entered the trade at an early
age as apprentices and could have had no opportunity for an
extended education: only one or two were university men,
who took up printing or publishing comparatively late in life,
having been originally intended for some profession. They
came from various classes of society: many were the sons
of earlier stationers or printers; others the sons of well-to-
do tradesmen or of smaller professional men. Christopher
Barker, the Queen's Printer from 1577 to 1588, owner of
what was probably the largest business of the time, is said
to have been related to a Garter King of Arms of the same
name, and at the time of his death was a person of considerable wealth. The brothers John and William Jaggard, the
latter of whom printed the First Folio of Shakespeare, were
the sons of a barber surgeon of London. Robert Dexter,
publisher of a large number of popular books, was the son
of a sailor of Ipswich. Richard Field, the printer of Shake-

speare's earliest works, Venus and Adonis (1593) and Lu-
crece (1594) was the son of a tanner of Stratford-on-Avon,
and it has been plausibly conjectured that it was owing to
his being a fellow townsman that these works came into his
hands to print.   He became one of the most important of
contemporary printers, was Master of the Stationers' Company in 1616 and 1622, and died in 1624.   Nothing is known
of his connexion with Shakespeare, and after the two early
poems he printed no more of his work.   As Field's output
consisted mainly of large and serious volumes, and as he
hardly touched popular literature at all, this fact has no significance.

        Turning now from questions of the trade in general,
let us consider the actual process of the publication of a
book in Elizabethan times.   It is first to be remarked that
there seems to have been a considerable circulation of works
in manuscript.   Not only was much verse circulated in this
form, without ever getting into print at all, but occasionally
larger works were thus handed about among the friends of
the author.   A well-known example is that of Sidney's Arcadia, which, written in the years 1580-3, was already famous by 1587, though it was not printed until three years
later.   There is evidence of a certain amount of trade in
manuscript copies of books, carried on by scriveners, but
this can hardly have been very large.   Comparatively few of
the manuscript copies of Elizabethan works which have come
down to the present time have the appearance of having been
written by professional scribes, though one would expect that
from their greater neatness and legibility these would have
been more valued and more likely to be preserved than private copies.   They would of course in comparison with
printed books have been very expensive, certainly no cheaper
than a transcript of a modern work of equal size made at
the present day; indeed, considering that writing was by no
means a universal accomplishment, it is reasonable to suppose that they would have been dearer.   On the other hand
printed books were, as we shall see, little more expensive
than they are to-day.

        Apparently transcripts of a manuscript were made
without restriction, [1] for although such copying was as illegal
as it is at present, detection was probably difficult and pros-
ecution certainly not worth while.   The same was probably
true also of the printing of such transcripts: we find frequent complaints that a work has been published without the
knowledge or consent of the author or his representatives,

but instances in which action was taken in consequence are very few. We do, however, hear of one work the publication of which was stopped for this reason. This was Sidney's Arcadia, and the fact is known to us from a letter written in November 1586, a month after the author's death, by Sir Fulke Greville to Sir Francis Walsingham. The writer states that he has learnt from one Ponsonby, a book-binder, that some one intends to print the work. Ponsonby, who is presumably identical with the bookseller of the name by whom the Arcadia was eventually issued, had inquired whether this was being done by the consent of Sidney's friends, and had advised that, if this was not so, notice should be given to the Archbishop of Canterbury or to Dr. Cosin, who had copies for perusal with a view to licensing. Probably representations were made and the license refused, for the book did not appear until 1590, but the course proposed for stopping publication strongly suggests that there was no regular or direct way of doing it, and that one who could not bring influence to bear with the licensers might have found difficulty in protecting his rights in similar circumstances.

Having obtained the manuscript, the publisher, before sending it to press, would have to see that the work was properly licensed and, if he thought fit, would enter it at Stationers' Hall. He would then, if not a printer himself, contract with one for the printing of the work. The printer might, if he had a large establishment, employ journeymen or apprentices to set it up in type on the premises, or he might, according to a curious and, one would imagine, most inconvenient system, give out the work to compositors to be set up in their own homes, only doing the actual printing himself. While the work was being printed the author would often visit the printing-house for the purpose of reading the proofs, and sometimes had the type corrected during the actual progress of the impression, with the result that differences frequently occur in copies of the same edition of a book, in some cases extending to the insertion or omission of whole lines. There is much of interest in the study of the actual processes of Elizabethan printing, a knowledge of which will often be found to throw light on points of textual criticism and even of literary history, but any attempt to discuss such matters here would lead us into technicalities alien to the design of the present work.

We may, however, notice in passing the employment from quite an early date of literary men as publishers' advisers, editors, or correctors of the press. In the economy of the Elizabethan printing-house such persons had never anything approaching the importance or status that they had on the Continent, but it seems clear that some of the chief printers had a connexion with one or more scholars or writers who assisted them when required.   Thus John Foxe, after being a reader of the press with Johann Herbst, or Oporinus, at Basle during Mary's reign, lived on his return to England for some time with the printer of the English edition of his Actes and Monuments, John Day, and took prominent part in his business.   We hear later of Gabriel Harvey, Barnabe Barnes, Thomas Nashe, and other literary men of the day as lodging in printers' houses, and we may suppose that the arrangement was a profitable one for both parties. Precise details on this point, as on so many others affecting the means of livelihood of Elizabethan men of letters, are, however, wanting.

The number of copies of a book which in Shakespeare's time formed an "edition" is another matter about which little is known.   In or about 1586 the Stationers' Company had ordered that no more than 1,250 copies of an ordinary book should be printed; if more were needed the type must be distributed and set up afresh, the object of this regulation being that work should be more evenly distributed between compositors and press-men.   An exception was made in the case of a few school-books and others for which the demand was very great: of these double the number, or even more, might be printed.   We may presume that in fixing the number 1,250 as a maximum, regard would have been had to the number of copies likely to be required of the most popular books, such as Robert Greene's pamphlets and the like, and a few favourite plays: more serious and more extensive works could hardly have had a sale approaching this.   It has been estimated that the number printed of the First Folio of Shakespeare's plays was from 500 to 600, but we have no direct evidence on the point.

To turn now to the question of price.   None of the very few booksellers' catalogues that have come down to us from early times makes any mention of price, and it is consequently very difficult to arrive at a clear idea of the average cost of new, and especially of the larger publications. We do not even know whether books, apart from certain service-books for which a maximum charge was fixed by the authorities, had any definite price at all, or whether the bookseller got what he could for them.   The absence of any established style of "publishers" binding--unless we regard

the common limp vellum covers as one--must have prevented
the better class of books from having a price absolutely
fixed, but it seems likely that the price of pamphlet literature was fixed. Occasionally, but very rarely, the price of
a book is mentioned in the book itself. Thus we learn that
The Forrest of Fancy, a pamphlet by H. C. published in
1579, was sold at a shilling, and that the quarto of Troilus
and Cressida, published in 1609, cost a testern, i. e. six-
pence. The first of these works is a quarto of 80 leaves,
that is to say of about twice the length of such a play as
The Merchant of Venice. The quarto of Troilus and Cressida is slightly thicker than the average play: it contains
48 leaves. A work of either Nashe or Harvey, probably the
former's Have with you to Saffron-walden (84 leaves), cost
five groats (1s. 8d.) and, according to John Davies of Hereford, was very dear at the price. There are numerous references to twopenny and threepenny pamphlets, but it is
doubtful whether these expressions are to be taken literally
or have merely a depreciatory sense. Even more caution
must be used in accepting the entries in diaries and accounts
of prices paid for books, for on the one hand it is seldom
certain that the book was a new copy, and on the other it
may have been in an elaborate binding, which would of course
add greatly to its value. On the whole we shall probably be
not far wrong if we suppose the ordinary quarto play to have
been sold, sewn or 'stabbed' at 4d. or 6d., or in a vellum
wrapper at 8d. or 9d. The greater part of the pamphlet
literature--Greene's, Dekker's, Rowlands's, &c.--would probably cost about the same. Of course if properly bound in
leather such books would be considerably more expensive,
but thin pamphlets would seldom, if ever, be bound in this
way, unless several were bound together.

Of larger works it is quite impossible to say anything definite. They were probably sold bound, and much
depended on the style of the binding. It has generally been
said that the First Folio of Shakespeare cost £1 when new,
but the statement should be received with caution, for it appears to rest on no more than a manuscript note cited by
George Steevens[2] as occurring in a copy then in the possession of Messrs. White, booksellers in Fleet Street. The
copy does not seem to be now known, and until it is found
we must not attach too much importance to Steevens's statement. It is not clear that the note of price is contemporary
with the original publication, nor do we know how the volume
was bound.

Assuming then that a play such as <u>The Merchant of</u>
<u>Venice</u> cost 6d. in Elizabethan money, we have to consider
what the equivalent value of this sum would be at the present day. We shall probably not be far wrong if we say
about 2s. 6d. or 3s. --in fact not very much more than the
price of a new play at the present time, and modern plays
are as a rule much shorter than Elizabethan. There seems,
on the whole, little reason to think that, so far as new books
were concerned, prices were appreciably higher than at the
present day. Whatever cheapening there has been is in the
reprints of standard works, for which nothing is paid to the
author.

The only other point which remains for discussion is
the question of the means taken by the publisher to bring
new works to the notice of the public. Caxton, as is well
known, soon after the establishment of his press in England,
printed an advertisement to inform the public where certain
service-books were to be procured, but after his time we
hear hardly anything of publishers' advertisements for a century and a half. About 1650 it became quite usual to add at
the end of a volume a list of other works to be sold by the
same stationer, and the practice has continued. A few service-books contain a statement of the price not only of the
book itself but of others, but with this exception there seems
in this country to have been nothing of the nature of a bookseller's catalogue until the appearance of the well-known
<u>Catalogue of English printed Bookes,</u> by the stationer, An-
drew Maunsell, of which the first and second parts were issued in 1595. These two parts contain the divisions of the-
ology and science: unfortunately the others, which would
have included poetry and imaginative literature, never appeared. But even this work is not to be regarded exactly
as a bookseller's catalogue, for, although Maunsell probably
intended it to serve the purposes of his business, it is not
merely a list of the books which he himself had for sale,
but one as complete as he could make it of all that had appeared in England. It is in fact an attempt to do for this
country what had been done for the learned literature of the
Continent in the <u>Bibliotheca Universalis</u> of Conrad Gesner,
or the condensed <u>Elenchus Scriptorum</u> of Wolffhart, and the
public utility of the work was recognized by the Stationers'
Company, who made to Maunsell a grant of money and books
for his "pains and charges" in compiling it. Although no
other catalogues from this time have come down to us, it is
not impossible that something of the kind existed, for otherwise it is not easy to explain Thomas Nashe's suggestion in

his Strange Newes (1592) that his enemy Richard Harvey had
stolen the names of certain authors whom he professed to
have read "out of some Bookseller's Catalogue." It may be
that booksellers kept manuscript catalogues in their shops
for the use of customers, or Nashe may be referring to
some foreign compilation. Had the date been a few years
later, one might have supposed him to refer to the famous
half-yearly catalogue issued in connexion with the great
book-fair at Frankfort, but this catalogue seems not to have
begun before 1598. It probably had some circulation in this
country, for in 1617 John Bill began to reprint it, and from
1622 to 1626 added to it a supplement of books printed in
England. From about this date also we begin to find other
evidence of the sale of books by such means. There are,
for example, at the British Museum two booksellers' catalogues, dating from 1628 and 1637, of works purchased in
Italy for sale in London.

It is then abundantly clear that, at the period with
which we are here concerned, the issue of catalogues was
by no means a usual or necessary part of a London publisher's or bookseller's business. He must have used other
methods than this to make his publications known. Seeing
that the area to which the trade was confined was so limited,
a great part of the sale would probably be to customers who
looked round the stalls and whose attention would undoubtedly be directed by the apprentices to anything new. "What
lack you, gentleman? See a new book come forth, sir! Buy
a new book, sir!" cries the apprentice in Rowlands's tract,
Tis Merrie when Gossips meete.

Various allusions point to a system of advertising by
printing copies of the title-page alone and fixing these up at
the recognized "posts" throughout the town--a practice which
would account for the frequency with which the address at
which a book is to be purchased is set forth on the title-
page, and for the fact that a title-page was sometimes kept
standing in type until a new edition of the book was required.
On the whole, however, we must suppose that the trade was
carried on with a very small expenditure on advertisement;
that, in fact, books became known chiefly by being talked of.
After all, the literary public was so small that it must have
almost formed one society, and the number of new books
was so limited that every one could be discussed.

Few words must suffice for the various arts or
trades subsidiary to printing, namely book-illustration, bind-

ing, type-casting, and paper-making.

The history of book-illustration during the first century of printing is of much interest, but in the period with which we are concerned there is far less to say about it. Indeed, one of the most remarkable facts connected with Elizabethan printing is the decline and almost complete extinction of the art of wood-cutting for the decoration of books. In the early part of the sixteenth century woodcuts were an important feature in a very large proportion of the books issued, and, rough as they were, they seem to have proved very attractive. These cuts, often copied from Continental cuts, are especially numerous in the work of Wynkyn de Worde and of Pynson, but they occur in practically all the more popular literature of the time. Printers seem, however, soon to have found them too costly an item in the production of a book, and almost from the beginning we find the same illustrations used over and over again, sometimes in the same work, to represent different subjects. Indeed, probably the less distinctly a cut represented a particular person or scene, the more useful it would be to its owner. Occasionally a printer would have a block newly cut from an impression of the old one--thus usually reversing the design--but often the actual blocks passed from printer to printer, until in the last stage of wear and decay they are found in chap-books or ballads of generations and even of centuries later. A notable instance of these "factotum" woodcuts is a set of figures which seem to have originally appeared in the Terence en François printed at Paris by Antoine Vérard about 1500. These cuts were used again in the elaborately illustrated edition of the first English translation of a famous compendium of astronomy, moral precepts, and rules for health, printed anonymously in Paris in 1503 as The Kalendayr of the Shyppars (i.e. Shepherds). This version was, however, in such curious English that when imported into England the volumes proved to be unintelligible, and a new one was therefore made and printed in London by Richard Pynson three years later. For this he copied the series of figures referred to above, and, once naturalized in England, they became very popular. Their great virtue seems to have lain in the fact that each figure had a scroll over its head in which could be inserted in type the name of the character whom it was intended to represent, and several printers had sets cut for their own use, and employed them constantly. They appear at the head of several early editions of interludes, such as Everyman, Youth, Hyckescorner, and Jacke Jugeler, to represent the various charac-

ters of the play, and in other works of a popular kind. It
need hardly be pointed out that the attempt which has sometimes been made to derive from them information about the
dress worn by the players in these interludes is absurd.

It may have been in some measure this economy of
material on the part of the printers and the consequent lowering of the standard of illustration that brought wood-cutting
out of favor, but other causes probably contributed. One
may have been the Reformation, for many of the early illustrated books were religious, and the cuts represented incidents in the lives of saints. All such pictures were by Edward VI and Elizabeth rigidly suppressed, and thereby a
large part of the field for illustration was at once cut off.
Another cause was perhaps that the printers found that books
might be decorated almost equally well by the use of ornamental letters and borders as by illustrations of the subject-
matter, and these could be freely used over and over again
without incongruity. A third cause may have been the introduction of copper-plate engraving, which, though much more
costly, could be used sparingly in the more expensive work,
and was regarded as infinitely superior to the current woodcuts. However this may be, pictorial illustrations, as distinct from diagrams, &c., became, early in Elizabeth's
reign, scarce in works of the better class. Such woodcuts
as we find are generally very rough, and occur chiefly in
books of a popular character, such as plays and a few
pamphlets, and even in these the illustration is generally
limited to a cut on the title-page. There are indeed exceptions. Foxe's Actes and Monuments (1563) has numerous
woodcuts, the first edition of Holinshed's Chronicles (1577)
has a few, repeated over and over again, and Spenser's
Shepheardes Calender (1579) has a series of twelve, one for
each of the months: but this is one of the last books of any
pretensions to be so decorated, and the idea of inserting
them may have been suggested by The Kalendar of the Shepherds from which Spenser borrowed the title of his work.

It must not be supposed that the going out of fashion
of woodcut illustration meant the disappearance of the wood-
cutter. His art was still in demand for many subsidiary
purposes. Ornamental initial letters were still cut, though
most of them are much inferior to the earlier letters, of
which they are often imperfect copies: woodcut title-pages
are fairly frequent, and a few, such as that of the second
edition of the Arcadia are good, but the majority, though
elaborate, have little artistic merit.

Besides such things as these, he cut also coats of arms, which are frequently to be found in works dedicated to members of the nobility, printers' devices and the like; while last, but by no means least, there was the constantly growing number of scientific works, herbals, books on natural history, medicine and physics, nearly all of which contain numerous woodcuts--intended, however, less to beautify the text than to render it intelligible.

The art of engraving on copper seems to have been practised on the Continent from about 1450, but it does not appear in England until about 1540, in which year was published Thomas Raynalde's Byrth of Mankynde, containing four plates of surgical diagrams. From that date the art grew steadily, though slowly, into popularity, but until towards the end of the century it was used chiefly for maps and diagrams. From about 1580, however, engraved portraits became numerous, and several engravers are known to have been working in London. The most ambitious book illustrated with copper plates that was published before the end of the century was perhaps Sir J. Harington's translation of Ariosto's Orlando Furioso, 1591, which contains forty-six plates, besides an engraved title. They are not of English design, but are copied from the plates of Girolamo Porro in the edition of Venice, 1584.[3]

From about 1600 elaborate engraved title-pages came into favour, especially for large and expensive works. Among them may be mentioned those of Coryat's Crudities, 1611 Drayton's Poly-Olbion (1613), the Authorized Version of the Bible (1611), Parkinson's Paradisi in sole Paradisus terrestris (1629), and the Works of John Taylor, the water-poet (1630). In nearly all such work, however, the artist seems to have aimed rather at elaboration of detail than at producing a harmonious whole, and the general effect is rarely pleasing.

Of bookbinding during the Elizabethan period there is no need to say much. It was evidently regarded as a trade, not as an art, and the names of very few binders have come down to us, while even those of whom we do find mention are generally known for some other reason than the excellence of their work. Some of the earlier bookbinders seem to have aimed at producing work of a distinctive style and to have made an effort to obtain good materials and well-designed stamps or rolls, but the decorations used in the later years of the sixteenth century are, with few exceptions,

commonplace, and indeed few books seem to have been decorated at all.   The most usual styles of binding were limp
vellum with ties for small or thin books, and plain brown
calf or sheep, often with clasps, for larger works.   Elaborate bindings of gold or silver, velvet or embroidery, were
occasionally executed for presentation to the Queen or other
exalted personages--it was no doubt of such a one that Shakespeare was thinking when in Romeo and Juliet (I. iii. 92) he
wrote of the book "that in gold clasps locks in the golden
story." There is testimony of a kind to the general existence
of a sentiment that books of value deserved to be bound well,
in the expression of scorn which Perdita bestows on a noble
work "vilely bound up" (Wint. Tale IV. iii. 22).   But as a
general rule there seems to have been little demand for dec-
orative work.

      The chief bookbinders may have had establishments
of their own, but the great majority were probably journeymen in the employ of stationers.   A few owners of large libraries, such as Archbishop Parker, kept private bookbinders in their employ, but there is no evidence that the
practice was at all common.

      In the early days of printing each printer seems to
have cast his own type.   There must from the beginning
have been a separate trade of cutting the punches used in
making the matrices from which the type were cast, for this
was highly skilled work and could not possibly have been attempted by the ordinary journeyman; but of the men who did
this nothing whatever is known.   So far as the present writer
is aware, the earliest person who carried on an independent
business in England as a type-founder was a certain Hubert
Danvillier, a Frenchman, who came to this country in 1553.
Whether from the beginning he worked independently or
hired himself out to printers is uncertain, but he evidently
had an establishment of his own in 1594, when Richard Watkins, a printer, placed one of his apprentices with him to
learn the art of type-founding.   One Antonius D'Anvillier,
also a type-founder, who is first heard of in 1562, was perhaps a relation.   In 1597, a certain Benjamin Sympson was
working independently as a type-founder; he seems to have
been the first Englishman recorded to have been employed
in the trade.

      None of the type used in England during the sixteenth
century was of a very high standard of excellence.   The best
was that used by John Day, who in this matter was by far the

most enterprising printer of his time.   To Day also belongs
the credit of cutting the first fount of Anglo-Saxon type,
which was used in an edition of a Homily of Ælfric edited
by Archbishop Parker in 1567.   A fount of Irish type was
cut in 1571, and was used in Dublin in that year.   Greek
had been used in single words or phrases since 1521, but
does not appear in any quantity until more than twenty years
later.   Hebrew is found in 1592.

The paper used by English printers during the reign
of Elizabeth was for the most part imported from the Continent, but this was not for want of attempts to make it here.
Lord Say's fifteenth-century paper-mill (2 Hen. VI, IV. vii.
41) appears indeed to have been imaginary, but there is
good reason to believe that one John Tate made paper at
Hertford from 1498, or earlier, to 1514.   He and others
who engaged later in a like attempt, seem, however, to have
met with little success, and in 1581 we learn that it had
been found impossible to compete in price with the paper
brought in from abroad, and that all manufacture here had
ceased.   In spite of this, John Spilman, of Lindau in Würt-
emberg, jeweller to the Queen, erected a mill at Dartford
in or before 1588, and in 1597 he obtained an exclusive pat-
ent to buy rags and make white paper for fourteen years.
He seems to have led the Privy Council to believe that he
had been the first to establish a mill in this country, but, on
the occasion of a dispute with the city authorities about the
persons whom he employed to collect rags, the Lord Mayor
stated that his claim was false and that previous to his time
there had been mills at Osterley, near Brentford, and at
several other places.   Spilman's mill was flourishing in
1605, when it was visited by King James and the owner was
knighted.

Notes

1.   Thomas Nashe, the satirist, complains in the dedication
     of his Terrors of the Night, that that work had--be-
     fore being printed--'progressed from one scrivener's
     shop to another, and at length grew so common that
     it was ready to be hung out for one of their signs,
     like a pair of indentures.

2.   The note seems to be first given in the Variorum Shake-
     speare of 1803, ii. 150, which appeared after Steev-
     ens's death.   It is not in his own edition of 1793.

3.   The fact that the engravings are only copies was pointed
     out by J. J. Jusserand: see his English Novel, Eng.
     trans., 1899, pp. 12-13.   He refers them to a Ven-
     ice edition of 1588 which I have not seen.   If the
     plates in this are identical with those of 1584, he
     seems, however, to go too far in saying that the Eng-
     lish engraver, Thomas Cockson, only drew the por-
     trait of Harington in the frontispiece, for several of
     the plates show considerable variation from the origi-
     nals; see, for example, plates 5 and 34.

     Bibliography. --The best general account of the print-
ing and publishing trade during the Shakespearian period will
be found in H. G. Aldis's chapter on "The Book Trade,
1557-1625," in The Cambridge History of English Literature, vol. iv.   Short biographies of all persons known to
have been connected with the trade are given in E. Gordon
Duff's Century of the English Book Trade, 1457-1557 (Bibliographical Soc., 1905), and A Dictionary of Printers and
Booksellers, 1557-1640, ed. R. B. McKerrow (Bibliographical Soc., 1910).   Much information on the subject of various
printers and of the trade in general will be found in The
Transactions of the Bibliographical Society, 15 vols., 1893-
1920, continued in The Library (4th Series), 1921, &c.   The
three volumes of wills of printers and publishers issued by
the same society throw some light on their business relations and circumstances: H. R. Plomer's Abstracts from
the Wills of English Printers and Stationers, 1903; Strickland Gibson's Abstracts from the Wills of Binders, Printers,
&c. of Oxford, 1907; and G. J. Gray and W. M. Palmer's
Abstracts from the Wills of Printers, Binders, &c. of
Cambridge, 1915.   For most matters connected with the
Stationers' Company the authority is A Transcript of the
Registers of the Company of Stationers of London, 1554-
1640, by E. Arber, 5 vols., 1875-94.   Concerning the pub-
lication of Shakespeare's works see A. W. Pollard's Shake-
speare Folios and Quartos, 1909, Shakespeare's Fight with
the Pirates, 1917, second edition (revised) 1920, and Sir
Sidney Lee's Life of William Shakespeare.   On questions of
copyright in early times see an article by W. F. Wyndham
Brown on "The Origin and Growth of Copyright" in The Law
Magazine for November 1908.   For wood-cutting see A. W.
Pollard's Old Picture Books, 1902, and for type-founding
T. B. Reed's History of the Old English Letter Foundries,
1887.

CHAPTER 6

THE USE OF THE GALLEY
IN ELIZABETHAN PRINTING*

It is well known that the usual practice of the modern
printer when putting a book into type is to set up the whole
of the copy in long or "slip" galleys, each containing from
two to four pages of type, and to take proofs from these before dividing the matter into pages.   This method has two
important advantages.   In the first place corrections can be
made much more easily while the type is standing in galley
than after it is in pages, and if the corrections involve the
addition of new matter or the cancelling of portions already
set up, this gives no special trouble, whereas were the matter already divided into pages a great part of that work
might have to be done again.   Secondly, if the type is to be
set up in long galleys it is possible to divide the copy among
a number of compositors who can work simultaneously, for
it is, of course, unnecessary that the amount given to each
should fill an exact number of pages.   Were the work cut up
into pages as composed it would, on the other hand, be necessary that each man's portion should end exactly at the
foot of a page, a thing which would hardly be ensured by the
most laborious counting of the words of the copy.

Now one of the many things that we do not know
about Elizabethan printers is whether they ever used galleys
in this way or not.   The question is perhaps not of the first
importance, but it has a certain interest from its bearing on
the further question of the circumstances in which a book
might be set up by two or more compositors working simul-

*The Library, 4th Series, Vol. 2, no. 2, September 1921,
pp. 97-108.   This is another article on early hand printing
based on physical evidence and observation.   Reprinted by
permission of the Council of The Bibliographical Society.

taneously and of the extent to which we are entitled to suppose such a distribution of the work in explaining the peculiarities of spelling and arrangement which are sometimes
met with in scattered portions of a text.

The point is not, of course, whether the Elizabethans
used galleys at all, for they must have used something of
the kind, but how they used them. The ordinary composing
stick--and pictures of early printing-houses show that they
used composing sticks--cannot have held more than some ten
lines of pica at most, for the weight of the type would have
made a greater depth of stick inconvenient to handle. [1] When
the stick was full the matter must have been transferred to
some receptacle or other, whether it was called a galley or
not is of no importance. What matters is whether it was
merely transferred thither to wait until sufficient material
was composed to form a page, or whether it was customary
to make setting in galley a definite stage in the work, so
that the matter of several pages might be standing in galley
at the same time before any of it was divided up.

There is, unfortunately, not much external evidence
as to the technique of Elizabethan printing. In fact, so far
as I know, there is no serious attempt whatever to describe
the art earlier than that contained in the second volume of
Moxon's Mechanick Exercises, 1683, but this, of course, is
both full and excellent. While it cannot be said, in view of
the date, to settle the question of Elizabethan practice, it is
not without significance that Moxon evidently had no idea at
all of the use of the galley to contain more than a single
page of type at a time. His galleys are of the shape of a
page and meant to contain one page each. He definitely lays
down that when a compositor has accumulated in the galley
the amount of type necessary for a page he should add a line
of quadrats and the first word of the next page (with, when
required, the signature). There is nowhere any suggestion
of setting up a quantity of matter in slip form and afterwards, cutting it up into pages.

Another passage of Moxon is perhaps worth noting in
this connexion. He advises that when a work is to be set in
an unusual measure, instead of each compositor using his
own stick, as was usual, one stick set to the required measure should be kept for the use of all the compositors employed on the job, who therefore must have worked in succession, not simultaneously. The assumption that the compositors would never be working simultaneously would hardly

be made by a man familiar with the use of long galleys.

Now it seems quite improbable that if setting in long galleys had ever come into general use it should have so completely gone out by 1683 that Moxon's treatise should ignore it altogether. But, after all, this is but negative argument, and I think that we can get positive proof that, at least, _many_ books were paged as set up. Unfortunately, however, as so often happens in bibliography, our evidence of what happened is all derived from errors. A perfectly printed book would show no trace of the method by which it came into being. The better-printed books, those, as a rule, which issued from the larger printing houses, contain little or no evidence as to whether they were set up page for page, or not, and it is precisely in such offices, with their larger quantity of type, that, if anywhere, we might expect to find the slip galley in use. Let us, however, consider what trace page by page composition is likely to leave when carried out by a not too careful printer.

After finishing a page the compositor would have to add the catchword and, when necessary, the signature, to tie the page up, and to place it in safety on the imposing stone or elsewhere. This would take an appreciable time, and if the compositor was a careless person who did not trouble to mark accurately the point of the manuscript at which he had left off there seems a possibility that when he came to start the next page he would have forgotten exactly where to begin. At any rate we should expect serious errors of omission or repetition--as of whole lines of verse-- to occur more frequently at a point where the work had been interrupted than elsewhere. Several such errors have been noticed[2] at the ends of pages, and so far as my experience goes they certainly seem to occur more frequently there than in other situations. It is, however, of course impossible, without examining a very large number of books for the special purpose, to obtain satisfactory proof of this, so the argument is not by itself conclusive.

A further point is that when a page ends with a passage in type different from that of the bulk of the book it is common for both the signature and the catchword to be in this type, though the rule is not invariable. Now this would save trouble to the compositor if he added the signature and catchword at the time of finishing the page, but it would add considerably to his trouble--without so far as we can see any gain in the result--if he made up into page from galleys and

for each catchword and signature had to consider and obtain
the appropriate type. Though therefore the variation of the
type of the signature line according to that of the text is not
conclusive evidence of setting straight in page, it is certainly more easily explained on such an assumption than otherwise.

We can, however, find much more satisfactory proof
of setting direct into pages when we consider the form of
the catchwords themselves. If a book is set up in long galleys, and then divided into pages, the catchword of any page
must necessarily be taken from the first word immediately
following the division, i.e. the first word of the next page;
there is no other possible source for it. Now suppose the
first word of this page happened to be incorrect, and yet a
real word (i.e. having in itself nothing suspicious and yet
wrong in its context), a compositor dividing, as we have supposed, long galleys into pages would have no idea that anything was amiss and would merely set up as catchword what
he saw. We should therefore never find a catchword correct,
while the first word of the following page was wrong, unless
indeed the error was one which the compositor of the catchword would necessarily recognize and avoid. On the other
hand, if the catchword was inserted immediately the page
was finished it would be taken from the manuscript or original copy, and therefore would have every reason for being
correct irrespective of whether the opening word of the next
page was afterwards set up rightly or wrongly.

The most significant of all errors in this connexion
are those in which a few words are omitted or repeated at
the beginning of a page, an error which, as has already
been said, is especially likely to happen when resuming composition after an interval, owing to carelessness in marking
the place in the copy where the compositor had left off.

Instances of correct catchwords followed by erroneous
page-opening are very numerous, and it requires little research to discover them. Those which follow may suffice
as examples. They are chosen from a couple of books which
I happen to have at hand, average examples of Elizabethan
printing, neither specially good nor specially bad.

(1) The Enimie of Idleness by William Fulwood, Henry
Bynneman, 1568.

B2 ends, "to suche maner of people it were" [catch-

word but]. B2^V begins "were but simplicitie to gyue instruc-
tions." Had the page been divided up from long galleys, the
catchword would necessarily have been the incorrectly repeated "were."

D4 ends a section describing how to write a certain
kind of letter. The next page gives an example of the letter in question. Such examples throughout the book are normally headed The Example, but this particular one is headed
merely Example. Nevertheless the catchword of D4 is The.

O5^V ends with "accepta-," the catchword being "ble."
The next page begins "vnto me," the rest of "acceptable"
having accidentally been omitted. On the theory of paging
from slip the catchword must have been "vnto."

O8 ends "that" [catchword "your"], the next page beginning, by accidental repetition "that your." The catchword "your" could only have come direct from the manuscript.

(2) The Golden Grove by William Vaughan, S. Staf-
ford, 1608 (second edition, enlarged).

In this work the numerous quotations are normally
printed in italics. Now sig. P7 ends with two quotations,
of which the first and so much as appears of the second on
this page are inadvertently printed in roman, the catchword
also being roman, but on turning the page we find that the
quotation is correctly continued on the verso in italics.
Evidently this catchword must have been added on completion of the page, for otherwise it would necessarily be taken
from the first word of the next page and be in italics.

There is another test which we can sometimes apply
in the case of plays, namely the form of the speakers'
names which appears in catchwords. Inspection of almost
any early play shows that very little attempt was made at
uniformity in the abbreviations used to represent the speakers' names. On the other hand, when in any particular passage a certain speaker's name recurs frequently, the compositor had, as we should naturally expect, some tendency
to keep to the same form. He would presumably have this
form in his mind, and while going straight ahead with his
composition would not trouble much about the form (often
perhaps only an initial) in which the name appeared in the
manuscript before him. If, however, any interruption oc-

curred in the work he might, so to say, make a fresh start
with a different form. It follows, therefore, that in a work
set up page by page, with the catchword added as each page
was completed, we should expect that whenever a catchword
included a speaker's name this name would be given the
same form as had been generally used towards the foot of
the page, without regard to the form of it with which the
next page opens. If, on the other hand, the work had first
been set up in long galley and cut up into pages afterwards,
the catchword, being taken from the first line of the following page, should follow this exactly, without regard to the
spelling used on the previous page, for the compositor would
have no alternative form in his mind, and indeed might not
know the name for which the abbreviation stood. He would
certainly have no inducement to alter it.

It may be worth while to summarize the results of an
examination of the catchwords of the First Folio of Shakespeare made from this point of view.

On 263 pages of the Folio the catchword (or the first
part of it) is a speaker's name.

Apart from three non-significant errors,[3] there are
82 cases where the form of the speaker's name occurring in
the catchword differs either from that previously used on the
page (or from the last form used on the page if there is
more than one) or from that used at the head of the next
page, or from both, but of these we may omit 12 from our
consideration on the ground that the speaker's name does not
occur previously on the page or that it occurs so far off that
the compositor is unlikely to have the form used in his mind
at the moment of setting up the catchword. We may also
omit a further five as being in some way peculiar.[4]

If we now classify the remainder we find that we have
24 cases in which the catchword differs from both the preceding and following form of the speaker's name, 26 where
it agrees with the preceding and differs from the following,
and 15 where it differs from the preceding and agrees with
the following form.

At first sight this seems rather inconclusive. It looks
as if the catchword was sometimes set up in immediate connexion with the last line of its page and sometimes (though
less often) taken from the first line of the next page; but
when we consider more closely the chances of agreement or

disagreement we see that our result is quite consistent with the theory that it was always set immediately after the last line, while it is evident that it sometimes must have been. We should not in any case expect perfect regularity. One method of setting should give merely a tendency to agreement with what has gone before, while the other should lead to a practical certainty of agreement with what follows. The evidential value of agreement or disagreement in the two directions is therefore very different. We have a considerable number of catchwords which would be almost impossible on the assumption of galley setting, against a much smaller number which are not quite what we should expect, but are still possible, if the pages were dealt with separately. The balance of evidence is thus clearly in favour of the page by page method.

When, however, we look at certain particular cases the evidence seems to be conclusive.

On K2^V the last three speeches of Hero have erroneously the speaker's name Bero, while the next page has correctly Hero. The catchword has Bero. This cannot therefore have been set up from the first line of the next page.

On d6 the name of Prince Henry's companion is given in the only two cases in which it appears as Pointz, and so also in the catchword. The first speech of the next page has, however, the form Poines.

On vv2^V we have a still more convincing case, for the catchword is Rodori. I, and in the Devonshire copy (Clarendon Press facsimile) these words do not appear at all on the following page, which begins "And hell gnaw his bones, Performances are no kin together." This was corrected in other copies, but it is evident that when the pages were being prepared for press there can have been nothing from which a compositor would take the catchword Rodori. I.

These three examples are in themselves sufficient proof that in the particular pages in which they occur the catchword was added immediately on completion of the page, and we may, I think, assume, until evidence is brought forward to the contrary, that the practice was followed throughout the whole book.

We have thus seen that three books taken from the years 1568, 1608, and 1623 show evidence that the matter

was put straight into page as composed, and was not first
set up in long galleys and cut up into pages afterwards; and
further that this was apparently the only system known to
Moxon in 1683. While we cannot, of course, say that such
evidence is sufficient to prove the universality of the method,
we must I think assume, until evidence to the contrary is
put forward, that it was the ordinary method in Elizabethan
printing, and that the use of the long galley was unknown.

Assuming then, that Elizabethan books were as a rule
set up page by page and that long galleys were not used, it
remains for us briefly to consider how this affects the question of the number of compositors who might be employed on
a single job. It is evident that whether it affects it or not
depends on the nature of the copy. When a printer had to
reprint a work already in type and was following his original page for page, it was open to him to give every sheet,
or even every page, to a different compositor, and all these
might work simultaneously (assuming a sufficient number of
type cases), for evidently each man's page would join on
properly to those before and after it. Even in the case of
a reprint which was not to follow the original page for page,
simultaneous composition by two compositors might sometimes be possible. A printer might, for example, wish to
reduce a book of ten sheets to one of eight, and might give
the first five sheets to one compositor and the second five
to another, instructing each to compress his five sheets into four. It is only when setting from a manuscript that such
division between two or more men would, without the use of
long galleys, involve such intricate calculation as to be impracticable. But even in such a case, though simultaneous
composition by a number of compositors is impossible, there
is clearly no reason why different men should not have
worked at the job in succession.

Many reasons might cause work begun by one compositor to be continued by another. The most likely is perhaps that the first man had emptied his type-cases and needed to replenish them. It was probably usual, as it still is,
that a compositor should himself distribute type into the
cases which he used. If he did not do this, he ran the risk
of the case being filled with letters wrongly distributed,
which would cause much loss of time when he next used it.
Now we have not sufficient evidence to enable us to calcu-
late accurately the amount of matter which one pair of
Elizabethan type cases would suffice to set up. Much depends on whether, as seems probable, a pair of cases or-

dinarily contained both roman and italic founts, and on
whether when setting verse the compositor had at hand an
additional supply of quads and spaces or was limited to those
which his case would normally contain. In general, however,
since the reach of an Elizabethan's arm and the length of his
fingers were pretty much the same as those of a compositor
of to-day, and since in 1580 the art was old enough for a
reasonably convenient arrangement to have been evolved,
there seems to be great probability that the dimensions of
the Elizabethan type-case were not much different from those
now customary. [5] On this assumption we shall, I think, be
fairly safe in supposing that at least three and not more than
five ordinary quarto pages could be set up from one pair of
cases. Probably we should not be far wrong in taking four
as a fair average number.

Of course a compositor might not be limited to one
pair of cases. On the other hand, the supply of type in all
save the largest printing-houses was probably quite small,
and each compositor would necessarily have the use of several (three at least) different sizes of book-type--probably
in black letter and roman--apart from the founts of excep-
tional sizes which would be used by all the compositors as
required. It seems, therefore, quite likely that one compositor might have the use of only two or three pairs of
cases, at most, of a particular fount. He would therefore
have to stop composition every dozen pages or oftener in order to replenish his cases by distributing work already printed off, and if there was another compositor available, and
the work was at all urgent, it would be natural for him to
take it over. There would accordingly be nothing surprising
if in a piece of Elizabethan printing we found indication of
two different compositors setting alternate groups of some
four to twelve pages. They would, however, have worked
alternately, not simultaneously.

As we do not know whether the compositor was always or usually a distinct person from the pressman or
whether each man took his turn at every kind of employment
in the office we can make no guess at the internal economy
of the Elizabethan printing-house or whether such a change
of compositor would be the usual thing or not. It may, however, be noted that distribution takes about a third of the
time employed in composition, and that a compositor would
almost certainly have had several other things to do besides
the actual composition, namely, to make up the formes, see
to the taking of proofs, if he did not himself pull them, and

make the necessary corrections. The total amount of time occupied in these subsidiary tasks might amount to practically the same as that taken in the actual straightforward composition, and the employment of two men at the case alternately might therefore not involve any loss of time.

Notes

1. The usual height to paper of modern English type is 0.92 in. I am indebted to Dr. Greg for the measurement of the only flat impression of an Elizabethan type that is known to me. This occurs in a copy of W. Lambarde's Άρχαιονομια, printed by John Day in 1568. The impression measures 0.97 in. The ink may have spread a trifle, but on the other hand as the paper was printed damp the impression would be slightly smaller than the type, so we can assume that 0.97 in. was about the actual height of the type and that therefore the weight of Elizabethan type differed only to a negligible extent from that of modern type of an equal body. Now the average weight of a square inch of modern type is taken as 5 oz. Ten lines of Elizabethan pica of the ordinary measure of a quarto book would therefore weigh some 25 or 30 oz., which with the weight of the stick itself would be as much as would be convenient to hold.

2. See Transactions, xii, p. 226.

3. A wrong speaker on A6 and transposed letters on S6 and mm5.

4. i.e. on E2^V, K2, and L2^V, the catchword departs from the form used immediately above, but the printer in these particular cases had purposely shortened the word to save space: O5, Shylock has been called Shy., but in the catchword and in the following page he appears as Iew. This change must be due to the manuscript: n4, catchword is Queene. She has previously appeared as Qu. and the next page begins Queen. It is difficult to know how to class this, as the printer seems to use anything from Q. to Queene, according to whether he had a long or short line.

5. The dimensions given in Moxon's Mechanick Exercises, 1683, are 1/2 in. longer, 2 in. wider, and 1/8 in. deeper

than those of the usual present-day case, but they would probably have been somewhat more heavily built and would have held hardly any more type.

CHAPTER 7

ELIZABETHAN PRINTERS AND THE
COMPOSITION OF REPRINTS*

In an article printed in The Library in 1921 I argued
that the Elizabethan printer composed his type page by page,
adding catchword and signature immediately it was completed,
and that the modern practise of having the matter of a number of pages standing in type at one time in long galleys and
cutting it up into pages as required for imposition was unknown, or at least unusual. It followed from this page by
page method that though a number of compositors may have
worked at the same book in succession, it was only possible
for one to work at it at a time, unless it could in some way
be ascertained in advance exactly at what point of the copy
each page should begin and end.

In the case of a prose manuscript such calculation is
impracticable, if not theoretically impossible. In the case
of verse it might be possible, though unexpected turnovers
might occur to throw the calculation out, and it would be seldom worth the risk and trouble. When, however, the copy
is itself printed matter the case is very different. It would
generally be possible, at the expense of a little trouble, to
ascertain the exact amount of copy which would be contained
in a page of the reprint, and of course when it is a case of
reprinting page for page there is no problem at all. For a
page reprint as many compositors as the printer could supply with type could be set to work at the same time. It is
therefore to be expected that the details of procedure will
differ in the case of a reprint from those followed when com-

*The Library, 4th Series, Vol. 5, no. 4, March 1925, pp.
357-64. This is an extension of the immediately preceding
article. Reprinted by permission of the Council of The Bibliographical Society.

posing from copy in manuscript. Let us consider how a
printer is likely to have dealt with a book that he had to reprint.

If it was not to be a page for page reprint the
chances are that he would proceed pretty much as if he were
dealing with a manuscript. The only difference would be
that if he was in a hurry, he could without any great difficulty divide up the work among two or three compositors
and set them at work simultaneously. Thus, suppose the
original print consisted of 24 sheets and he wished his reprint to be in 18 sheets he might divide it among three compositors with the instruction that each was to reduce his
eight sheets to six. Within each of the three sections the
work would proceed as if the compositor were working from
a MS., i.e. the pages would have to be composed in the
numerical order, and the whole of a gathering would have
to be in type before any printing could be done.

Suppose, however, the reprint was to be page for
page, everything would be different. It is to be noted that,
of course, "page for page" merely means with the same
amount of matter in each page. It does not imply the same
size of page or the same type or the same signatures or
even a correspondence line for line. The essential point is
that, the matter in any page being fixed in advance, the
pages can be composed in any order most convenient and by
any number of compositors working simultaneously.

There is, however, the question of the amount of type
required and the necessity of so adjusting composition to
machining that both compositors and pressmen shall be continuously employed. The printer's purpose would normally
be to keep the type standing for as short a time as possible.

Now let us suppose a printer to be starting on a reprint page for page, about which he is not in any special
hurry. If it is a folio there are three possible courses open
to him. Let it be a folio in sixes. He will, of course, in
any case have to compose 6^V before he can print 1, and 6
before he can print 1^V, and so on. He may therefore (1)
treat the gathering as if it were MS. and put all the twelve
pages into type before proceeding to print, or (2) set up
first 1, 1^V, 6, 6^V, completing each sheet of the gathering
before touching the next one, or (3) he may set up all the
outer formes 1, 6^V, 2, 5^V, 3, 4^V, and print these before
starting on the inner ones.

Were the book a quarto or octavo he would have merely the choice of composing all the pages in the normal order
or of composing first all those of one forme and printing this
before starting on the other.

It seems clear that in either case composition in the
numerical order of pages is the least economical of type,
as nearly double the number of pages required for printing
must be composed before any go to press.   At the same
time other considerations might easily determine the printer
to follow this method, and we cannot say that it would on
the face of it be unreasonable.   Can we find any evidence
as to the procedure that was actually adopted?

Frankly, in the vast majority of cases we cannot.
The order in which the pages were set up in type leaves no
evidence whatever by which we can trace it.   Suppose, however, that we could find some book in which the same illustration or block of an initial letter--which must, of course,
be recognizably the same block and not merely a similar de-
sign--was frequently repeated, the repetition might tell us
something.   We should not, for example, expect to find the
same block twice in matter which was all standing in type at
the same time, and the intervals between the repetitions
might give us some idea as to the amount that was kept
standing at once.

Even here, however, we must interpose a caution.
If a block were absolutely necessary to the illustration of
two particular passages in the same sheet of a book, while
it could not, of course, appear twice in the same forme, it
might appear in both formes even if these were set up in
the normal page-order, for it would not be difficult for the
compositor when setting one of the pages on which it was to
appear to substitute another block of the same size and ex-
change this for the correct one when the latter had been released after printing the other forme.   I have noticed what
may be an instance of this in an Italian edition of Sacro-
bosco's Sfera del Mondo, Lyon, 1582,[1] which has the same
block of a necessary diagram on i 3 and i 6.   This would,
however, have been a particularly easy block to move from
one forme to another after the type was set, as it occupies
the whole width of the page.   But it is probably only in
cases of this sort where a diagram or illustration is necessary for clearness that a shift of this kind--always more or
less troublesome--would be made.   When the block under
consideration is merely an initial letter of no particular im-

portance or significance, and the printer has several blocks
of the same letter, it is most unlikely that he would trouble
to make provision for the use of a particular one in a particular place.

Now let us imagine that we have a folio book in sixes
in which many initial letters are used and which is a page
for page reprint of an earlier edition, and see what effect
the different methods of composition can have on the recur-
rence of particular initial blocks.

1. Suppose the printer composed his pages in the
normal order. He could not then begin to print at earliest
until he had composed sigs. 3^V, 4, and it seems unlikely
that he would print until the whole 12 pages of the quire
were in type. Even, however, assuming that printing was
begun at the first possible moment, pages 3^V, 4 would hardly have been distributed in time for any of the material to
be used in the remaining pages of the gathering. We may
say that by this method it is perhaps just possible, though
very unlikely, that material used in 3^V, 4 might be again
used in 6 or 6^V, but that it is only in these pages that we
could expect to find material used twice in a gathering.
Note, that if we did find material used twice there is an
equal chance for it to be used twice in the same kind of
(outer or inner) forme, or once in an outer and once in an
inner forme.

2. Suppose he set up first 1, 6^V; then 1^V, 6; then
2, 5^V; then 2^V, 5, &c., printing each forme as he composed it. By this method he could have perfected each
sheet as he went along, a method which, if the ink dried
quickly, might have been convenient.

If he had done this an initial might easily be released from one forme in time for it to appear in another
forme of the same gathering, but as the two formes of
each sheet were composed in immediate succession, no initial could appear on both sides of a single sheet, unless indeed each forme was printed and distributed before the composition of the next was begun, a method hardly likely to be
adopted unless only a single workman was available both for
composition and machining, and one which would make the
progress of the work intolerably slow. Further, by composition of the pages in this order there would be, as before, an equal chance of a block used twice in one gathering appearing once in an outer and once in an inner or
twice in similar formes.

3. Suppose he first set up all the outer (or inner)
formes of a gathering, 1, 6^V (or 1^V, 6), 2, 5^V (or 2^v, 5),
3, 4^V (or 3^V, 4), and then all the inner (or outer) ones.
In this case, even if the formes were sent to press immediately upon composition, it is unlikely that material would be
released from one outer (or inner) forme of a gathering in
time to be used in another outer (or inner) forme of the
same gathering. On the other hand, if all the inner formes
were composed after all the outer ones of the gathering it is
quite possible that some of the material from the outer
formes might be used again in some of the inner formes (or
vice versa). There will at any rate be a much greater probability of material which is used twice in a gathering appearing in opposite formes than in the same.

Suppose that the method was to compose, print, and
distribute all the outer (or inner) formes before touching the
inner (or outer) ones, the same will be true except that material used twice in a gathering must always be in opposite
formes.

Having gone thus far with theory let us turn to the
particular example which gave rise to this little inquiry,
namely a Barker's folio "Bishops" Bible of 1591. This
Bible, like several others of the larger Bibles, contains a
great variety of initial letters, of which most of the larger
ones are much-worn wood blocks, a few are evidently cast
metal letters, and some may be either wood or metal. To
any one turning over the pages of this Bible it must be evident that many examples of what are certainly the same
block occur in close proximity to one another, and especially that the same initial is not uncommonly found on both
sides of a leaf. [2] It seemed to me that it might be worth
while to look into this matter more closely on the chance of
its yielding something of interest as to the order in which
the pages were set up, and I therefore made lists of the occurrences of certain of the blocks. It happens that, at any
rate in the early part of the Bible, the letter A occurs with
great frequency as the initial of a chapter. I therefore took
eight different initial A's of each of which the printer appeared to have only a single block, and followed them
throughout the book. The results were at least curious. I
find that I have recorded 266 appearances of these eight initials, an average of over 33 times each, two of them being
used 41 times each, and at the other end of the scale two
of them respectively 22 and 21 times. Six of the initials
are probably wood, two probably metal, but it seems to me

fairly certain that of these latter the printer only had a
single block of each design.

In three cases, namely in signatures 4 G (twice) and
4 I, I found the same block used thrice in a gathering; in
41 cases twice in a gathering; but the interesting point is
that in 37 out of the 41 cases the two occurrences of the
block are in opposite formes (one in an outer and one in an
inner forme), and only in four cases in similar formes.[3]
In 19 cases out of the 37 the initial occurs on opposite sides
of the same leaf, and in a further three cases on the page
forming part of the same forme as the opposite page of the
leaf.[4]

Apart from these I have noted down some 35 cases
of other initials being repeated on two pages of a leaf, and
these are taken from a portion only of the Bible.

Now, as we have seen, the only method of composition which would make it much more probable that if any
block occurred twice in a gathering it would occur in opposite formes, is that of first setting up all the outer (or inner) formes and then all the inner (or outer) ones, and it
seems clear that this was the method followed in this particular book.

But can we go further? Can we account for the very
frequent occurrence of the same block on both sides of a
leaf? I think that we can, though here, it must be confessed,
we are treading on somewhat unsure ground. It seems, however, possible to infer that though the outer (or inner)
formes must all have been set up before the inner (or outer)
ones, the process cannot have been to get them all in type,
print them and distribute before beginning the opposite
formes, for in that case an initial would be equally likely to
occur again in any page of the opposite formes, and out of
our 37 cases of an initial occurring twice in a gathering,
only six or seven should show it on both sides of the same
leaf (as each might equally well be in any of six pages), instead of the 19 that we found. Printing and distribution
must therefore have gone on concurrently with composition.

Actually, I think we may say that the process must
have been something like this. The composition--which
must obviously always have proceeded at the same average
rate as the printing, must always have been on the average
three formes ahead of the distribution, so that at one mo-

ment one would have had, say, 1, 6^V just distributed, 2, 5^V
and 3, 4^V at press, or in process of correction, and 1^V, 6
being composed. The compositor of 1^V, 6 has probably the
material of 1, 6^V, which perhaps he himself has just distributed, immediately before him. If he needs an initial
similar to one which has just been released from that forme
it is probably at hand, and he is more likely to take it than
another. Similarly, when it comes to composing 2^V, 5 the
material of 2, 5^V will just have been distributed, and the
initials will similarly be available; and in the same way with
3^V, 4 and the materials of 3, 4^V. Thus, and, I think, only
thus, can we explain that especial tendency to use the same
initial on both sides of a leaf, which we meet with in this
Bible.

Notes

1. It is, however, possible that this was a page for page
    reprint of another edition, and was set up by <u>formes</u>
    and not in normal page order--but even so there
    must, one would imagine, have been an original edi-
    tion in which the pages were composed in numerical
    order, and in which the block must have been changed
    from forme to forme as I have supposed.

2. To give a single instance. In gathering 3 L the same
    I is found on both pages of leaf 1, another I on both
    pages of leaf 2, and an A on both pages of leaf 3.

3. The most interesting gathering from this point of view
    is perhaps 2 H, where initials are repeated in the
    following pairs of pages: 1, 1^V; 2, 5; 3, 5; 3, 3^V;
    2^V, 5^V. In the last case the initial is cast and the
    identification of the block perhaps doubtful.

4. i.e. such pairs as 1^V, 6^V, where 6, 6^V are opposite
    pages of a leaf, but 1^V would necessarily be in type
    and be printed at the same time as 6.

CHAPTER 8

BIBLIOGRAPHICAL TERMS*

SIR. --The reviewer of Mr. H. C. Hutchins's "Robin-son Crusoe and Its Printing," in your issue of October 22, ends his interesting discussion of the meaning of the terms "edition," "impression," and "issue" with the suggestion that "distinct states of a book which cannot... be distinguished as different-editions should be called different im-pressions if the type has been reset; and different issues if they are (in the main) from the same type." He thus apparently makes the literary contents and not the method of production his criterion for distinguishing the "edition" and the "impression"; indeed, his "new edition" might conveniently be defined as one of which a free copy would, under the Copyright Act, have to be sent to the British Museum. But is it fair to put on the bibliographer the onus of deciding exactly how much alteration is necessary to constitute a new edition? One foresees endless differences of opinion.

Surely it is a pity now that the use of these terms has been more or less agreed upon, or at least in this country, to introduce new meanings for them. The definitions officially put forward by the Publishers' Association accord exactly in spirit with the practice of almost all modern bibliographers, though it might be difficult to devise a form of wording equally applicable to the earliest printed books and to those of to-day. Briefly, an "edition" is understood to be the whole number of copies of a book printed at any time or times from one setting of type, including copies printed from stereotype plates or electros made from this

---

*The Times Literary Supplement, October 29, 1925, p. 719. McKerrow presents the standard definitions of "edition," "impression" and "issue." Reprinted by permission of Malcolm B. McKerrow.

one setting.   An "impression" is the whole number of copies
printed at any one time.   The meaning of "issue" can best
be deduced from the Publishers' Association definition of a
"reissue" as "a republication, at a different price or in a
different form, of part of an impression which has already
been placed on the market," i. e., it implies the using-up
of existing sheets of a book without reprinting the main part
of it.

Of course such definitions do not cover all possible
cases, but turning, as they do, on definite and generally as-
certainable facts, whether or not there has been a new
printing (matching), and whether or not there has been a new
setting up of type, they do at least afford a good basis to
work on, even in the case of early books when the vagaries
of the printer often render any simple description of this
sort impossible.   We do indeed want one quite non-commit-
tal word to describe certain differences in books of the same
impression, for which we now have to use "variety" or
"type," both objectionable words, the first because it may
seem to imply a norm which is varied from, the second because of its other associations in bibliography.   Such a word
would cover a number of minor differences, such as the
cases in which parts of an impression bear different publishers' names, and those in which for economy in machining the printer has had a few odd pages at the end set up
twice over, so that, while there is only one impression,
these pages are from different settings in different copies of
the book.   I venture to suggest that, thus supplemented, the
words "edition," "issue," and "impression" in their generally accepted senses should go as near as any single terms
can to satisfy the requirements of bibliographers in describing things which often have to be considered not as wholes
but as more or less fortuitous collections of much smaller
parts.

CHAPTER 9

BOOK REVIEW

Specimens of Books Printed at Oxford with the types given
to the University by John Fell. Oxford: at the Clarendon
Press in the Centenary Year 1925. pp. viii, 128. Three
guineas net.

The purpose of this volume is, as we learn from the
preface, firstly to do honour to John Fell, and secondly to
furnish students of printing with convenient examples of the
famous types which have come to bear his name. It certainly fulfils this twofold purpose. It is a most handsome
and worthy tribute to the memory of one of the greatest
benefactors of the Oxford University Press, while at the
same time it serves to bring home to us that whatever high
hopes Bishop Fell may have had in making his bequest, they
have been very amply realized in the work of the press which
he did so much to establish. That it will be of use to students of typography goes without saying, but there is another
way in which the book will especially interest many members
of the Bibliographical Society.

We have recently listened to a discussion on the reproduction of early books in facsimile. Now there are of
course two principal ways in which a book can be reproduced. Either we can facsimile our original, by photograph-
ic or other methods, as nearly as possible as it now appears
with all the blemishes of age and accident upon it, or we can

*The Library, 4th Series, Vol. VII, no. 2, September, 1926,
pp. 225-27. This is an example of a typical McKerrow review with concise comments on "type-facsimiles" and the Fell
type. Reprinted by permission of the Council of The Bibliographical Society.

remake it from the beginning, setting it in type as exactly
as possible resembling that first used, and print it on good
paper with all the neatness and regularity of modern press-
work; in short, we can reproduce it in "type-facsimile."
By the one method we shall produce something which in
many respects is inferior to our original even at present,
and which is probably much inferior to that original as it
came from the printer; by the other method something better.   Which method is preferable in any particular case depends on the purpose of the reproduction, and it is not of
course by any means always that the second is practicable.
We cannot make a type-facsimile of an incunable, for the
necessary type does not exist and the expense of cutting
punches and casting it would generally be prohibitive.   The
true occasion for this method is in such a book as the one
before us, when the purpose is not to reproduce a text but
rather a design, to show not so much what the original
printers did, as what they tried to do and what, had they
possessed the resources of to-day, they would have done.
When, as in the present case, it is possible to use type actually cast from the original matrices the method is not only justified but results in a work of very great interest.

Most of those who examine the pages here displayed
will, I am sure, agree with me that the Fell type is better
than they thought it was.   Especially is this the case with
the various sizes of italic, which look unexpectedly well in
the mass.   I confess that, for my own part, I have always
disliked the smaller sizes of Fell italic when used as a dif-
ferential type in roman texts.   It has, at least to my mind,
an odd suggestion of mixed founts, and even here in the
specimens given on p. 79 of this book from Mr. Dobrée's
Restoration Comedy, I find it difficult to convince myself
that the C of The Country Wife on "p. 81" is really small
pica, while that of Chedreux near the foot of "p. 73" is
long primer.   But certainly the varied slopes of the letters,
which seem to be unpleasantly accentuated when we have
single words among the strictly vertical roman, are far
less noticeable in a page printed entirely in italic.   At the
same time it must be conceded that the Fell italic accords
better in colour with its roman than is the case with many
other italic founts.

The specimens here given of course show the Fell
type to the best advantage, and the best is very good, but
it may be noted that there is considerable difference between the different sizes.   The best of all is, I think, the

double pica (pp. 10 and 11), for the peculiarly large v, x
(and z), which to some extent disfigure the great primer
(see "hazard," "ʃoever," and "perplexity" near the foot of
p. 7) are not here apparent, and the h and ʃt are upright.
In the two pages 112-13, one of which is solid and comparatively widely spaced, while the other is leaded and narrow
spaced, I should give my vote for the former as on the
whole more readable as well as more pleasant in appearance.

The preface refers to Horace Hart's study of the
Fell type in his Century of Typography, 1900, but it is to
be wished that for convenience of reference a brief summary
of the facts had been given here, especially in regard to the
pica.   The type-specimen of 1693 includes a pica "Bought
by the University 1692" as well as another which is presumably the type presented by Fell.   This latter, though matrices of both roman and italic and some punches of the
roman still exist, seems not to have been cast in modern
times, and it is the other, the "bought" type, which is used
in the book before us and, I suppose, in all modern "Fell"
books printed in pica.   It is also apparently the "Fell pica"
in the specimen given in Some Account of the Oxford University Press, 1922, though its claim to this description seems
at least doubtful.

The get-up of the book is admirable.   Pages of
smaller size than folio are cut out and mounted on a dark
mount, the only possible way of giving them anything like
their actual appearance in a book.   I am not sure that pairs
of pages mounted flat in this way are quite right as one
misses the effect of the fold in the inner margin: an "opening" never looks flat like this.   But it is difficult to see
how else they could have been treated unless they had been
folded and only one leaf attached to the mount, a method
which in practice is most inconvenient however sound it may
be in theory.

CHAPTER 10

BIBLIOGRAPHY: TWO LETTERS*

SIR. --Professor J. E. Spingarn makes my Introduction to Bibliography for Literary Students and your review of that book the occasion for some remarks on the meaning of the word "bibliography." With his general contention that it would be better if there were separate words to distinguish the study of the material form of books (generally known as "bibliography") from a list of books by a particular author or dealing with a particular subject (generally termed "a bibliography") most people would, I think, readily agree--though whether any real inconvenience is caused by the use of the same word for two different things is a matter of opinion. But when he says that my Introduction is not concerned with books, on the ground that a book is not, or not only, "the physical dress in which it is given to the world" but "a spiritual entity of some sort," and that "the word 'bibliography' properly belongs only to the study of this spiritual entity," I must be allowed to differ from him. If he will be at the pains to look up to word "book" in the N. E. D. and read the examples there given, he will, I think, quickly be convinced that the earliest and at all times the predominant sense of "book" has been the material object and not the "spiritual entity" (has a book ever been any less a book for consisting of blank pages?). Similarly the earliest meaning of the word "bibliography" seems to have been "the systematic description and history of books, their authorship, printing, publication, editions, &c.," and not a list of books of some particular kind; just as "geography" means the systematic description of the earth and not a list of

---

*The Times Literary Supplement, January 26, 1928, p. 62. This and the following letter (TLS, March 22, 1928, p. 221) deal with McKerrow's use of the term "bibliography." Reprinted by permission of Malcolm B. McKerrow.

92

countries having certain characteristics in common. While, therefore, I would not venture to emulate Professor Spingarn in laying down rules for the use of the English language--a matter of generally allowed custom in his own country as well as here--I would submit that the sense in which I have used "bibliography" has at least as good authority as that which he would give to it, and that if a new word is to be coined it would be more reasonable to find a fresh title for "the selection of books to illustrate a given subject" than to usurp for this one section of the "science" the term now commonly applied to the study of books as a whole.

SIR. --In your issue of January 19 Professor Spingarn charged me with misusing the word "bibliography" in the title of my Introduction to Bibliography for Literary Students, and stated that the word had "properly" quite a different meaning. In reply, I referred him to the N. E. D. He now retorts that the advance of a science is not to be attained by consulting a dictionary (did I ever suggest that it was?) and that the lexicographer is not "the final arbiter in any fundamental discussion de rerum natura" (but surely we are discussing the names of things, not their nature) and quotes the use of the word "bibliographic" in two French works and a German one to show that I am wrong. I am quite well aware that the current meaning of "bibliographic" differs from that of "bibliography," and if my book had been written in French or German I should not have used that word in the title: there are many words the meaning of which differs from that of words of similar form or derivation in other languages. In any case, if we in England are to change our usage of English words at the dictation of scholars (in Professor Spingarn's sense of the term) we can hardly be blamed for waiting until the scholars of our own country give us a lead.

CHAPTER 11

EDWARD ALLDE AS A TYPICAL
TRADE PRINTER*

It is, I think generally recognized that the printers of the Elizabethan period may be divided into two groups, according as they themselves published and sold the bulk of the work they printed—the so-called printer-publisher, or printed mainly or entirely for others--the so-called trade printers. The two groups cannot, it is true, be sharply differentiated, for a number of men combined both kinds of business, doing a certain amount of publishing on their own account and occupying their press between whiles by printing for others; but nevertheless the distinction is in the main a perfectly sound one. For example, John Day, Richard Tottel, and Christopher Barker seem never to have printed for any one else; Bynneman and John Wolfe very seldom; while on the other hand some men, such as Henry Middleton, Arnold Hatfield, John Windet, and Humphrey Lownes, printed almost entirely for others and perhaps never dealt directly with the public, or at any rate never kept anything of the nature of a bookseller's shop. Their trade was in fact very much the same as that of most printers of the present day.

Naturally enough, almost all the work that is good from the typographical point of view was executed in the houses of the printer-publishers. The fact that these could afford the outlay and risk incidental to publishing implies a certain amount of capital. They were thus in a position to spend time and trouble in the improvement of methods of

*The Library, 4th Series, Vol. X, no. 2, September 1929, pp. 121-162. This is a major illustrated article in which McKerrow's conception of the Elizabethan printer is advanced with the example of Edward Allde. Reprinted by permission of the Council of The Bibliographic Society.

production and in beautifying their books, and in their case
such expenditure would be worth while, for they would themselves reap the benefit of increased sales.   The result has
been that it is these printer-publishers who have attracted
the greatest amount of attention in modern times--so far at
least as any printer later than 1550 has been studied at all
--while little or no work has been done on the trade printers.   And yet from some points of view these latter are the
more important.   While many of the larger volumes of history, law, divinity, and the like came from the presses of
the publisher-printers, the great bulk of the popular literature seems to have been financed by the booksellers and
printed for them by the trade printers.   For example, there
are some forty-five Shakespearian quartos dating from before the First Folio.   All except three of these are stated
to have been printed for some one or other--that is to say,
they were the work of trade printers.   Of these three, two
are 1619 piracies, The Merchant of Venice and Midsummer
Night's Dream, the other being the first and very imperfect quarto of Romeo and Juliet ''Printed by John Danter,''
a man who was indeed both printer and publisher, but, if
we may judge from the Parnassus Plays, of the less reput-
able sort.

        And as with Shakespeare, so with almost all the oth-
er dramatic writers and poets.   A very large proportion of
the play-quartos, the smaller volumes of verse, the prose-
pamphlets, and the popular literature in general was printed
by these trade printers, many of whom, it may be said,
give a great deal of trouble by their casualness in the matter of imprints and dates.

        It therefore seemed that it might be worth while to
take one of the trade printers and to attempt an examination of his work on the chance of something useful coming
to light.   There are several besides Allde who call for
study, such as John Windet, Richard Bradock, Ralph Blower, and the rather mysterious persons Robert Raworth and
John Monger, who bought Islip's business in 1606 and were
almost at once suppressed, but who, nevertheless, are said
to have continued to print.   I strongly suspect that a comparatively small amount of work devoted to such minor
people as these would help us very greatly in identifying the
house of origin of many books which bear no printer's name.

        I chose Edward Allde not because of his importance
but because he seemed to me to be an average sort of per-

son; just a typical commercial man with no pretensions to
be anything else. He was never particularly prominent in
the trade, in spite of his long connexion with it. The only
honour which befell him--if indeed it was an honour--was to
represent, with others, the Stationers' Company at the Lord
Mayor's Banquet in 1611, 1616, and 1624. On the other
hand, he was not, on the whole, by any means a disorderly
person. He did indeed get into trouble in 1597 when certain
materials used in printing "a popishe Confession" were found
at his house and he was in consequence forbidden to print by
order of the Company, but the suspension was evidently quite
short, and his output of books for the year in question does
not seem to have suffered greatly, though for a few years
after this date his recognized production was on a somewhat
smaller scale. In 1600 he was fined 5s. for his share in
printing a disorderly ballad of the Wife of Bath and was apparently also condemned to imprisonment for the same of-
fence, but a note states "And ther Imprisonment is respited
till another tyme." In 1602 he was fined 6s. 8d. for printing a book without entrance, and there are records of one or
two other minor offences as well as of complaints brought
against him by other members of the Company. But
troubles of this kind happened to most of the printers of the
time, and they do not suggest any great moral obliquity.

Beyond what we can gather from his books and from
the records of the Stationers' Company there is, so far as
I know, not a fragment of external information about Allde.
We have not even any of those scraps of useless personal
detail which we have about several of the other printers of
the period--no one seems even to have charged him with piracy. He seems to have been simply a fairly competent
commercial printer, who having inherited a small but sound
business from his father, gradually enlarged it, worked it
for nearly fifty years, and, dying, left it to his widow.

What, then, apart from his being such an average
sort of person, are the special reasons which seem to make
it worth while to investigate him? In the first place he appears to have had the bad habit of frequently omitting his
name from his productions. A large number of books, at
least sixty-three, have already been identified as coming
from his press, by the ornaments, initial letters, &c.,
which are used in them, and I suspect that there are a good
many more still waiting identification. It seemed that it
might be useful to collect and reproduce as many as possible
of the ornaments which he used in his acknowledged books.

Secondly, as his output seemed to be fairly constant
throughout his career--there are at least no important
breaks in it, though there are some odd fluctuations in quan-
tity--it seemed to me that we might be able to derive from
an examination of it some idea, however rough, of the average yearly output of one of the smaller Elizabethan printing-
houses. For many reasons we cannot expect to get exact
figures. Many books printed by him may have disappeared
altogether--as we shall see later, some certainly have--
and, as I have said, many more may be still unidentified.
Nevertheless, we may at least see what can be done in this
direction.

There are two different ways in which we can consider a printer's output. We can look at it either from the
point of view of the compositors or of the pressmen, assess-
ing it either in pages of type composed or in sheets of paper
printed we should require to know the size of the edition of
each book, a thing at which we can only guess in the rough-
est way, but seeing that the work in all printing-houses was
necessarily so organized that, as far as possible, both compositors and pressmen were kept fully or equally occupied,
there must always have been, on the average, a fairly constant relation between the number of pages composed and
the number of sheets printed; and if we know one we shall
be able to infer the other with some approach to accuracy.
It must be remembered that there was none of the reprinting from standing type or stereotype plates, which often so
badly upsets the economics of modern printing-houses, caus-
ing at one time the composing-room, at another the machine-room, to be standing more or less idle. The number
of pages composed per year will therefore afford a fair
measure of the printer's whole business.

Now it is of some importance that we should have an
idea of the average output of the smaller Elizabethan printers. As every one knows, during the greater part of the
Elizabethan period the number of printers, or of presses--
I am not certain which--was strictly limited. Thus in the
Star Chamber decree of 23 June 1586 it was enacted that no
new presses were to be set up until the number of existing
ones was reduced, and though no doubt this regulation was
not observed with absolute strictness, the returns of presses
which have been preserved, from the years 1583, 1586, and
1615, show that the number was fairly constant. The figures are as follows: For 1583, 23 printers, 53 presses (including 2 not in use and 2 secret presses); for 1586, 25

printers, 53 presses; for 1615, 19 printers, 33 presses.
The 1615 return, however, omits Robert Barker, the King's
Printer. As this business was undoubtedly the largest of
all and had had in 1586 six presses, while in 1615 it probably had even more; and as on the other hand the earlier
lists include two or three people who were either type-
founders or engravers and whose presses were presumably
not used for printing books, it would, I think, be reasonable
to suppose that at any rate between 1583 and 1615 there
were in London never more than about 24 master printers
owning a total of some 50 presses.

Now there can be no doubt, I think, that if it was
necessary to restrict the number of printers and presses,
the possession of a press and the permission to use it must
have been a valuable asset, and that no reasonable person
who enjoyed this permission would allow his press to stand
idle. There would thus seem to be something very suspicious about any one claiming to be a printer and not producing a reasonable number of books--such an average number
as might be expected from a printer of his class. When we
find such a printer, we must, I think, either suppose that he
was one of those people who printed many books without putting his name to them, in which case his ornaments, initials, &c., will need to be studied carefully, or alternative-
ly that the books which he claims to have printed were actually only printed for him and he was not a printer at all.
I fancy that further investigation will show that in a fair number of instances this is the true explanation. However, I
need say nothing further on this point at present, beyond
suggesting that the very imperfect figures of output which I
shall give you for Allde should be checked as soon as possible by work on one or two other of the smaller printers.

Edward Allde's business came to him from his father,
John Allde, who had been apprentice to the printer Richard
Kele. This Richard Kele, on his death in 1552, left the
lease of his business premises, "the Long Shop in the Poultry under St. Mildred's Church wall," to his brother John
Kele. John, though he was in business as a stationer up to
1571, does not appear to have done any printing and probably made over the premises to John Allde either in 1555
when he took up his freedom or shortly afterwards. John
Allde is not, however, known to have begun business on his
own account until 1561, in the latter part of which year he
took an apprentice and had several small books or ballads

entered to him in the Register. The first actually dated
book bearing his name seems to belong to 1562, and the
first which bears the address of the Long Shop in the Poultry
to 1563. From that date, however, he worked there regularly, the S.T.C. containing books dated in, or attributed to,
every year until 1582, when he either died or retired. John
Allde was, I may mention, particularly lax in dating his
books, 32 out of the 58 which he is known to have printed
being without a date.

The name Allde is just a little puzzling. In Kele's
will it is spelt "Aldey," and in the Stationers' Register generally "Aldee" or "Alldee," though occasionally with only
one e. In their imprints both John and Edward spell it with
one final e--Alde or Allde. From 1617 onwards, however,
that is, during the last ten years or so of his life, Edward
regularly spelt it with a hyphen, "All-de." So far as I have
been able to ascertain he never spelt it thus before 1617,
though Hazlitt does indeed record one book, The Antient,
True, and admirable History of Patient Grissel, 1607, in
which, according to him, this spelling appears. I have not
seen the book, and as this seems at present to be untraceable, I think that we may retain an open mind about it and
regard all books in which the hyphen is used as probably not
before 1617. From that date, as I have said, Allde used
the hyphen regularly. Not quite regularly, of course--or
he would not have been an Elizabethan, or a printer--but
reasonably regularly. At any rate the large majority of
books printed by him after this date, and by his widow Elizabeth after him, have this hyphenated form. What led to its
sudden adoption I cannot say. The purpose evidently was to
lay stress on the fact that his name was disyllabic, and not
"Ald." The only suggestion that I can make is that some
confusion may possibly have arisen between him and the
printer George Eld, but this is perhaps hardly a likely explanation, seeing that Eld had been printing for some thirteen years before the change was made.

"Allde" in two syllables does not sound quite like an
English name, and it seems possible that the family may
have been of Dutch origin.

John's son Edward was made free of the Stationers'
Company "by patronage" on 18 February 1584, and in the
same year he issued two books and a broadside. One at
least of these is stated to have been "Imprinted at the Long
Shop adioyning vnto Saint Mildreds Church in the Pultrie."

From that time until 1588 there is evidence that Allde
printed at that address, but, so far as I have been able to
discover, not one of Allde's books after that date contains
any statement as to where it was printed, though many give
Allde's residence and some say where they are to be sold.

Whether or not Allde continued to print at the old
premises in the Poultry, he had evidently ceased to reside
there by 1590, in which year two of his books, The Quin-
tessence of Wit, by Francesco Sansovino, and The Safegarde
of Saylers, bear a new form of imprint, namely, "Printed
by Edward Allde, dwelling without Cripplegate at the signe
of the guilded Cuppe." In his article on the Long Shop in
the Poultry in Bibliographica Plomer described the Gilded
Cup as in Fore Street, which is probably correct, though I
do not know whence he derived the information. It was certainly there or thereabouts.

In 1597 we find an edition of the Book of Cookery
"printed by E. Allde dwelling in Aldersgate street over
against the Pump" (Hazlitt, III. 47). So far as I have observed this address does not occur in any other of his books.

According to Hazlitt's Handbook, p. 508, Allde printed
in 1600 The Booke of mery Riddles, giving as his residence
"Little Saint Bartholomewes, neere Christ-church." Unfortunately this book does not seem to be at present traceable,
and as although Allde certainly lived at that address later,
there is no other evidence of his connexion with it at this
date, we may, I think, fairly suspect that something is
wrong here.

In 1604 we find him dwelling in Lombard Hill, near
Old Fish Street, a place at which he apparently remained until 1611, moving in that year, or possibly in 1612, to a new
address "near Christ-Church." This, which is generally
given in the fuller form "dwelling in little Saint Bartholomew's near Christ-Church," occurs fairly frequently in his
later books. It served him for the remainder of his life
and, after his death, which probably occurred in 1628, for
his widow Elizabeth.

There is indeed in the Dialogues of Posselius, printed
in 1623, a statement that the books were "printed by Edward Allde, and are to be sold by Christ-Church greater
South doore," and it is perhaps possible that Allde had a
shop there for the sale of his goods, for Little Saint Barth-

olomew's, his usual address, although in the immediate vicinity, would, I think, hardly have been thus described. Unless, however, the same thing can be found in other books, it seems much more likely to have been the address of some one for whom the book was printed, possibly the Edward Rive who translated it into English.

We must now return for a moment to the Long Shop in the Poultry. As I have said, Edward Allde printed there until 1588, and for anything I know to the contrary he may have continued to print there for many years longer, though residing elsewhere, for even in Elizabethan times a printer did not, I suppose, necessarily live over his printing-house. The shop itself had, however, perhaps been left by John Allde to his widow Margaret, for in 1601 we find a broadside entitled A living remembrance of Master Robert Rogers "Imprinted at London for M. Allde, and are to be solde at her Shop vnder Saint Mildreds Church in the Poultry" (Hazlitt, I. 363), and in 1603 A Lamentable Dittie composed vpon the death of Robert Lord Deuereux late Earle of Essex, also printed for her, was to be sold "at the long shop vnder Saint Mildreds Church in the Poultry" (Hazlitt, I. 148). There seems, therefore, no reason for supposing that Margaret Allde's shop was any other than the original "Long Shop" which had been her husband's.

Here, however, there is a little difficulty that I have not been able to clear up. In his article in Bibliographica Plomer stated that in 1602 Margaret Allde transferred her business to Henry Rocket, a stationer who in that year had taken up his freedom in the Company. Rocket certainly had books printed for him in 1602, 1603, and 1605 bearing the statement that they were to be sold "at the long shop under S. Mildred's Church in the Poultry." We have, however, seen that in 1603 Margaret Allde had a broadside printed for sale at precisely the same address, and as this and another ballad were entered in the Stationers' Register to her in that year, she was clearly still in business. What, then, was the relation between the two people?

I cannot go into the story in detail. It involves some curious changes in the form of Rocket's address in the years 1606 and 1607, which suggest that for a time--possibly after the death of Margaret Allde--Rocket was occupying other premises though still in the Poultry. In 1607, however, Allde printed two books, one, Bradford's Godly Meditations, bearing Allde's name alone, and the other, Gervase Mark-

ham's English Arcadia, being printed for Rocket. The remarkable thing is that the first of these has a colophon stating that it was to be sold "at his [namely Allde's] shop vnder Saint Mildred's Church in the Poultrey," while the other
was "to bee solde by Henrie Rocket, at his shop vnder Saint
Mildreds Church in the Poultrie" (Hazlitt, III. 154); what appears to be the same address being described in the one
book as Allde's, in the other as Rocket's. This address
does not seem to occur, as his, in any of Allde's later
books, but Rocket continued to use it.

     Unfortunately the form in which what seems to be
meant for the same address is given continually varies.
Sometimes it is "the long shop" and sometimes not; it may
be "under" or "adjoining unto" St. Mildred's Church, and at
times it seems to be "under the Dial." There was certainly more than one shop near the church, for from 1579 to
1590 the address of the bookseller William Wright was "In
the Poultry, the middle shop in the row, adjoyning to St.
Mildred's Church." On the whole, however, the probability
seems to be, that the shops occupied by Margaret and Edward Allde and by Henry Rocket (save possibly in 1606-7)
were one and the same, and that from 1602 onwards until
1607, with perhaps the short interval mentioned above,
Rocket was trading there under some sort of arrangement
with the Allde family. From 1607 onwards the shop may
have passed into the hands of Rocket alone, or if the premises contained both a printing-house and a shop for the sale
of books, Rocket may have taken over only the shop and
Allde continued to have his press there. I have come
across no evidence which would enable us to settle the
point, which is indeed not of any great importance.

     We may now consider the nature of Edward Allde's
business. In the first seven years, 1584-90, this business
was evidently quite a small one, and was that of a printer-
publisher rather than of a regular printer for the trade. In
these seven years Allde printed some 29 books, an average
of hardly more than 4 per year, and of these, 22 bore his
name alone, 6 being for other booksellers (the full imprint
of one is not known to me). This is in striking contrast
with what seems to have been his busiest period of seven
years, 1604-10, when he printed 95 books, of which only 14
were for himself and as many as 80 were for others (again
there are doubts as to the imprint of one of the books).
Between these two periods he had evidently perceived the advantage of working as a trade printer for other men, and of

getting, we may suppose, immediate payment for his work--
even though at a lower rate of profit--rather than taking the
risks of publication.   The change over in the nature of his
business seems indeed to have occurred in or soon after
1591, for from that date onwards there are only some four
or five years--and those generally years of small known out-
put--in which his work for others does not greatly exceed the
books which bore his name alone.   Taking his career as a
whole, the books at present traced to his press amount to
some 368, of which 63 are attributed to him on the grounds
of the printing material used in them, ornaments and initial
letters, but do not bear his name.   Of his whole known output, a trifle more than two-thirds was printed for sale by
some other bookseller, the other third either bearing his
name alone or in a very few cases no name at all.

    And here, by the way, I should like to say that all
figures given in this paper are to be regarded as incorrect.
I hope that they are more or less near to the truth, but the
only thing certain about them is that they are not and cannot be exactly right.   Allde's books are almost all exceed-
ingly scarce.   I do not know any considerable printer of his
time examples of whose work seem to be so difficult to obtain at a moderate price--probably a result of the popular
and ephemeral nature of a great part of his output.   Many
books printed by him are only known from single copies.
Some which he entered in the Stationers' Register and probably printed are not now known to exist, and of others editions have certainly vanished.   My figures of Allde's output
are based on the Short Title Catalogue, supplemented by
some very valuable notes given me by Mr. Ferguson of Allde
books which he has seen, and by notes taken from Collier,
Hazlitt, and others of books the whereabouts of which is not
now known.   I have little doubt that it would be possible,
could one spare the time, to add an appreciable number of
books which at one time or another have been recorded as
bearing Allde's name, and a much larger number which
were certainly printed by him though his name does not appear.   But it was not part of my intention to compile a bibliography of Allde's work, even had I the time to attempt
any such thing.

    Looked at from what I may call the publisher's point
of view, the books which either bear Allde's name alone, or,
bearing no name of printer or publisher, are attributable to
his press, that is to say, those books which he did not print
for any other bookseller, may be divided into two groups of

very different character. There is first the larger group
of books which have the appearance of profitable speculations, popular best-sellers in fact, or what we can well suppose he meant to be best-sellers, such things as news-
pamphlets, giving accounts of murders, witches, and the
like, plays, gardening and cookery books, and pamphlets
such as those of Samuel Rowlands and John Taylor, not for-
getting certain popular works of devotion. To these we will
refer presently. Secondly there is a smaller, but still considerable, group of books which, I think, we can only suppose to have been printed by Allde on commission for their
authors and at the expense of the latter. In some cases we
can be sure that this was so, for it is made clear in the
book itself, but there are many others of which the same
thing is almost certainly true.

     For example, there is a medical treatise of William
Clowes on the cure of struma, the King's Evil, printed by
Allde in 1602 with a colophon stating that it was to be sold
at Master Laybourne's, a Barber Surgeon near Billingsgate.
I have no doubt that Laybourne commissioned Allde to print
the book for professional purposes.   There is a little tract
by one Thomas Proctor, printed in 1607, entitled A worthy
worke profitable to this whole kingdome. Concerning the
mending of all high-waies, as also for waters and iron
workes, in which I cannot but suspect the enthusiasm of the
author rather than of the publisher.   Evidently, indeed, it
failed to sell, for the sheets were reissued with a new title
in 1610.   There is a pamphlet entitled London Triacle, Being the enemie to all infectious diseases; as may appeare by
the discourse following, 1612 and a new edition in 1615,
which seems to be nothing else but an elaborate advertisement of a particular "Triacle" sold by one William Besse in
the Poultry at the price of 2s. 8d a pound or 2d an ounce.
There is a prayer to be said at Christ's Hospital which Allde
printed in 1614 when he was living in that neighbourhood;
and there is the curious and interesting little book entitled
Seabrookes Caveat, or his Warning piece to all his ...
Countrymen, to beware how they meddle with the Eyes,
1620, a strange medley of excellent common sense and medieval remedies written by an oculist of King's Lynn, who
tells us that he is now 72 years of age and has been in
practice since his youth.   This book has, I think, every sign
of having been printed for its author, including as it does a
conspicuous notice of his address facing the table of contents.
And besides such things as these there are a certain number
of technical and Latin treatises, the sale of which we can

hardly suppose to have been sufficiently rapid to make them worthy of a bookseller's attention.   Such are the tract De fide, by E. H. , 1592, an answer to Peter Baro's tract of the same name; A copie of the Speache made by the Mathematicall Lecturer [T. Hood] at the house of M. T. Smith, 4 nov. 1588; John Dickenson's Deorum concessus, 1591; Thomas Rawlin's Admonitio pseudo-chymici, c. 1610; John Maxwell's Carolanna, 1619.   I will pass over several other volumes which seem equally unlikely as the speculations of a publisher of popular literature and mention only the important group of text-books of the mathematical teacher John Speidell, dating from 1616 to 1628.   One of these, A Geometricall Extraction, or a Compendious Collection of the Chiefe and Choyse Problemes, Collected out of the best, and latest Writers, is definitely stated to have been "Printed by Edward Allde, and are to be solde at the Authors house in the fields betweene Princes streete and the Cockpit, 1616," while in others similar information is given, and those desirous of learning mathematics are advised to repair to the author's house, where they can be instructed "in the best and briefest ways."   Speidell's works must have been a valuable property--one, the New Logarithms of 1619, reached a sixth impression by 1624--and it is possible of course that Allde financed some of them, but I cannot help thinking that they are far more likely to have been Speidell's own speculation and that Allde merely printed them for him. Possibly also the Dialogues of Posselius, to which I have previously referred, belongs to this class of book printed to order.

It is worth noting that none of the books which I have mentioned, except two of Speidell's and the Dialogues of Posselius, seem to have been entered in the Stationers' Register, a fact which possibly indicates that Allde did not feel himself concerned with the copyright of them.   On the other hand, the omission may have been due merely to carelessness.

It is indeed quite possible that a larger part of Allde's printing than is now apparent may have been work of this sort, commissioned by authors who desired to put something before the public that would hardly be saleable in the ordinary way.   In the absence of libraries on which they could be planted by force, such private ventures would tend to become almost as scarce as books of the most popular kind, not because they were thumbed to pieces, but because very few copies would ever get out into the world at all and the

bulk of the edition would finally be scrapped. Of most of
the books just mentioned only one or two copies seem to be
known. Many which would have fallen within the same class
may well have perished altogether.

Apart from the books which we may suppose to have
been printed on commission for their authors, those which
bear Allde's name alone are for the most part of a popular
kind, such as were likely to give a good and quick return to
their publisher. These were partly ephemeral productions,
such as news-pamphlets and the like, and partly longer and
more solid works for which there seems to have been a
good demand. These included Thomas Hill's book on the
Art of Gardening which, having been repeatedly printed from
1563 onwards, was re-entered to Orwin in 1591 and appears
with Allde's name alone in 1593 and in 1608, when the second part was printed by Ballard; and the Safeguard of Sailors, an important work of practical navigation which was
printed by Allde in 1587, 1590 [in 1600 by Islip], and "newly corrected" by Allde in 1605 and 1612.

There are also the two volumes of Homelies which
Allde printed in 1595. The second of these, containing 304
leaves in quarto, was Allde's largest single piece of work.
He seems to have been allowed to print these volumes by
some special arrangement, for they would surely by normally the copyright of the Royal Printer. The entry of the book
to him in the Stationers' Register (S. R. , ii. 659) authorizes
him to print only one impression and requires him to allow
6 d in the pound to the use of the poor.

Another of Allde's most profitable books may have
been the Book of Cookery, by W. A. , of which the earliest
known edition, described as "now newly enlarged," was
printed by John Allde in 1584. There existed editions printed by Edward Allde in 1587, 1591, and 1594, and seeing
that only a single copy of each of these is recorded in the
S. T. C. it is quite likely that there may have been other editions which have perished.

Allde may possibly have made even more out of his
rights in certain devotional works by John Bradford. His
Godly meditations upon the Lords prayer, the Beliefe and
ten commandments, which had been the copyright of John
Allde, was printed by Edward in 1597, 1602, 1604, 1607,
1614, and 1622, and by Elizabeth Allde in 1633.

The books which have been mentioned were either of some size or were frequently printed. Allde, however, also produced a number of small ephemeral publications which while individually bringing in less must in the mass have been an important source of income. There were, for example, certain plays and pageants, such as Peele's Device of the pageant borne before Woolstone Dixi, 1585, Preston's Cambises, c. 1585, Fulwell's Like will to Like, 1587, and Daniel's Royall Masque, 1604. Further, there were some pieces of popular literature such as The Booke of mery Riddles, 1600 [?], Rowlands's Guy of Warwick, 1609, and Anthony Copley's Wits, fittes and fancies, a reprint of 1614. There is, by the way, a little problem about this last book. There appear to be two editions by Allde, both dated 1614 but differing throughout except in the first two leaves. As, however, the previous edition had been, so far as there is any record, as long before as 1596, it can hardly be supposed that two new ones were needed in 1614. It may be suspected that one of these editions represents simply the using up of sheets of an earlier one.

From 1612 onwards Allde printed a number of John Taylor's tracts, some for the bookseller Henry Gosson, others apparently for himself.

Other small tracts which Allde seems to have printed for himself include two or three books by Anthony Nixon, The dignitie of man, 1612 (and probably 1616), A straunge foot-post, 1613, A mery jest of the frier and the boy, 1617, and The historie of Frier Rush, 1620; to which may be added a number of news-pamphlets, such as The apprehension and confession of three notorious witches at Chelmsford, 5 July, 1589. True news concerning the winning of ... Corbeyll by the French King, 1590. The honourable victorie obteined by Grave Maurice [1597]. A Prayer for the... Earle of Essex in Ireland, by John Norden, 1599. A true relation of Gods wonderfull mercies in preserving one [J. Johnson] alive which hanged five days [1605?]. The King of Denmarkes welcome, 1606. News from Perin [or Penryn] in Cornwall: of a murder, 1618. The lamentable burning of the citty of Cork, 1622, and so on.

None of these bear any name of a bookseller and we must, I think, suppose that they were Allde's own speculations.

But, as I have said, the great majority of Allde's

output, some two-thirds of the whole number of titles--and
a good deal more than two-thirds if we count the number of
leaves, for a large proportion of Allde's own books was
merely pamphlets of broadsides--was done for other publishers.

Allde seems to have printed for some 86 different
booksellers, for some 55 of which he only produced a single
book.   There were, however, five or six with whom at one
time or another he seems to have been particularly closely
associated.   By far the most important of these associations
was with Edward White senior and junior, whose dates are
given as 1577-1612 and 1605-24.   With these two Allde was
associated throughout almost his whole working life, printing in all more than fifty books for them from 1587 to 1621,
about which date Edward White junior probably died.   Mistress White, who may have been either his widow or his
mother, assigned her property in a number of books to E.
Allde on 29 June 1624 (S.R., iv. 120).

Other men with whom Allde was especially associated
were the two nautical booksellers, Hugh Astley and John
Tapp.   Hugh Astley, bookseller, 1588-1609, carried on a
business in nautical books at St. Magnus Corner (Thames
Street, near London Bridge), and from 1592 to 1596 Allde
printed six books for him, all dealing with nautical matters.
John Tapp, originally a member of the Drapers' Company,
having begun by re-editing Richard Eden's Art of Navigation,
in 1596, printed by Allde and sold by Hugh Astley, transferred in 1600 to the Stationers' Company and, it would seem,
started to sell his own works, for in 1602 he produced the
Seamans Kalender, which was printed by Allde for John
Tapp, and to be sold at his shop in Tower Hill.   This last
was several times reprinted and the association with Allde
continued, for Allde printed for him in all eighteen books,
both before and after he had succeeded Hugh Astley at his
premises at St. Magnus Corner.

In the later part of his life, from 1608 onwards,
Allde printed some nineteen books, mainly the writings of
John Taylor, the water poet, for Henry Gosson, but these
were mostly small and do not form any important part of
his output.

Others for whom he printed six books or more were
William Ferbrand (12), Nicholas Ling (6), Nathaniel Fos-
brook (8), Nathaniel Butter (9), Thomas Archer (12), and

Nicholas Bourne (6), five of those for Archer and Bourne belonging to the year 1622 when the two of them seem to have been trying to run a regular news-intelligencer.

In 1604-5 Allde printed three almanacs for the Company of Stationers. It is, I think, probable that other almanacs dating from about the same period were also from his press, but the workmanship of these books has often so little that is characteristic of a particular house that identification is difficult.

Of the other booksellers for whom Allde printed it need only be said that they include a very large proportion of those who were dealing at the time in the more popular literature.

Now I confess that I began this paper with the hope of being able to put before you some fairly close estimate of the yearly production of Allde's press. I had indeed visions of some sort of graph such as is to be found in Mr. Madan's book on the Oxford Press, but the difficulties proved to be much greater than I had anticipated. In almost every year there are books the collation of which I have not, with the time at my disposal, been able to ascertain, and even when it is possible to guess at the size of these with some approach to accuracy, we have still to reckon with that part of Allde's output which waits identification. It may, however, be worth while to give such figures as I can, on the understanding that they are not intended as more than quite rough approximations.

I have taken the quarto page as the standard and have counted a page in octavo as half, and one in duodecimo as one-third of this. Broadsides I have taken as equivalent to four quarto pages.

On this basis the identified output of Allde's second year of printing (1585) amounts to 160 quarto pages (five books). In 1587 the quantity had risen to 484 pages, in 1590 to somewhere about 560, and in 1592 to about 680 (nine books).

The following year, 1593, is remarkable in that Allde is only known to have printed a single book, Hill's Profitable Arte of Gardening, 280 pages in 4to, but of course there may have been other anonymous work belonging to this

year; and although six books are assignable to the year which
followed, their equivalent in quarto pages is only 304.   Perhaps, however, part of this year's production was held over
until the following year, 1595, when Allde's two books of
Homilies together amount to 800 pages and with other publications give a total of some 1,150 pages, a number which he
does not seem again to have reached for another ten years.
In 1596 production is still high with 1,026 pages; from this,
however, the number falls off rapidly until 1601 in which he
only produced a single book of 48 pages--so far at least as
is known--his output in this year reaching its lowest point.
From 1602, it rises again to 1,108 pages in 1605 and 1,636
pages in 1607, his maximum.

        I do not propose to give you the figures year by year
for the rest of Allde's business life.   This would be unneces-
sarily tedious, and besides I have not been able to work
them out to my satisfaction.   In almost every year there are
queries of one sort or another.   In general, however, I may
say that such information as I have been able to collect
seems to suggest an output in the neighbourhood of 800
quarto pages per annum from 1608 up till about 1618, with
a gradually diminishing production during the ten years which
followed, when, though Allde continued to print a fair number
of books, there was a high proportion of very thin ones
among them.

        Omitting these last ten years of Allde's career, I
find in twenty-eight years, for which I have figures which
seem to me likely to be not too wildly wrong, a total of
17,550 quarto pages, giving an average of 627 pages per
year.   This figure includes several years in which his production seems to be abnormally small, indicating, I think,
either that for some reason or another his business was
temporarily interrupted or that a large part of the work of
those years has disappeared without leaving any trace.   The
latter is perhaps the more probable explanation.   We know
indeed of editions of certain books of which no copies are
now traceable.   Thus, take Tapp's Seamans Kalender which
first appeared in 1602.   Three other editions are known, the
third in 1608, the fifth in 1615, and the ninth in 1625.
Here, then, are five editions of a 4to book of 92 pages, all
probably printed by Allde, which have completely disappeared.   So also we may suspect lost editions of Bradford's
Godly Meditations, and of the Safeguard of Sailors, and perhaps of other books which were Allde's copyrights and were
obviously popular.   In these other cases, however, the ex-

isting editions are not numbered and we have therefore no clear indication of how many are lost. It would of course only take the addition of a few lost editions of books of this kind to the apparently lean years of Allde's output to bring them up to the average.

As I have just said, the known production of twenty-eight years between 1584 and 1618 averages 627 pages per year, while that of the years 1608-18, when his business was fully established and he was still in middle age, seems to have been in the neighbourhood of 800 pages. Allowing for a reasonable number of lost and unidentified books, we might, I think, assume an average for Allde's whole career, except the first few years and the last few, of 800 pages, rising to 1,000 or 1,200 at his best period round about the years 1605-10.

Would this be a reasonable amount of composition to come from a small press? If we assume that the functions of compositor and pressman were never combined in one person, as perhaps we may at the time with which we are dealing, then no press could well have had less than one whole-time compositor, or, to put it somewhat differently, if the press were to be economically run, its output must have been not less than the amount of work which could be done by a single compositor.

If, further, we are entitled to assume that a normal book, other than a reprint, was commonly set up by a single compositor or by two working alternately but not simultaneously, the rate at which a book could be put through the press is the rate at which one compositor could compose. It happens that we have information as to the rate at which at least three books passed through the press in the early or middle seventeenth century. The evidence shows a curious agreement and all points to one sheet a day as a maximum but not unreasonable rate. The extract from Sir Thomas Urquhart's odd book entitled Εκσκυβαλαυρον of 1652, printed by Mr. Percy Simpson in a recent part of the Transactions of the Oxford Bibliographical Society, suggests that a good rate of composition for an expert compositor was one sheet a day. From a paper by Mr. G. W. Wheeler in the same volume of Transactions it appears that the 1604-5 Catalogue of the Bodleian Library was also composed and printed at the rate of one sheet a day. In both cases, however, there seems to have been some especial haste, so we must evidently regard this as the upward limit of ordinary

work rather than as an average rate of production. Lastly
we are informed that the composition of Isaac Casaubon's
De rebus sacris et ecclesiasticis exercitationes, 1614, was
at the rate of one sheet (four folio pages) per day (Patti-
son's Casaubon, p. 386). This at least was Casaubon's
reckoning at an early stage of the printing: actually it did
not proceed quite so quickly, though it appears that there
may have been other causes of delay besides the rate of
composition.

If, then, particular books, set up, we may suppose,
by a single compositor, or by two compositors working alternately but not simultaneously, could be set up, under
pressure, at the rate of one sheet (eight quarto pages) per
day, it seems to follow that the rate of composition in the
smallest printing house when fully occupied might approxi-
mate to 2,000-2,400 quarto pages in a year of 300 working
days, an amount well in excess of Allde's known output in
any one year. This suggests that the books which have
come down to us, or that have been identified as Allde's, do
not represent the whole of his production.

But for a printing business to be carried on economically there must be a definite correspondence between the
rate of composition and the output of the machine-room. In
The Library, 2nd series, vii. 43, an opinion of Mr. C. T.
Jacobi is quoted to the effect that the old wooden presses,
with two men to each, could turn out about 1,000 sheets per
day, printed on one side, equivalent to 500 perfected sheets.
If this applied to Allde's pressmen, and if the average number of copies of a book printed was 1,000, one compositor
could, working hard, have kept two presses, each with a
pair of pressmen, busy. But if I interpret correctly Moxon's figures in his Mechanick Exercises of 1683--and I am
not sure that I do interpret them correctly, for Moxon is by
no means a lucid writer--Mr. Jacobi greatly underestimates
the rate of machining. According to Moxon, what he calls
a "token" of paper was an hour's work for the press, and
we find elsewhere in his book that a token for "half a
press," namely a press worked by a single workman, was
5 quires, or for a whole press (two workmen) 10 quires.
Now if two pressmen could work 10 quires (half a ream) per
hour, they could work 4 reams per day of eight hours.
This of course was working the sheets on one side only, and
is therefore equivalent to 1,000 perfected sheets per day,
exactly double Mr. Jacobi's figures. I think, however, that
Moxon was only considering the time actually taken in pulling

the impressions, whereas the pressmen had many incidental
tasks which would occupy a large portion of their time;
there was not only the actual making-ready of the forme,
but often adjustments to the press, besides the preparation
of the tympan, frisket, and of the ink, and the washing down
of the type after use, while it would seem, from what Moxon says, that they might even be called on to remove the
forme which was being worked in order to print proofs--
though in his own day many printing-houses had a separate
press for proofing. All these jobs would cut so much into
their time that possibly Mr. Jacobi's 500 impressions for a
day's work may not be so much below the mark as would
appear.

In the later part of his career Allde had two presses.
The output of these, each worked by a pair of men, would
be on the lower estimate 1,000 sheets a day. If this represented the average number of copies in the impression, it
obviously calls for an average composition rate of one sheet,
or eight quarto pages a day, say, 2,400 a year. This is
considerably more than double what we have taken as Allde's
average rate of composition, namely 800-1,000 pages a year.
Here again, therefore, we seem to have evidence that Allde's business, assuming it to be economically run, should
have had a much greater output than we can now assign to
it. We may perhaps suppose either:

(1) That Allde's books were much more numerous
than we are aware of, i.e. that a great part of his work is
unidentified or lost; or

(2) That though Allde had two presses he did not keep
them nearly fully occupied. He might of course possibly
have used one as a proof press; or, lastly,

(3) He may have done a good deal of printing that
was not book-printing at all. Seeing how well recognized
was the custom of pasting-up advertisements on certain so-
called posts, it is surely to be assumed that a number of
various announcements would be printed. Then, too, there
were programmes of various events, descriptions of cere-
monial processions, funerals, &c., announcements of lot-
teries, lottery-tickets, and perhaps price-lists like the list
of binding-prices in the collection of the Society of Anti-
quaries. Indeed there must have been a large amount of
printing done which was not book-printing, and of which only a minute proportion would survive, but which must have

given a good deal of work to the smaller trade printers. [1]
So perhaps there is not after all so great an inconsistency
between Allde's possession of two presses and the number
of book-pages which his composing-room seems to have
turned out as we might at first suppose.

Let us now turn for a moment to the financial side
of the matter. Neglecting all possible printing of other
things than books, at the existence of which we can only
guess and of which we really know nothing at all, what, on
the assumption that he produced 800 pages in quarto yearly,
would he make out of his business? Frankly, it is rather
absurd even to attempt to answer--we know far too little of
the conditions of the time. But it seems to be generally
agreed that for the early part of the seventeenth century it
is not unreasonable to take the average price of new books,
unbound or simply stitched, to the public, as 1 d per sheet,
and to take 1,000 as representing an average edition. Popular books were likely to be printed in larger numbers,
1,250 or 1,500 to the edition, but books of a heavier kind
might well run to only 500. Two-thirds of Allde's books
were printed for the booksellers; all of these would naturally be taken off his hands at once. Suppose that of the remaining third--his own publications--he also sold all that he
printed, not of course immediately but in a few years, so
that the average sale was at the same rate as the average
production. This of course is not likely to be strictly true;
he must occasionally have made a bad speculation and found
himself with a book that was unsaleable, but to judge from
the sort of books that he published for himself and what we
can infer as to the conditions of the Elizabethan trade in
books, I doubt whether these few exceptions would be worth
taking into account. If we ignore them, his 1,000 copies of
800 quarto pages would sell to the public at 1,000 times 100
pence, i.e. 100,000 d or £416 13 s. 4 d. Of course this
would not be all profit. There are the whole of his ex-
penses in paper, type, wages of his workmen, and so on,
and on two-thirds of the output there is also the profit of
the booksellers for whom the books were printed. But assuming that Allde sold a good proportion of the remaining
third to the public at their full price and he himself worked
in the business, as he presumably did, it seems not extrava-
gant to assume that he would get for himself something like
20 per cent of what the public paid for his output--though I
admit that this is a mere guess and that I should be sorry
to be called upon to justify it. If, however, it is correct,
Allde's 800 pages per annum would give him £83 6s. 8d.

Multiplying this by 6 to give the 1914 equivalent, or by 10 to give a present-day figure, we arrive at £500 or £833 6s. 8 d. respectively--not indeed princely, but, I think, not unreasonable for one of the smaller printers of the time, and of course we have taken no account whatever of any income derived from the printing of other things than books.

I ought perhaps to apologize for the somewhat speculative character of the last few pages, which are indeed hardly based on the firm foundation which we have a right to expect in bibliographical work; but it is, I think, useful at times to attempt a more general view of a subject than the evidence strictly warrants. Such a view may enable us to see how far the a priori conception which we have formed of what is likely to happen is contradicted by the extant evidence on particular points, and at the same time may bring into greater prominence those points on which further evidence is needed. We may now pass to the more matter-of-fact question of Allde's printing material.

Allde's types. Of Allde's types there is little to say. He had a normal range of black-letter, roman, and italic of the faces used by most of the smaller printers of his time. So far at least as I have observed, there is nothing in the types used which serve to distinguish Allde's work from that of a dozen other printers, and it seems therefore better to leave any discussion of them until the types of the period are dealt with as a whole.

Devices. In my book on Printers' Devices I mentioned three devices and one compartment as found in use by Allde, but of these only the compartment (No. 360), one with four armillary spheres, which was presumably cut for use in almanacs and which bears the initials E. A., has any obvious connexion with him. It was used from 1607 to 1609. Of the other three, one, a fleur-de-lis with In Domino confido (No. 270), had formerly been Waldegrave's and had passed to Allde in 1603 or 1604 (cf. below under Ornaments, Nos. 9 and 13). It was used, but only occasionally, by him and by his widow Elizabeth after him. The second, a griffin segreant (No. 284), had apparently belonged to Thomas Gubbin, who traded at the sign of the Griffin, and passed to Allde in 1598-1600. The third (No. 290) and a fourth (No. 343), the ownership of which I had been unable to determine, were probably cut for J. Harrison, for one of them bears his rebus of a hare, a sheaf of rye (?), and the sun, while the other, of similar design, still has the sun, though the

ovals which should contain the other portions of the rebus
are empty. I have found neither of these in use by Harrison, but both were, I think, undoubtedly owned by Allde during practically the whole of his career. No. 290 was used
by him from 1592 and by his widow after him, while No.
343 is found in 1594 in The Wars of Cyrus, printed by E.
A. for W. Blackwal, as well as in Grimellos fortunes,
1604, and J. D. B.'s Eclogue ou chant pastoral, 1627, which
have no printer's name but contain evidence of coming from
Allde's press.

   Ornaments. The ornaments used by Allde are a miscellaneous collection of little merit or interest except as a
means of identifying the output of his press; and, unfortunately, even for this purpose they are not all that could be desired in view of the doubt whether several of them are woodcut or metal.

   Those which are here reproduced include, I think,
all of which Allde made frequent use. There are, however,
many of his books which I have not seen, and it is probable
that a few other ornaments are to be found in these. For
the same reason it must not be assumed that the dates which
I have given to the various blocks accurately represent the
time during which they were in his possession. The notes
which follow are to be regarded as very rough. I have made
no attempt to trace the ultimate source or to work out a
complete history of the blocks, a thing which indeed could
only be economically and effectively done as part of a study
of the ornaments of the period as a whole. For convenience
I give first the ornaments which he used in a number of
books and which may be regarded as his regular stock.
They fall into three groups according to the dates when they
appear to have come into his possession. The earliest
group may possibly have been part of his father's printing
material, as were certainly some of the initial letters which
he used, but such books of John Allde as I have seen contain no ornaments whatever.

   The earliest ornament that I have found in Edward
Allde's work is the sun and cloud block, No. 1, which he
had by 1591. Possibly at the same time he possessed Nos.
2, 3, and 4.

   About 1604, he seems to have obtained several fresh
ornaments, four of which occur in The Wit of a Woman,
printed anonymously in 1604 but identified as Allde's by the

presence of No. 4. These four, Nos. 5, 6, 7, 8, are all
found later in work bearing Allde's name. About the same
date he became possessed of two which had formerly been
used by Waldegrave at Edinburgh, namely Nos. 9 and 13,
as well as Nos. 10, 11, 12, and 14, all of which he had by
1605 at latest.

A little later come Nos. 15, 16, and 17 (1607), 18
(1608), and 19 (1610). After this last date he seems to have
acquired nothing further for some years, but towards the end
of his life we find one new one, No. 20.

At least nine of the ornaments commonly used by him
are to be found later in books printed by his widow, and
there seems to be no evidence of any of his ornaments passing into the possession of other printers during Allde's lifetime.

Allde's regular ornaments

1. (21.5 x 68 mm.). The sun rising clear of clouds in
    centre: cherubs at sides.
    This is probably the ornament of which Allde made
    most frequent use and it seems not impossible that it
    was an attempt at a punning device having reference
    to Allde's name, taken as equivalent to spelt 'All-
    day'. It is found from 1591 and was used during the
    whole of his career and by his widow Elizabeth after
    him.

2. (18 x 45 mm.). Winged torso of somewhat Mongolian
    aspect holding ends of volutes.
    Found from 1593 and still in use by Elizabeth.

3. (17 x 60 mm.). In centre a winged torso: two mon-
    sters' heads: two cornucopias.
    Found from 1593 to 1624. By the latter date it was
    badly worn, and it is possible that it was then dis-
    carded.

4. (21.5 x 72.5 mm.). In centre a winged torso rising out
    of a heart-shaped object. Two cherubs with rabbits:
    volutes with foliage.
    Found from 1593 and still in use by Elizabeth. This
    much resembles an ornament used in Marlowe's Ed-
    ward II printed by R. Bradock in 1598 and in the

Allde's ornaments 1–5

1594 edition of the same book without printer's name but presumed to be also printed by him.

5.   (70. 5 x 84. 5 mm.).   Large tail-piece with lion's head in centre on dotted background: vase of fruit above. Found from 1604 to 1617.

6.   (20 x 92 mm.).   Head-piece with satyr's head in centre, squirrels, and birds' heads. Found from 1604 and later used by Elizabeth Allde. The break at the left end appears in all prints known to me.

7.   (37 x 92 mm., with aperture 12 x 69 mm.).   A head-compartment with two dragons above. Found in 1604 and 1605.   In the example reproduced, the only clear print found, it is used upside-down.

8.   (37 x 57 mm.).   A coarsely cut ornament with a lion's head in centre. Found from 1604 to 1614.

9.   (15 x 45 mm.).   A strip with a blank shield in centre. Used from 1604 and, after Allde's death, by Eliza-beth.   It is the upper portion of a compartment used by John Wolfe in 1597 in The Charter of Romney Marsh, where it had the arms of London in the shield. This compartment passed to Robert Waldegrave and was used by him in T. Cartwright's Answer to the Preface of the Rhemish Testament, Edinburgh, 1602, where the shield is voided as here.   It was presum-ably brought back to London by Waldegrave in 1603 and the upper portion, if not the whole, came into Allde's possession after Waldegrave's death a few months later, as did Ornament 13, as well as Device No. 270.   The lower portion of the same compart-ment, containing a fleur-de-lis, was used in 1632 by W. Jones and in 1640 by T. Payne.   I have not found this in Allde's books, and it is possible that it passed from Waldegrave into the hands of Blower, some of whose material seems to have come into the posses-sion of Jones. [2]

10.   (36 x 36 mm.).   An ornament of lines. Found from 1605 to 1612.

(continued on page 122)

To the Reader.

Allde's ornaments 6–11

12

13

CAVALARICE.

14

15

16

Allde's ornaments 12–16

11.   (39 x 47 mm.).   A Medusa head.
      Found from 1605 to 1615.   A bad block which seldom
      gives a satisfactory impression.

12.   (17 x 84 mm.).   A head-piece of foliage with two
      snails at top.
      Found from 1605 and later used by Elizabeth.

13.   (16 x 69 mm.).   A winged boy facing to left and hold-
      ing in his right hand a wreath and in his left one end
      of a festoon of flowers.
      Used by Allde from 1605 until, at least, 1626.   This
      appears to be identical with the block used by Walde-
      grave at Edinburgh in 1590 in J. Davidson's D. Ban-
      croft's rashnes, and in 1591 in King James's Poeti-
      cal Exercises.   Compare No. 9.

14.   (36 x 93 mm., with aperture 11.5 x 69 mm.).   Head-
      compartment with two-headed eagle at top and parrot
      below.
      Used from 1605 to 1617.

15.   (11 x 89 mm.).   Head-piece.   Two-tailed boy with out-
      stretched arms holding ends of foliage.   Half-horses
      at ends.
      Used from 1607, and later by Elizabeth.

16.   (27 x 98 mm.).   In rule.   Vase between two boys;
      head below: at ends rabbits and wyvern's (?).
      Used in 1607 in the Tragedy of Claudius Tiberius
      Nero, which has other Allde ornaments, and until
      1627.

17.   (37 x 48 mm.).   An ornament of lines.
      Used in 1607-8.

18.   (14 x 90 mm.).   Head-ornament.   Woman's head in
      centre with crescent in hair, two snails, and foliage.
      Used from 1608, and later by Elizabeth.

19.   (62 x 60 mm., or 60 x 62 mm.).   An ornament of
      conventional foliage.
      Used from 1610 to 1614.

20.   (14.5 x 91 mm.).   Head-piece with winged head in
      centre, rather coarsely cut.
                                        (continued on p. 124)

Allde's ornaments 17–20

What appears to be the same block is found in use
by W. White (e.g. in U. Regius, Sermon...on the
way to Emaus, 1612).   It seems only to occur in
Allde's later work, from 1624, and was afterwards
much used by his widow.

Occasional ornaments

I am doubtful whether the following were Allde's
property, though they occur in books stated to have been
printed by him.   In some cases further investigation may
perhaps show that the books in which they occur were printed
for him by others.

21.   (11.5 x 74 mm.).   Head-piece, with a woman's head
      in centre and snakes striking at her.   Cornucopias
      at ends.
      Probably a cast ornament.   It is found in 1590 on
      the title-page of The Serpent of Division, which bears
      Allde's name as printer.   Similar ornaments appear
      in G. Chapman's Seaven Bookes of the Iliades of
      Homere, J. Windet, 1598, in the Fisher quarto of
      Mids. N. Dream, 1600, perhaps printed by R. Bra-
      dock, and in books printed by J. Legate at Cam-
      bridge in 1607, by J. Barnes at Oxford in 1613, and
      by J. Beale in London in 1637.   In spite of the fact
      that certain breaks or imperfections in the design,
      notably small gaps in the double spiral projecting
      from below the left-hand cornucopia, and below the
      head of the right-hand serpent, seem to occur in all
      the prints, we can hardly suppose that they are all
      from the same block, and we are therefore driven to
      assume that we have to do with a number of blocks
      cast from the same, slightly defective, pattern.   On
      the other hand, it seems not impossible that the Ser-
      pent was actually printed for Allde by Windet; cf.
      No. 22.

22.   (17 x 72 mm.).   Torso of a bald-headed boy grasping
      two human-headed quadrupeds by the tails.
      Used in Sansovino's Quintessence of Wit, 1590, with
      Allde's name as printer.   What appears to be the
      same block occurs in Sir Gyles Goosecappe, printed
      by J. Windet in 1606, but a block which I cannot dis-
      tinguish from these was in use by F. Kingston in
      1628 and 1630.   As printing material is not known

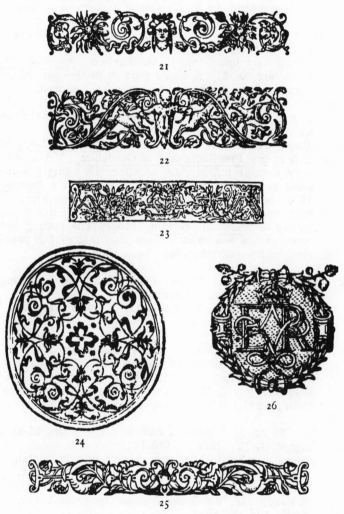

Ornaments occasionally found in Allde's books

to have passed from Windet to Kingston, it is possible that this, like No. 21, is a cast block. It is a
close copy of a foreign ornament, which occurs, for
example, in the edition of the Mythologia of Natalis
Comes printed by S. Crispinus at Geneva in 1612.

23.   (11 x 58 mm.). An ornament of foliage and mouldings
      within a rule.
      I have only found this in W. Perkins, A golden Chaine,
      1591, sig. A 3. A small portion of the top rule,
      shaved off in the original, has been restored.

24.   (52 mm.). A circular ornament of conventional foliage
      within a triple rule.
      Found on the title of T. Hill's Ordering of Bees (sig.
      Y 3 of his Profitable Art of Gardening, 1593). A
      very similar but slightly smaller (49.5 mm.) orna-
      ment occurs on the title-page of Marlowe's Edward II,
      1594, believed on the evidence of other ornaments to
      have been printed by R. Bradock, and of the Fisher
      quarto of Mids. N. Dream, 1600. The cutting of that
      ornament is somewhat neater than that of the present
      one, which may therefore be a copy.

25.   (10 x 87.5 mm.). Conventional foliage and mouldings,
      a ball with horns in centre.
      Found in 1608 in T. Hill's Art of Gardening, sig. X
      4.

26.   (37 x 37 mm.). Wreath with E. R. crowned.
      This must of course be an old block, but I have not
      traced it earlier than 1620, when it occurs on the
      title-page of R. Crowley's School of Vertue (Bagford
      Coll., Harl. 4910, pt. iv. 29).

27.   (24 x 68 mm.). Head in centre. Two coats of arms.
      Signed G. H. (See p. 130.)
      Found only in J. M[elton], A sixe fold Politician,
      1609, sig. A 2. I have not identified the arms.
      They might, I think, be those of a Derbyshire family
      of Hardwicke, but I can find no connexion between this
      family and the book.

28.   (23 x 83 mm.). The sill-piece of a compartment with,
      below, three faces having drapery hanging at sides.
      (Not illustrated.)
      This compartment was used in 1553 by R. Grafton in

T. Wilson's Rule of Reason, and in 1554 by R. Caly
in T. Martin's Treatise declaring that the marriage
of priests is forbidden, but I know nothing of its
after-history until in 1614 the sill-piece was used by
Allde in A. Copley's Wits, fittes and fancies. It
was again used by him in 1626 and later by his widow.

Cuts, &c. Apart from these devices and ornaments
Allde possessed a certain number of woodcuts, though none
of any particular distinction. A couple of very similar cuts
of a ship in full sail (see next page) are frequently used on
the title-pages of his nautical books, and these also contain
a number of geometrical diagrams, representations of land-
falls (in the Safeguard of Sailors), and the like. He also
possessed a few old almanac cuts, "anatomical men" and
other oddments, but so far as I have seen, not a single
block of any particular merit or interest. There is indeed
on the title-page of one book which he printed, the Trigo-
nometry of Bartholomew Pitiscus, a really pleasing compartment of the pictorial kind, with ships at the base and men
engaged in taking the altitude of the sun, heaving the lead,
and in other nautical pursuits, but this, I feel sure, belonged to John Tapp, for whom the book was printed, rather
than to Allde.

Initials. Many printers of the period seem to have
made use of a great variety of old and worn initial blocks.
Allde, however, though he possessed a few oddments for use
when a special size was required, throughout the whole of
his career made general use of only three alphabets. I imagine that all three of these alphabets were cast in metal
and it would therefore, in the present state of our knowledge,
be quite unsafe to attribute a book to Allde's press on the
evidence of the initials alone. The alphabets are the following:

1. c. 31 x 30 mm. This seems to have been the
earliest used by Allde and was used by many printers of
his time. Any one who compares these initials as used by
Allde with the same letters in the work of other printers
(e.g. in the first volume of the 1587 Holinshed), paying attention especially to the distribution of the lines of shading,
will, I think, have no doubt that they are cast from the
same matrices.[3]

A

B

Allde's two ships

Types of Allde's initials

2. c. 22 x 23 mm. in a double-rule border. Perhaps also cast, though I am not sure. This series was used
by John Allde and by Edward from 1593 at least. It eventually passed to his widow, though Edward seems to have made
comparatively little use of it in the later years of his life.

3. 19.5 x 19.5 mm. A small, neat alphabet which
from its clear-cut appearance must surely have been cast,
though I can offer no evidence of this. It appears in Allde's
later work, and was much used by his widow after him.

The only one of Allde's miscellaneous initials which
seems to demand notice is a rather elaborate A with a
crowned rose and two cherubs as supporters (Fig. 4), which
was used by him in 1610 and thereabouts. It evidently at
one time had the initials E. R. which have been altered to
I. R. This initial seems to be a copy of one which appears
in the 1587 Holinshed, vol. iii, at the beginning of the reign
of Elizabeth (p. 1170). That had Semper Eadem in the pan-
el below.

Allde made use of three or four factotums of which
one, 23 x 21.5 mm., represents two nude figures holding a
wreath between them. This is within a rule and was probably a cast block, for a similar one, but without the rule,
is found in use by Waldegrave at Edinburgh in 1591.

ornament 27

Notes

1. In the Court Book of the Stationers' Company we find un-
    der date 29 October 1595 a complaint of Thomas Pur-
    foot against Allde "for printing of breues aperteyninge
    to the seid Thomas." It was agreed that he should
    desist from printing "any breve or breves of letters
    patentes" belonging to Purfoot, and that he should not
    print "other brieues as for starch or otherwise" not
    belonging to Purfoot without their first being entered
    and allowed to him. I confess that I am not very
    clear what these "breves" were, or the amount of
    business that they represented, but it is evident that
    Purfoot's rights in them were of value or he would
    hardly have troubled to bring a complaint.

2. Would it be fantastic to suggest that at a printer's death
    his ornaments may sometimes have been given to his
    friends as keepsakes? It seems difficult otherwise to
    account for the curious dispersal of ornaments which
    seems sometimes to have taken place even when a
    printer's business, with, we may presume, the bulk
    of his material, passed to a successor.

3. Initials which seem undoubtedly to be from the same ma-
    trices as those in Holinshed may be found in the work
    of Field, Bynneman, and Islip, and probably of many
    other printers. There were, however, other sets of

the same design and very similar in general appearance which were probably either woodcut copies or
cast from different matrices, e.g. Newbery had a
set some of which differ in having closer lines of
shading while others are almost, if not quite, indis-
tinguishable from the Holinshed ones.

CHAPTER 12

BOOK REVIEW

Bibliography, Practical, Enumerative, Historical. An Introductory Manual. By Henry Bartlett van Hoesen, with the
collaboration of Frank Keller Walter. Illustrated. Charles
Scribner's Sons: New York, London. 1928. Pp. xiii+519.
27 s. 6d net. *

   I frankly admit that at first sight I disliked this book
extremely. What good could there possibly be in what is described by the publishers as "a comprehensive work in com-
pressed form covering the entire field of bibliography in all
its aspects," and which on inspection proved to deal with
such varied things as the formation of correct habits of reading, preparation of manuscripts for the press, publication--
incidentally we learn that the usual royalty paid to an author
in U.S.A. is 10 per cent., is this really so?--subject bibliographies, library science, special bibliographies, the history of writing, printing, book-decoration and the like? It
did not seem possible that writers who attempted to cover
so vast a field could succeed in dealing efficiently with any
part of it, an impression strengthened by a consideration of
the "bibliographical appendix" which seems to have some
quite odd inclusions and omissions.

   Closer inspection has, however, convinced me that
the book, in spite of inequalities, contains much that is of
value. Few students engaged in any branch of research
could fail to benefit by consulting it, though it is hardly a

---

*Review of English Studies, Vol. V, 1929, pp. 493-96. Mc-
Kerrow's clarity and objectivity may be seen in this re-
view. Reprinted by permission of The Clarendon Press,
Oxford.

book for any but the most omnivorous to read through.
That it is at times exasperating is less the fault of its authors than of its subject, or rather of the confusion of several subjects which are included under the term bibliography.   The authors define bibliography as "the science of
books. " I am not quite sure in what sense one can have a
"science" of material objects, but granting that one can,
there seems to be a confusion of thought between books and
the information contained in books.   The purpose of many
bibliographies and of most libraries is to facilitate the discovery and use not of books, but of information contained
in books, and it is unfortunate that we have no word for the
study of sources of information, whatever they may be,
whether books, monuments or men.   The fact that we have
no such word tends on the one hand to strengthen the common idea that books are the sole sources of information,
and on the other to obscure the fact that the treatment of
"bibliographies" must be very different according to the purpose aimed at.   That the authors fully recognise the danger
of the confusion is clear from their note on p. 154, but
they cannot help the fact that in a great part of the literature with which they are dealing the distinction between the
"bibliography" as a list of books and as an index of information is not fully recognised.

        The parts of this book which will be most useful to
students are the account of the most important bibliographies
of the various subjects which occupies pp. 46-132, and of
the general reference books, special bibliographies, etc.,
occupying pp. 172-258, and the Bibliographical Appendix at
the end, the latter especially for its references to recent
American bibliographical work, information about which is
extremely hard to come by in England.   It would have been
very helpful if the author had added some indication of the
number of pages each work contains.   As they themselves
say, "If you have not seen a book ... it is worth while to
know whether it is an encyclopaedic work or a ten-page
pamphlet. " It is certainly very well worth while to know
this when the work in question happens to be a foreign one
and to obtain a sight of it will cost one a considerable expenditure of time and money.   To be of real use to a student, a bibliography should, of all books not to be found in
any decent library, invariably give the size, price and publisher.   These things together will often give one a better
notion of whether a book is likely to be of use to one than
an average review.

In a few places a slight amount of touching up would
make things clearer. I doubt, for example, if any one who
did not know the Browne system of library entry would get
much light upon it from the description on p. 136.

> In the Browne system each book has a 'book-card,'
> inserted in a pocket inside the cover, and two or
> more separate pockets for each borrower (accord-
> ing to the number of loans permitted to each indi-
> vidiual). When a book is loaned, the book-card is
> inserted in one of the separate pockets and the
> pocket is filed by date.

Assuming that some words, such as "are provided"
after "separate pockets" have been accidentally omitted, one
sees glimpses of a system, but how does the librarian know
what or how many books a borrower has out save by a complete search through the whole file of separate pockets?

It is interesting to know that the custom of indexing
members of the peerage under their family name rather
than under the title is an illustration of "English conserva-
tism" (p. 145).   Surely it is rather due to a common-sense
objection to scattering a man's writings under two or more
catalogue headings as he changes his title. His surname
may well be the only permanent designation that he has.

On p. 150 the authors' choice of John Drinkwater's
Abraham Lincoln as an instance of a book requiring in a library catalogue the addition of an indication that it is a
play, not a biography, is an unfortunate one, for the words
"A Play" happen to form part of the title, at any rate as
the book was first issued.

Should another edition be called for, it would be well
that the sections of the Bibliographical Appendix should be
submitted to scholars with a special knowledge of the particular subjects. At present it is often very difficult to see
any principle in the selection--especially is this so in the
"English" section--and the placing of certain items is clearly wrong. I am doubtful in what section I should expect to
find Dr. Greg's Calculus of Variants, but I am quite sure
that the one headed "History of Book-trade, Copyright, Censorship" is not the right place for it.

The final chapters on the history of writing, of
printing, book-decoration, etc., are naturally in more read-

able form than the rest of the book and will provide useful summaries for those who have no opportunity of consulting more special works. It is a pity that the printing of the illustrations, rather a haphazard collection, as the authors seem to be aware, made it necessary to use a different paper from that of the rest of the book.

To sum up, the book is one which contains much that is useful and to which it would be well that every student who contemplates research should have access. On the other hand, it can, I think, hardly be recommended to beginners, nor is it, so far at any rate as English bibliographical work is concerned, by any means exhaustive.

CHAPTER 13

"EDITION" AND "IMPRESSION"*

SIR, --as my name has been mentioned several times
in the articles and correspondence which you have recently
printed concerning "Edition" and "Impression," may I be allowed to say that, while, as a bibliographer, I see nothing
wrong with the current usage of these terms in bibliographical work, I happen also to be a member of a publishing
firm, and, as a publisher, am by no means convinced that
the Publishers' Association are right in advocating the use
of the term "edition" in the bibliographical sense in trade
descriptions of current publications?   (The firm to which I
belong, Sidgwick and Jackson, Limited, has, however, always followed the association's ruling on the subject: and
I think that if Mr. Symons will look on the verso of the title-
page of our books he will find all the information which he
states that no firm except Messrs. Methuen and Co. gives.)

To the bibliographer a book is a material object made
up of paper, printer's ink and other things; but besides this
it is also a vehicle for imparting instruction or entertain-
ment, and it is in the later capacity that modern books are
generally sold by their publishers: the purchaser as a rule
buys a book with the intention of reading it, not in order to
study its bibliographical peculiarities.

The average reader is not in the least concerned with
how a book came into being, but merely with it as it now is;
on the one hand with its literary content, and on the other

---

*The Times Literary Supplement, October 1, 1931, p. 760.
McKerrow presents further distinctions in the terms "edition" and "impression" not only from the point of view of a
bibliographer but also of a publisher.   Reprinted by permission of Malcolm B. McKerrow.

with its material form, its size, elegance, legibility and so on, and its price. The publisher's business is to sell books to the reader, and for that reason, it seems to me, he would be wise to accept the reader's point of view, and in describing the books which he has for sale, to use terms which will convey to him the information about them which he requires.

To this average reader a book is a "new edition," not when the type is set up again--a thing about which he generally cares nothing at all--but when either the literary content or the form is altered. Thus in the case of new books (including, of course, modern reprints of old ones) it seems advisable for a publisher to talk of a "new edition" when, and only when,

(1) the literary content is altered;

(2) the form is altered by a change in size, type, quality of paper, binding, &c.

If this practice were followed, a mere re-setting of a book word for word in the same type would not be called a new edition (it is, of course, a new impression, as any reprint is), while a re-issue of the original sheets, cut down and in a cheaper binding, would be so called; this being, of course, the direct opposite of the bibliographical usage.

"Edition" would thus be used quite differently in a bibliography (whether of old or modern books) and in a publisher's catalogue; but I do not see that any confusion could result. "New" in a "second-hand" bookseller's catalogue means something quite different from the same word in a publisher's advertisement, but no one fails to understand.

It is true that the words "new edition" as applied to a book reprinted without change are by some publishers regarded as having advertising value; but it may be doubted whether the public is much impressed. If it is desired to stress the fact that a book has been successful, it is always possible to indicate how many copies have been sold by describing a particular impression as say, eleventh-fifteenth thousand, as the French and Germans do. This is a much more informative and indeed, I think, "selling" description than would be, say, "third edition" to possible customers who have no idea whether the first and second consisted of 500 or 10,000 copies.

It is, of course, very desirable that both bibliographers and publishers should agree among themselves as to the meaning of the terms which they use; but it seems doubtful whether there is any gain in attempting to find a formula which will suit two parties whose way of looking at the whole matter is necessarily quite different.

CHAPTER 14

THE ELIZABETHAN PRINTER
AND DRAMATIC MANUSCRIPTS *

Abuse of the Elizabethan printer is perhaps not so
common as it used to be. Pope, in the preface to his edition of Shakespeare, wrote of the "excessive carelessness of
the press: every page is so scandalously false spelled, and
almost all the learned and unusual words so intolerably
mangled, that it is plain there either was no corrector to
the press at all, or one totally illiterate." He was, of
course, referring especially to the printing of Shakespeare's
works, but the charge seems to have become generalized
and many since Pope have written as if any piece of English
sixteenth-century printing might be expected to swarm with
errors.

The impression is not an unnatural one, for most of
those who have concerned themselves with question of textual accuracy in Elizabethan printed books have approached the
matter by way of the study of the dramatic work of the period, and it would be absurd to deny that there are many passages in the early editions of Elizabethan and Jacobean plays
which cannot possibly represent with any approach to accuracy what their authors wrote, and cannot indeed represent

_____

*The Library, Vol. XII, no. 3, December 1931, pp. 253-
75. This article is based on McKerrow's 1928 lectures as
the Sandars Reader in Bibliography at Cambridge. Greg
says of it, "In this he developed the important theory that
confused texts of many plays (apart from the recognized 'bad
quartos') are due to their having been printed from the 'foul
papers' or rough drafts of the author, the fair copy being
used as the prompt-book and remaining in the hands of the
actors." Reprinted by permission of the Council of The
Bibliographical Society.

what could be in the manuscript of any reasonably intelligent
copyist. It may well, to one who only knows the early
printers from such texts as these, seem as if they were an
utterly careless and incompetent crew of rascals.

So much attention is now paid to textual work on the
plays of Shakespeare and his fellow dramatists and to inquir-
ing into the textual errors which undoubtedly exist, with a
view to correcting them, that it seems worth while to examine this question of the accuracy or inaccuracy of the sixteenth-century printers a little more closely, for obviously
it is of importance to us to determine, if we can, whether a
bad text is likely to be a bad reproduction of a good manuscript, or a good reproduction of a bad one. We should approach the question of emendation quite differently according
to which of these two alternatives is likely to be correct.

Further, supposing that we find that, in the case of
non-dramatic books, Elizabethan printers reproduced with
reasonable accuracy the manuscript before them, can we infer that the same would be the case with the dramatic texts
and that therefore a bad printed text of a play means that
the printer had an incorrect manuscript to work from? The
answer to this question must, of course, depend on whether
there is likely to have been anything about the dramatic
manuscripts supplied to the printers which made them more
troublesome to the compositor than the average non-dramatic
manuscript. I shall have some suggestions to make on this
point later.

Our first question is, however, were the Elizabethan
printers reasonably good? Did they in general reproduce
the text that they saw before them with substantial accuracy?
I think that without question, but within fairly definite limits,
they did, and I believe that any one who examines a few non-
dramatic books of the period from this point of view, reading them as he would read modern proofs for press, will
find that he ends his task with a much higher opinion of
Elizabethan printers and press-readers than he started with.
Certain allowances have of course to be made. They were
not all competent linguists, and Latin phrases or foreign
names evidently puzzled them at times--they had not the easy
means of reference to dictionaries and gazetteers that we
have--and further, we must allow something, perhaps a good
deal, for the inferior proofs that the correctors probably had
to work on. Worn black-letter type, or for the matter of
that worn roman--and much of the Elizabethan type was very

badly worn--could not be expected to give a clean impression unless carefully pulled on paper of the correct degree
of dampness, and proofs roughly pulled from type not properly locked up in the chase may often have been much less
legible than they should have been. A worn c and a worn
e, an over-inked or slurred u and n, l and i, for example,
might often have been difficult to distinguish, and a proof-
reader may well be forgiven for passing over errors of this
kind. But on the whole there is extremely little to grumble
about.

        Now I do not wish to weary you with lists of mis-
prints, or with comparative statistics of the accuracy of
early and modern printing, but I have examined a number
of sixteenth- and seventeenth-century books from this point
of view, and must mention one or two examples to prove,
or at any rate support, my contention. I may say that the
books which I chose for investigation were taken entirely at
random, or rather because they happened to be most easily
accessible. Let us take first, as an example of non-dramatic verse, Spenser's Faery Queen. In the "Oxford Spenser" the text of the Faery Queen, edited by Mr. J. C.
Smith, is based on the 1596 edition printed by Richard Field,
one of the better, though by no means the best, of the Elizabethan printers. In this edition books IV to VI appear for
the first time. If we examine book IV, the first of these
new books, we shall find that the editor has thought it necessary to depart from the text as printed by Field in not
more than twenty-one places. Now of these twenty-one errors three at least, and probably four, must, I think, be
straightforward mis-readings of the manuscript--whether by
the compositor or by a copyist we cannot of course say,
namely, "bravelike" for "beamlike," "nearest" for "mean-
est," "guest" for "quest" and "virtues" for "virtuous."
One error, namely "three" for "seven," is probably a slip
on the part of the author or copyist, as may be a "her" for
"his." Of the others eleven consist of a single letter wrong,
omitted, or superfluous, such as "worst" for "worse,"
"said" for "sad," "repayred" for "repayed." In passing we
may note that all these errors form real words, or in the
case of the four proper names included among them, what
may have seemed to be real words, a fact which indicates,
I think, careful but not very intelligent proof-reading and
suggests a doubt whether Spenser read the proofs himself,
though he is supposed to have been in England at the time.
Now these twenty-one errors are perhaps not quite all. In
some half-dozen other cases emendations have been pro-

posed, and some of these may be correct, but the text as
it stands is nowhere else so obviously corrupt that the Oxford editor felt called upon to emend it.   Further, there
may be a few errors of punctuation and possibly some other
trifling mistakes which the editor has not thought it worth
while to record, but even if we allow that there may be
some thirty or thirty-five errors, we still have the remarkable fact that in the whole of this book, consisting of 5,391
lines of verse, there are not more than two passages which
contain such serious faults that an editor who had before
him no other text than this first edition of 1596 need have
had any real doubt as to the correct reading; and even in
these two he might have guessed without any very great risk
of error.   And this, as I have said, is in a text of 5,391
lines, whereas, I need hardly remind you, the average length
of Shakespeare's plays is only some 2,800 lines--the longest,
Hamlet, having less than 4,000.

I will next take a pamphlet which there seems no
reason to suppose to have been printed with any unusual
care, namely Greenes Newes both from Heaven and Hell,
printed by an unidentified printer in 1593.   I choose this
simply because I once edited a reprint of it and happen to
have made a list of its misprints.   The pamphlet--a quarto
--contains sixty-two pages, and being in prose must contain
somewhere about the same number of words as an average
play.   Now when we look at the list of errors we find that
the most serious are two examples of words omitted, "continue the" for "continue in the," "doo vse" for "doo you
vse":   three cases of words repeated, "not not," "the the"
and "you you"--in the first two cases one of the words ends
a line and the other begins one; and one case of "any" where
the sense seems to require "my," one of the commonest of
misprints.   The remainder are eight cases of single-letter
misprints: "camber" for "chamber," "lytttle" with three
t's, "with" spelt "whith," and so on; some four queer spellings
which may or may not be actual errors, such as 'fraudelent" for
"fraudulent," and lastly some half-dozen errors of punctuation, such as a colon in place of a full stop at the end of a
sentence.   In the whole pamphlet there is not, I think, a
single error which could cause a moment's difficulty in reading.   If only the dramatic texts had been of this order of
correctness what a world of trouble we should have been
saved!

Lastly, for the purpose of comparison with the First
Folio of Shakespeare, it seemed well to look at some book

from the same printing-house and not far off in date.   I
therefore took the second volume of the prose compilation
entitled The Treasurie of Auncient and Moderne Times which
was printed by William Jaggard in 1619, and read ten pages
with as much care as I am capable of, noting down every
misprint, however trivial, that I found.   The book is a folio
and ten pages contain some 7,500 words.   In the pages
chosen I noted eighteen errors, of which only one is at all
serious.   The others consist of such trivial faults as the
omission of commas in series of names, so that Suidas
Strabo appears to be a single person, of single erroneous
letters in Latin names so that one has Titesius for Tiresias
and Nenius for Neuius, an "n" for "u" in "seuenth," and the
apparent mistaking of the English word "sea-side" for a Latin place-name "Seasia."   Considering the large number of
classical and foreign names in this book, I think that we have
here little cause for complaint.

        The three books which I have mentioned are, I believe,
quite fair samples of non-dramatic texts, and they certainly
seem to show a very decent level of accuracy in printing.   I
have no doubt that one might find, here and there, examples
of really bad work, but I cannot say that--except among dramatic texts--I have ever come across anything remarkable;
any text, that is, of which one could say with confidence that
in many places it cannot possibly represent the author's intention, as one can say of many of the printed plays.

        If then the Elizabethan compositors habitually set up
the manuscript before them with a high standard of accuracy,
are we to assume that in the case of the dramatic texts they
were supplied with manuscripts so careless as to contain
passages of evident nonsense, and if so why; whence did
these manuscripts come and who supplied them: or can any
other reason be suggested for the badness of some--not, of
course, all--dramatic texts?

        And here, by the way, I must interpose a caution.   I
am not referring to "bad" texts in the sense of deliberately
altered ones.   A play may be cut; it may be adapted; gag
may be added; incidents foreign to the story may be inserted
--it may be damaged from the artistic point of view in a hundred ways, but this is quite a different kind of badness.
Such a text may quite accurately represent the adaptor's intention.   It may be perfectly intelligible, correctly spelt and
punctuated, and be only bad from the point of view of what
the author originally wrote.   Nor, on the other hand, do I

refer to that small group of exceptionally imperfect texts
such as the First Quarto of Hamlet, which, without doubt,
were set up from bad copy surreptitiously put together from
the recollections of actors or from some such irregular
source. The kind of bad text to which I refer, and of which
I feel that some explanation is needed, in view of its inferiority to other work done by the same printers, is the text
which, while the bulk of it seems to represent fairly enough
the author's intention, contains passages which make no intelligible sense, in which words evidently meant to rhyme
do not rhyme, passages which should be verse are printed
as prose, or prose passages as verse, in which speeches
are assigned to the wrong persons, or in which there are
evident omissions or repetitions such as could hardly occur
either in a reasonably good manuscript or in the play as
actually staged. It is this sort of badness that we often find
in dramatic texts. We have seen that there was a reasonably high standard of accuracy in Elizabethan printing as a
whole. Why does Coriolanus in some 3,400 lines contain,
apart from many errors or irregularities in punctuation and
line arrangement, at least twenty-one passages in which
conservative modern editors have had either to emend the
text or admit their inability to do so? Why does the second
quarto of Hamlet, printed "according to the true and perfect
Coppie," contain at least a dozen passages of similar incor-
rectness? Was it that printers thought it not worth while to
take any trouble about plays, or can any other explanation
be suggested?

        Let us consider the normal history of a work that
was to be printed. The first necessity was the production
of a correct and legible manuscript. This was, for two
reasons, even more important than it is at the present day.
In the first place it had, at least in many cases, to be licensed and it can hardly be doubted that a licenser would
deal more rapidly with, and look more favourably upon, a
legible manuscript than one which gave him a lot of trouble
to decipher. In submitting a manuscript to the licenser the
author would therefore take pains that it should be tidy and
readable, as all but very foolish people do nowadays if they
have to submit their work to the judgement of a publisher.
Secondly, the method of printing sheet by sheet as composed
meant that an author, even if, as seems to have been customary, he attended at the printing-house to read his proofs,
had far less opportunity of touching up what he had written
in the proof stage than he has at present, and it was thus
even more important than it is now that the manuscript

should be correct in every detail. If the author was a good
penman and experienced in preparing a book for the press he
probably made a fair copy himself: if he were not, he
would have it done, as a rule, by a professional scribe, or
by a secretary. When the fair copy was ready he would no
doubt read it through to see that it was correct.

We get a few quite definite references to this copying
for the licenser or for the press. Thus Henry Chettle tells
us that he transcribed Robert Greene's Groatsworth of Wit,
which had been left by Greene at his death. As he says,
"it was il written, as sometime Greenes hand was none of
the best; licensd it must be, ere it could bee printed, which
could neuer be if it might not be read. To be briefe, I
writ it ouer; and as neare as I could, followed the copy."[1]
Here we have an admirably plain statement of what happened
in one particular case. A fair copy was required for the
licenser, and though this is not actually stated, it is im-
plied that it was from this copy that the work was afterwards printed, for Chettle's purpose is to make clear that
he had no share in the work save as copyist, and that,
though he omitted a few passages, he added not a word of
his own. It all seems very reasonable and natural, and I
think we may take it as a general rule that a legible copy
would be submitted to the licenser and that this legible copy
would afterwards be used by the compositor for putting the
work into type.

It would be interesting if we could determine to what
extent it was customary for an author to get his work pro-
fessionally copied for the licenser and the printer, and to
what extent the actual preparation for the press, the adding
of headings, the marking of passages for special type, and
the like, was part of the work of the copyist, but the probability is that there was no more rule in the matter than
there is at the present day when some authors send their
work to a publisher in manuscript, but the great majority
send it typewritten either by themselves or by a professional typist. It probably depended then, as it does now, mainly on whether the author was a good writer and experienced
in setting out his work for the printer or whether he was
not.

References to the matter are, I think, few, but if the
procedure was usual we should not expect many. In A
Briefe Explanation of the Prouerbs of Salomon, by Robert
Cleaver, 1615, we are informed in the Errata that certain

faults occurred "when the copie was written out, and made
ready for the presse," and much later--in 1674--we find the
Cambridge Platonist, Henry More, informing a correspondent that he is setting two more scribes on his copy (that of
book on which he had been working) that he may have it all
fitted for the press before a journey which he is shortly to
take. [2] He writes as if such fair-copying were the usual
thing, but it should be mentioned that More himself wrote
an abominable hand.

On the whole a compositor might, perhaps, be expected to produce the best possible text from a fair-copy
made by a professional scribe and afterwards corrected by
the author. It is, I think, most people's experience that
they do not make perfect copies of their own work. Its fa-
miliarity causes one to pay less minute attention than one
would to a strange piece of writing. One has perhaps in the
first draft hesitated between two words or two forms of expression: in copying one accidentally goes back to the
wrong one--or mixes the two up. One tries to improve as
one writes; and the improvement clashes with something else
that one has overlooked, and so on. And even harder than
copying one's own draft is, I think, reading over the copy
when finished--at least unless a considerable time has
elapsed since it was written. Thus a writer's own fair-copy
is perhaps on the whole likely to be somewhat less good than
one made by a competent professional copyist and read over
by the author, while at the same time one would expect it to
be less legible. Either author's copy or corrected scribal
transcript should, however, give a perfectly good text for
the compositor to work from.

Nor would, as a rule, those books which were printed
without the knowledge, or at any rate without the co-opera-
tion of their author be, from the compositor's point of view,
any more troublesome. The copy for such books would usually be either professional transcripts or have been made
privately by a friend of the author. If they were professional they would at any rate be legible, and if they were copies
made for sale--and there seems to have been a regular trade
in such copies--we may be sure that they made sense, for
undoubtedly if they did not the purchaser would have com-
plained. He would not be nearly so lenient to faults in a
relatively expensive manuscript copy as he would to those in
a cheaply printed text. So, too, we might expect legibility
and intelligibility in a copy made privately by a friend of the
author--at least if he were handing this copy over to the

printer. We might in either case get departures from the
original in the direction of simplification, for a copyist will
often substitute an easier reading for one which he does not
understand and thinks must be wrong, but in neither case is
the copy for the printer likely to contain obvious blunders.

   Now the point which I wish to make is that in the
case of all ordinary books, and especially of all those which
were submitted to the licenser, the text sent to the printer
is likely to have been clearly written and--whether conform-
ing exactly to the author's original manuscript or not--at
least intelligible and free from evident mistakes. To the
printer it would be a straightforward job, for to the Elizabethan compositor the writing of his day was presumably as
easily legible as the writing of our own time is to us--a
thing that seems sometimes to be overlooked--and he would
produce from it, as we have seen that he did, quite a reasonably correct piece of printing. We certainly do not find
in the ordinary, non-dramatic, texts of the time those
puzzles which are so frequent in the texts of some of the
dramatists, of which editor after editor is forced to say
that the reading is obviously corrupt and no satisfactory
emendation has been proposed. Was there then something
peculiar about the manuscripts of dramatic works sent to the
printers which caused them to be specially troublesome? It
seems to me that we are driven to suppose that there was.

   But why should this have been? One must suppose
that a play as written, and as played on the stage, was intelligible. There is indeed very little wrong with the texts
of those plays which were issued under the supervision of
their authors, such as Ben Jonson's or Daniel's; nor, with
certain exceptions, such as Sir Thomas More, a quite special case, is there anything wrong with the text of the few
plays which have come down to us in manuscript. In fact
I think that it can fairly be said that--apart from the damage
caused by time and ill-usage--the texts of these plays are
almost entirely free from verbal difficulties or manifest errors.[3] Why, then, the peculiar badness of certain prints
of plays of the popular stage, most if not all of which seem
to have come to us by means of the theatrical companies?
Surely the companies themselves must have had good manuscripts of the plays which they owned, seeing that in every
case a legible copy must have been produced for the perusal of the censor.

   I suggest that the explanation is a very simple one,

namely, that in the case of plays the printer very often did
not get anything like so clean a copy to work from as he did
in the case of other books; he did not in fact get a fair-copy
at all, but as a general rule, the author's original from
which the fair copy had been prepared. Consider what would
naturally happen. It seems clear that a dramatist usually
disposed of his plays outright to the theatrical company, who
became the sole owners of all rights in them. If the author's original was a good and legible fair copy, as in the
case of Massinger's Believe as you List, and perhaps The
Two Noble Ladies, this would presumably be submitted to
the Master of the Revels for his approval and on its return
would become the theatre's official copy and be used as a
prompt-copy. If, however, the author's copy contained revisions or corrections, or was not clearly written, we may
suppose that a transcript would be made from it by a scrivener regularly employed by the company for the purpose and
practised in dealing with dramatic copy. It would, no doubt,
be his business to regularize and, when necessary, expand
the speakers' names, see that the entries and exits were
properly supplied, and, in short, to some extent edit the
play. This professional fair-copy would, of course, be the
one to be submitted for licence and would in due course become the prompt-copy. It is a point that must be insisted
on that no copy but a good, orderly, and legible one could
possibly serve as a prompt copy. In view of the frequent
change of repertory, the Elizabethan actors must have often
needed prompting, and it would have been perfectly impossible for a prompter to make use of a copy which was in
any way, either on account of bad writing or of revisions,
difficult to read. As a matter of fact, most, if not all, of
the extant manuscript plays which appear to be actual
prompt-copies, such as Believe as you List and The Welsh
Ambassador, are such good and legible scripts as could
easily have been used in the theatre.

Now if a theatrical company, falling perhaps on hard
times and wishing to make a little further profit out of
plays which had passed their first youth, decided to let the
booksellers have them, they would surely have been reluctant to hand over the actual prompt-copy to the printer, for
this--bearing, as it usually would, the licenser's signature
--was their authority for acting the play, which they might
still wish to do at a future date; and further, it contained
prompter's notes which might then be useful to them. I am
of course aware that an opposite view is held by several authorities, notably by Professor Pollard and Professor Dover

Wilson, and that the former denies any weight to the argument that the prompt-copy was too valuable to be lent to the printer. He admits, however, that it would have to have been edited for the compositor and descriptive stage directions written in to replace the managerial ones, and I cannot help feeling that this treatment would so much have injured the copy from a prompt point of view, [4] that, other things being equal, the handing over of the prompt copy would generally have been avoided. I do not of course say that this was never done, for several of the Beaumont and Fletcher plays, as well as a few others, seem undoubtedly to have been printed from the actual prompt-copies, but it still seems to me that if any other copy was available it is likely that this would be given to the printer rather than the theatre's official copy itself. And as a rule there would, I think, have been another copy--namely, the author's original manuscript. [5] No sentimental value would have been attached to an author's manuscript in those pre-collecting days, and it would have been the natural thing to use it, while if it was a normal author's draft, edited as it probably would be by the company's producer, and perhaps revised by the author in consonance with the producer's suggestions, before being fair-copied, it is easy to see that although an experienced theatrical scrivener might find it easy enough to make a fair-copy from, it might well puzzle a compositor used only to working from clean manuscript.

My suggestion is, then, that one of the reasons for the badness of dramatic texts is that they were often set up from the author's original manuscript and not from a fair-copy such as would be usual in the case of other books. And we must remember that the original manuscript of a play would not have been written with any thought of the press. It was not intended for the study, or for the minute discussion of students three hundred years away in the future. It was not a literary document at all. It was merely the substance, or rather the bare bones, of a performance on the stage, intended to be interpreted by actors skilled in their craft, who would have no difficulty in reading it as it was meant to be read. To a compositor, however, it may well have been much more confusing than any literary manuscript, even in the author's original draft.

Now there are two obvious objections which may be brought against this view, namely, that plays appear in the Stationers' Register as licensed for the press, and that if they were to be licensed a fair copy would presumably have

to be made for the licenser as was done in the case of other
books, and that this would have been the copy for the compositor to work from; and further, that it has been recently
held that many of Shakespeare's comedies, including some
that show decidedly bad texts, were printed from prompt
copies. I have something to say on both these points.

   In the first place, I doubt very much whether it was
regarded as necessary for plays which had been licensed for
performance and had been regularly performed for years to
be actually perused again by a licenser for the press before
printing. The point is, I admit, not altogether clear. The
evidence of the Stationers' Register tells us very little.
Some plays were not entered at all, but many were. Omitting records of transfer, some 120 plays were entered between 1584 and 1607: in about fifty of these entries the
name of an official licenser appears, [6] the remainder being
simply entered under the hands of the Master or Wardens
of the Company, or without any mention of authority at all.
We cannot, however, argue from this that the latter were
not officially licensed, for entries in the Register were in
the main a trade matter, and had for their chief purpose
the prevention of disputes as to copyright between members
of the company, and at any rate at certain periods the clerk
does not seem to have troubled to enter the licenser's name
even when a book had been duly approved. As I have shown
elsewhere, [7] out of nineteen books by Richard Robinson, all
of which were, according to his own statement, duly "perused and allowed," either in the case of religious books by
the ecclesiastical authorities, or in that of secular ones by
the Wardens of the Stationers' Company, only eight appear
in the Register at all, and of these eight, six of which had
been licensed by the ecclesiastical authorities, only three
entries give the name of the licenser. It is therefore quite
possible that every play printed during this period had been
read in accordance with the law.

   But is it likely? Surely then, as now, the possible
harm done by a play being performed was regarded as much
greater than could be done by its being read. If it had
been passed for the stage there could be nothing against its
being printed, and whether or not a licence was formally
necessary I think we may take it as highly probable that
proof that a play had been already licensed for the stage
would be regarded as sufficient. After all, the Elizabethans
were practical people, and no one who has to read manuscripts wants to read any more of them than he must. I

have been a publisher's reader myself.

The matter seems even clearer after 1607 when the entries of plays in the Stationers' Register appear always-- or practically always--under the hand of the Master of the Revels.   As he, or one of his predecessors, had licensed them for the stage, he was not in the least likely to want to read them again for the press.

I think, therefore, that we may conclude that there is at any rate no evidence that a fresh fair-copy of a play would be needed for the licenser before it was printed.

Now as to plays being printed from prompt-copies. As I have said, a prompt-copy must have been a good, leg- ible and correct copy, for otherwise it could not have been used to prompt from, and if it was all this we should have expected the compositor to produce from it a good and cor- rect text.   But were prompt-copies used to print from?   For the reasons already given I doubt it, except in a few cases, and in every one of these we do, I think, get a text consid- erably above the average.

In the extraordinarily interesting and valuable sections on the copy for the various plays which Professor Dover Wil- son has included in the volumes of the "New Shakespeare," and which, by the way, remain as interesting and valuable by reason of their acuteness and subtlety whether one agrees wholly with them or not, he has argued that most of the comedies were printed from theatrical prompt-books, sever- al of them being from Shakespeare's manuscript, used as a prompt-book.   In one case, however, Twelfth Night, he con- siders that a copy of the prompt-book has been used which was not in Shakespeare's hand.   "On the contrary," he says, "the cleanness of the text"--it is almost entirely free from verbal cruxes--"suggest that the printers handled a very readable manuscript, and if we are to judge from texts like Love's Labour's Lost, Hamlet (Q2), Coriolanus, and Antony and Cleopatra, all of which seem to have been set up from autograph manuscripts, Shakespeare's papers were not at all easy reading for contemporary compositors."

Now is not the true explanation of the matter that-- whether Twelfth Night was from a prompt-book or not, none of the others were; though they may have been, and, I think, probably were, Shakespeare's autographs?

The evidence adduced by Professor Pollard in his
Shakespeare's Fight with the Pirates, and by Professor
Dover Wilson in the sections on the "copy" in the various
volumes of the "New Shakespeare," in support of their contention that certain of Shakespeare's plays including Romeo
and Juliet, Midsummer Night's Dream, Much Ado, The
Tempest, Love's Labour's Lost, As You Like It, and the
second part of Henry IV, were printed from prompt-copies,
is the fact that they contain stage directions in the imperative form such as "Ly downe," "Sleepe," "Winde horne" in
Midsummer Night's Dream, in which Professor Dover Wilson considers that "we hear the managerial voice giving
real 'directions' to the players," or "Wrastle" and "Shout"
in As You Like It; and what Mr. Pollard calls "characteristic prompter's notes" such as "Enter Romeo and Juliet aloft.
Play Musicke" in Romeo and Juliet; and, secondly, the occasional appearance of the names of actors instead of those of
characters as when Kemp and Cowley appear in place of
Dogberry and Verges in Much Ado, or when in the second
quarto of Romeo and Juliet (iv. v) we have "Enter Will
Kemp" in place of "Enter Peter." But this surely is but
weak evidence when set against the admitted fact of the irregularities and anomalies of the copy used for the majority
of these plays, which would have totally unfitted it for use
as a prompt-book. The question is of so much importance
that we must examine it a little more in detail.

What are the characteristics of a prompt-copy of a
play, that is to say of a copy used or prepared for use at
a theatre by a prompter or stage-manager? Fortunately
there can be little doubt as to this, for we have a few manuscripts which undoubtedly represent prompt-copies, as well
as several printed plays which correspond so closely in certain peculiarities with these that it seems clear that they
must have been printed either from actual prompt-copies or
from close transcripts of them. It is true that none of these
are very early, but there seems no reason for supposing
that there would be any essential difference between prompt-
copies of, say, 1590 and of 1620 or 1630.

In a genuine prompt-copy we should expect to find
some of the following things:

1. Warnings, either of actors who are to be ready
for entry, or of properties which are required for use later.
Thus in the manuscript of Believe as You List, two actors
are to be "ready to open the Trap doore for Mr. Taylor,"

Antiochus is to be "ready: vnder the stage," others are to
be "ready for the song at ye Arras," and so on.   In the
printed Chances, iv. ii, we find the direction "Bawd ready
above" in preparation for her appearance in the following
scene.   In Love's Pilgrimage, iv. i, we have the marginal
note, "John Bacon ready to shoot off a pistol"--the shot being fired some sixty lines later, and so on.   Similarly we
find properties mentioned as to be ready.   Thus in The
Spanish Curate we find in Act III, sc. iii, the note, "chessboard and men set ready"--the chessboard being required
for scene iv, and in Act v, sc. i, "A Table ready covered
with Cloath Napkins Salt Trenchers and Bread," and "Dishes
covered with papers in each ready" for use in scene ii, while
in Act iv, sc. vi we have a still more purely theatrical note,
"Pewter ready for noise," the explanation of which is to be
found in the following scene where we have the direction,
"A great noise within."   Similar things are to be found in
The Two Noble Kinsmen, a play which must have embar-
rassed the property-man by reason of the number of hearses
which he was required to produce.   There we find in the
quarto of 1634 the marginal note in Act I, sc iii, "2 Hearses
ready with Palamon: and Arcite: the 3 Queenes.   Theseus:
and his Lordes ready."   These hearses were required for
scene iv.   In that scene there is another note, "3 Hearses
ready," the second lot being required in scene v for the hus-
bands of the three queens.

    2.   A second mark of genuine prompter's copies is
the mention, at the time of the entry of a character, of
properties which he will require later in the scene, but either
must not or need not exhibit to the audience at the time of
entry.   Thus, in Beaumont and Fletcher's Cupid's Revenge,
1615, at the head of Act v, sc. iv, we find the direction,
"Enter Leucippus with a bloody handkerchief."   The purpose
of the handkerchief appears some sixty lines later when Ur-
ania is killed and Leucippus displays it stained with her
blood.   In the same play a handkerchief is mentioned in another stage direction (II, ii), though here it is only required
to dry someone's tears.   Similarly in The Spanish Curate
(II. i) there is the direction, "Enter Leandro (with a letter
writ out)," though the letter is not exhibited until 112 lines
later.

    3.   A third mark of prompter's copies is the men-
tion of actor's names as a gloss.   This is important.   So
far as I have noticed, the name of the actor in a prompt
copy always appears in addition to the name of the charac-

ter, not substituted for it.[8] Thus in Believe as you List
we have "Ent: Demetrius--Wm. Pattrick," or "Ent: Len-
tulus: Mr. Rob: wth a letter." Similarly in the printed
Wild-goose Chase (III. i) we have "Enter Leuerduce, alias
Lugier, Mr. Illiard"--Leuerduce, or rather "Leuerdure" be-
ing apparently the name originally given to "Lugier." In
The Two Noble Kinsmen (IV. ii), we have "Enter Messenger.
Curtis," in the first part of Antonio and Mellida, iv. i, "En-
ter Andrugio, Lucio, Cole and Norwood," where Cole and
Norwood were evidently the actors who played the parts of
Andrugio and Lucio.

I believe that there is no case in any play having the
clear marks of being, or being printed from, a prompt-copy,
of an actor's name being given alone without that of the character whom he was to represent, as that of Kemp appears in
Romeo and Juliet, or of an actor appearing in the speakers'
names as Kemp and Cowley do in Much Ado.

4. Finally, a mark of a print from a stage copy is
the entry of characters before the proper time. This I suppose means that what was intended as a warning to be ready
to enter has been printed as an actual entrance. Thus in
Cupid's Revenge, which we have had other grounds for thinking to be printed from a prompt copy, many of the stage directions are placed much too early. The same is the case
with the entry of the revellers in Act III, sc. ii. There was,
however, much likelihood of such things being corrected in
the course of printing, and it goes without saying that they
are always altered in a modern text.

Such marks of a prompter's copy are, however, not,
I think, to be found in the Shakespeare texts which have, of
late, been regarded as based on such originals. The characteristics which have been relied on as indicating a stage
origin are of what may be called a much less definitely theatrical kind. They are, as we have seen, stage directions
in the imperative mood, such as "Enter Romeo and Juliet
aloft. Play Musicke" or the "Winde horne," &c., in Midsummer Night's Dream, or the occasional mention of actors'
names instead of characters. I am not sure whether Mr.
Pollard, who gives these examples, would attach much importance to the phrase "Enter aloft." There is no doubt, I
think, that an Elizabethan print of a play was regarded as a
play--a thing the rightful place of which was the boards of
a theatre, and not the study, and that hence, though stage
directions were generally, in author's manuscripts and fre-

quently even in prompter's copy, given in a descriptive
form, little care was taken to rid the printed text of a theatrical atmosphere.   Thus I do not think that we should regard the use of the words "within," "aloft," or "above"--
though, of course, they belong properly to the language of
the stage--as in any way suggestive of actual stage copy.
Nor should we attach any importance to oddly phrased entries, such as "Enter Tigranes in Prison," "Enter Mistris
Frankeford in her bed," "Enter a corpse," and so on, where
"enter" means of course no more than that a curtain is
drawn aside and the character discovered.   Such forms
would certainly appear in prompt-copies, but there seems no
reason to doubt that an author might use them in his own
manuscript.   The same is the case with directions for characters to enter or exit by particular doors.   In one play at
least, namely, Nabbes' Covent Garden, which appears to have
been printed under the direct supervision of the author, we
find every entry and most exits particularized as "Enter ...
by the right Scoene," "they goe forth by the left Scoene," or
"by the middle Scoene."   This kind of thing means no more
than that the author had in his mind a clear idea of how his
play was to be staged.   Of even less significance are surely
the occasional directions in the imperative form such as the
"Winde horne," "Ly down," &c., already referred to.   What
could be more natural than that a skilled dramatist closely
connected with the theatre and writing, not with any thought
of print, but with his eye solely on a stage production, should
give stage directions in the form of directions to the actors
(as they might appear in a prompt-book), rather than as descriptions of action viewed from the front of the theatre?
Probably he would use either type of direction as it happened
to occur to him, just as we find them mixed in the manuscript of The Two Noble Ladies, which is held to be in the
hand of its author.   There we find, on the one hand, descriptive directions such as "Cantharides bites him," "The fiends
roare and fly back," and on the other, directions of the
prompt-book type, such as "Drag her in," "Kisse," "Crye
within, help help," all in the hand of the author.

Even the occasional mention of the name of an actor
seems to me far from unnatural in the manuscript of such a
dramatist as Shakespeare, who was writing for a particular
company with which he was closely connected.[9]   Psychologi-
cally it is, I think, just what we should expect.   To a man
with a good power of visualization such as every successful
dramatist must have, and who knows in advance what actor
will fill each of the more important roles, the actors them-

selves must have been more or less constantly present in
his mind as he wrote. I suspect, indeed, that this fact was
responsible for the extraordinary vitality and vividness of
of some of Shakespeare's minor characters. Dogberry and
Verges were so life-like because they were not merely a
constable and a watchman in the abstract, but actually the
Kemp and Cowley whose every accent and gesture Shakespeare must have known, <u>playing</u> a constable and a watchman. And if this is so, what more natural than that
Shakespeare, who was notoriously careless about the names
of his minor characters, just because they were, I think,
to him his friends and fellow-actors playing such parts,
should momentarily forget the names which he had assigned
to the characters and put down instead the much more familiar names of the actors themselves?

It thus seems to me that the origin from prompt-
books of the texts of A Midsummer Night's Dream and the
other Shakespearian comedies to which we have been referring is far from being proved, and that until this is done
we may continue to assume that they were printed from the
author's own manuscript, or at any rate from a rough copy
of one sort or another. If this was so, and if this indeed
was what generally happened when a popular play was sold
by a theatrical company to the bookseller, it affords, I
think, a very natural and reasonable explanation of the irregularities and low textual standard of many printed dramas in comparison with the general level of printing of the
time, namely, that whereas in the case of most book-copy
of the time the operation of the licensing laws brought it
about that the compositors had a careful fair-copy to work
from, in that of the plays they were far more likely to be
furnished with an author's rough draft much corrected and
never put in order for the press.

Notes

1. "To the Gentlemen Readers" prefixed to <u>Kind-Harts</u>
    <u>Dreame</u>.

2. <u>Conway Letters</u>, ed. Nicolson, p. 384.

3. Other than a few trifling and easily corrected slips of
    the pen.

4. At the same time it must be admitted that, as Profes-

sor Pollard has pointed out (Shakespeare's Fight, 1917,
pp. 68-9), printed quartos seem to have been at times
used as prompt-copies. A printed book would surely
have been easier to prompt from than any manuscript,
but which was used would probably depend on the
fancy of the prompter and the condition of the original prompt-book. In the case of popular plays this
may have worn out with much use. Mr. Pollard
tells me that he fully agrees that "the handing over
of the prompt-copy would generally have been avoided"; but that in trying to prove that some plays of
Shakespeare in the ordinary course of business would
have been printed from his own manuscript he was
anxious not to put his case too high. In arguing
against a general belief in the "stolen and surrepti-
tious" origin of the early quartos he was content to
show that they came from the theatre, and he is very
willing to believe that more than he had hoped were
printed from Shakespeare's autograph.

5.   As in the case of Bonduca; see Dr. Greg in The Li-
     brary, vi. 152-3.

6.   Including in the number a few in which a note is made
     that further licence was required before printing was
     permitted.

7.   The Library, xi. 173.

8.   In some cases only an actor's name is given when he
     is merely required to open a trap-door, shoot off a
     pistol, or sing a song, without being a named char-
     acter of the play.

9.   Since this paper was in type my attention has been
     drawn to two important articles by Professor Allison
     Gaw which appeared in 1925, namely "John Sincklo
     as one of Shakespeare's actors' (Anglia, xxxvii) and
     "Actors" names in basic Shakespearean texts" (P. M.
     L. A., xl, no. 3), which I failed to see on their ap-
     pearance, or, if I saw them, had failed to remem-
     ber. Professor Gaw concluded, as I have done, that
     the presence of actors' names in first printed texts
     is due to the author, and not to a prompter, though
     he seems to accept the view of Professor Dover Wil-
     son as to several of Shakespeare's comedies having
     been printed from prompt-copies. He makes the im-

portant point that the actors whose names occur in
the Shakespearian texts were, so far as their history
is known, associated with the company for which
Shakespeare was writing at the time when the plays
in question were written.   If they had been added by
the prompter (or, as I should say, if we had here to
do with a prompt-copy), it is not most improbable
that these names should have been allowed to stand
unaltered for some twenty to thirty years when the
parts must, if the play continued to be performed,
have been taken by other actors?   They might, however, well have remained in the original draft, which,
once fair-copied, need not have been used again.

CHAPTER 15

THE TREATMENT OF SHAKESPEARE'S TEXT
BY HIS EARLIER EDITORS, 1709-1768*

The last few years have seen so much new work done on the text of Shakespeare, so much development in critical method, and so many fresh theories involving ever greater concentration on the minute study of the earliest forms in which his plays were printed, that there seems to have been of late a disposition to ignore, as something out of date and wholly superseded, the work done by the editors of the eighteenth century, and to forget the thanks which are due to them for their share in making Shakespeare accessible to the reading public.

It is perfectly true that in a sense their work, like that of all pioneers, has been superseded, and that almost any person of quite moderate attainments and experience could nowadays, working from the early editions and with the aids now available in the form of dictionaries, concordances, grammars, and the like, produce a text of Shakespeare which would be regarded by scholars as far superior to those of the eighteenth-century editors. So far as pure scholarship is concerned we might now, without more than such moral damage as a lack of decent gratitude can do one, forget them altogether and let them and their too numerous quarrels rest in peace. But in the matter of literature, scholarship is not

---

*From the Proceedings of the British Academy [Annual Shakespeare Lecture of the British Academy, 1933]. London: Oxford University Press, [1933]. Reprinted by permission of The British Academy. Of this lecture Greg says, "In this he demonstrated how great a debt the current text owes to the critics of the eighteenth century from Rowe to Capell and defined more clearly than before the characteristic contribution of each."

everything. Besides and apart from the few who study the
work of Shakespeare, there are thousands in all parts of
the world who read him solely for pleasure. Such readers
have, as a rule, no need for the kind of edition which appeals to the modern scholar. What they require is rather
what the eighteenth-century editors aimed at producing, and
did in fact produce, a text which is easy to read and intelligible, without asperities either of grammar or of metre,
and provided with all those helps in the way of stage directions, indications of locality, and the like which enable the
lazy-minded to fathom the meaning without puzzlement and
the lover of literature to savour the poetry without distrac-
tion. In spite of the work of the last 150 years, Shakespeare, as he is known in the literature, not only of our
own country, but of the world, is still in the main the
Shakespeare of Rowe, Pope, Theobald, Johnson, and the
other eighteenth-century editors; and let me emphasize this
afternoon that if it had not been for the less careful, I
might almost say less respectful, treatment accorded to him
by these earlier editors, he might never have reached the
position in the world's esteem which has made the later
scholarship seem worth while. Let us therefore pay a tribute of gratitude to them by attempting to study, so far as is
possible in a brief hour, their attitude towards the text of
Shakespeare and the work which they did upon it.

     As you will remember, the folio volume of 1623, the
"First Folio," contained all the plays generally attributed to
Shakespeare with the exception of Pericles. This volume
was thrice reprinted--in 1632, the "Second Folio"; in 1663,
the "Third Folio"; and in 1685, the "Fourth Folio." In the
later issue of the Third Folio, and in the Fourth, were included seven additional plays attributed to Shakespeare, of
which only one--Pericles--is generally printed in modern
editions. Previous to 1623 nineteen plays (including Pericles) had been printed separately in quarto, and two or
three were reprinted from one of the folios as quarto play-
books later, but even at the end of the seventeenth century
any one who wanted to read Shakespeare would for almost
half his plays have had to turn to the inconveniently large
two-columned folios. While he certainly was read in these
folios, the more handy and readable editions produced in the
eighteenth century undoubtedly had a great influence in widen-
ing the circle of Shakespeare's readers, while in its turn
this greater popularity itself led to the multiplication of editions. As against the four folios of the seventeenth century
from 1623 to 1685, we have in sixty years of the eighteenth

century, from 1709 to 1768, editions by Rowe, Pope, Theobald, Hanmer, Warburton, Johnson, and Capell, and as most of these were reprinted at least once and some much more frequently, the total number of editions of Shakespeare's complete plays issued during the period amounts to twenty-five or thereabouts, indicating a very great increase in the attention paid to him by the reading public.

When we consider the editions of Shakespeare from the First Folio of 1623 to the edition of Pope a century later, we see very clearly the transition between the simple reprinting of an author regarded as contemporary and the "editing" of one who has become out of date and somewhat difficult to understand, in order to present his text in as sound and intelligible a form as possible to a later public to whom he is no longer one of themselves.

The alterations made in the three later folios of 1632, 1663, and 1685 are for the most part merely the kind of alteration generally made in reprinting a contemporary or definitely recent author. They consist almost entirely of two kinds. Firstly, the correction of such misprints as happened to be noticed--we need say nothing about the introduction of new ones, for these were presumably unintentional--and, secondly, the normal modernizations in spelling and in various points of typographical practice which have at all times been usual in reprinting any book in which exact reproduction is not regarded as important.[1]

When, leaving the folios, we come, in 1709, to Rowe's edition, we find this normal modernization still continuing,[2] and indeed being carried somewhat further than in mere spelling, for Rowe frequently substituted modern forms of words for older ones, "whilst" for "whiles," "been" for the old unemphatic form "bin," "an" for "and" in the sense of "if," "he" for "a" in such phrases as "a rubs himself with civet," and so on; but with Rowe the more serious attention to the text as a whole begins to overshadow the mere local corrections of a kind that might be made by a compositor or proofreader. What we understand by the "editing" of Shakespeare has begun.

At the time when Rowe's edition was put in hand the position as regards the text of Shakespeare was as follows. There were on the one hand the four folio editions with their progressive modernizations, and on the other a number of quarto editions of single plays. These were of two kinds.

There were, firstly, the original quartos printed before the
date of the First Folio and for that reason representing an
authority superior to, or at any rate different from, that of
the folios. Some of these had continued to be reprinted up
to Rowe's time as theatrical play-books. Thus there were
Hamlet quartos of 1676, 1683, 1695, and 1703--indeed more
than these, for three of these dates are found on two separate editions, one in each case being possibly a piracy.
There were Othellos of 1655, 1681, 1687, 1695, and 1705,
a Merchant of Venice of 1652, and a Lear of 1655. These
all go back to the original quarto texts, though with a good
deal of minor alteration. They are in fact, as stated on
several of the title-pages, the play "as it is now acted."
But besides these quartos there were also two or three
which were merely reprints of the folio text. Thus there
had been a Taming of the Shrew in 1631 and later there
were quartos of Julius Caesar and Macbeth.

It seems to have been generally realized at the time
that the printed texts of Shakespeare were bad, and also
that there were differences between the folio and quarto versions. No serious attempt had, however, been made to
work out the bibliography of the Shakespeare plays, and
nothing better existed than the rough lists in Gerard Langbaine's Account of the English Dramatic Poets, 1691, and
Lives and Characters of the English Dramatic Poets [1699].
Between them these mention quartos of nine plays, including The Tempest, Macbeth, and Julius Caesar, but the only
dates given are late in the seventeenth century, with the odd
exception of Titus Andronicus which Langbaine dates as 1594,
a date which was proved to be correct more than two hundred years later by the discovery of a copy in Sweden in
1904. How vague the knowledge on the subject was at the
time and even later may be inferred from the fact that in
1722 Jacob Tonson, the publisher, was, in view of Pope's
forthcoming edition, advertising for editions of The Tempest,
Macbeth, Julius Caesar, Timon of Athens, King John, and
Henry VIII printed before 1620. [3]

Nothing seems to be known as to the reason which
moved Tonson to bring out a new edition of Shakespeare,
but the matter is probably simple enough. In the early
years of the eighteenth century there was, owing to the great
amount of piratical printing and the uncertainty of the law,
much agitation about copyright, and eventually an Act was
passed for the regulation of this, more or less on present-
day lines, coming into force in April 1710. Tonson, who

was one of the largest London publishers, had some years
earlier obtained the rights in the folio text of Shakespeare
by purchase from the publishers of the Fourth Folio of 1685,
and it seems not improbable that the edition of 1709 was undertaken, partly at any rate, with a view to calling attention to his possession of these rights.   Nicholas Rowe was
probably as good a man as Tonson could have found to act
as editor.   Originally trained for the law, he had early devoted himself to theatrical affairs and for some ten years
had been known as a writer for the stage.   He had interested himself in Jacobean drama to the extent of producing
an adaptation of Massinger's Fatal Dowry, and must altogether have seemed quite a suitable person to edit Shakespeare.

As Tonson appears to have paid Rowe only £36 10 s.
0 d for his work on Shakespeare, which even considering the
higher value of money at the time was not much, we may
doubt if anything very elaborate was looked for.   The edition was clearly intended as a popular one, for in spite of
the forty-five engravings with which it was embellished, the
price of the seven volumes was only thirty shillings.   Probably a considerable part of the remuneration paid to Rowe
for his edition was for the Life of Shakespeare which he prefixed to it.   This remained for many years the standard and
indeed only "Life" and was reprinted in almost all the editions of Shakespeare down to the "Variorum" of 1821, and
its admitted importance, in spite of the vast number of
statements contained in it which have since been discredited,
seems to some extent to have distracted attention from
Rowe's treatment of the plays themselves.

Let us consider first what Rowe professed to do, and
then what he actually did.   His intentions are set forth in
his Dedication to the Duke of Somerset, where having referred to the particular pleasure which he had heard the
Duke express in "that Greatness of Thought, those natural
Images, those Passions finely touch'd, and that beautiful Expression which is everywhere to be met with in Shakespeare,"
he continues with a thoroughly eighteenth-century gesture:

> And that he may still have the Honour to entertain
> Your Grace, I have taken some Care to redeem
> him from the Injuries of former Impressions.

He admits that it is impossible to restore the text to
the exactness of the author's original manuscripts, as these

are lost. He has, however, compared the several editions
and, as well as he could, has given the true reading from
thence, thus rendering very many places intelligible that
were not so before. He continues:

> In some of the Editions, especially the last, there
> were many Lines (and in Hamlet one whole Scene)
> left out altogether; these are now all supply'd.

This is a large claim, but we must see what he actually performed. By the "last edition" he presumably
meant the folio of 1685, and as regards Hamlet, the only
play specifically mentioned, he carried out more or less
what he claimed to do. He evidently collated one of the
later quartos, that of 1676 or one still later, with the Fourth
Folio, though perhaps rather hastily. As is well known, the
folio texts of Hamlet from the first onwards omit many lines
which are found in the second and later quartos. Of the
lines omitted--some 231--Rowe restored about 131, including 59 lines in Act IV, scene iv, which is presumably the
whole scene which he states to have been omitted in the
"last edition," though actually the folios give the first eight
lines of it. The other 100 lines omitted by the folios which
Rowe did not restore include a speech of 22 lines in I. iv.
17-38 regarding the drunkenness of the Danes,

> This heavy-headed revel east and west
> Makes us traduced and taxed of other nations:

and 41 lines of Hamlet's talk with Osric in v. ii. 109-50.
These at least must, I think, be intentional omissions,
though some of the shorter passages Rowe may simply have
overlooked.

So much for Hamlet, but what of the other plays? It
was long ago remarked that in Romeo and Juliet Rowe printed
a prologue that is only found in the quarto editions. As,
however, he printed this prologue, not at the beginning of
the play, where the quartos have it, but at the end, it has
been argued that the quarto must have only come to his
knowledge while the play was actually being printed.

So far as I have observed, there are no other clear
proofs of Rowe having used any of the early quartos;[4] but
there is one insertion of his which does ultimately come
from a quarto though not from a genuine Shakespearian one.
In the fourth act of Macbeth, the scene of the witches' cav-

ern, there occurs in the folios--there is no old quarto text
of this play--a stage direction "Musicke and a Song. Blacke
Spirits, &c.," the song itself not being given: Rowe here
inserts the following song:

> Black Spirits and White,
>   Blue Spirits and Gray,
> Mingle, mingle, mingle,
>   You that mingle may,

having in all probability taken it, with the trifling substitu-
tion of blue spirits for red ones, from Davenant's adaptation
of Macbeth, first printed in 1674, Davenant himself having
taken the song, with other matter, from Middleton's play of
The Witch, a play the relation of which to Macbeth is still
an unsettled problem. As, however, Rowe did not give the
words of another song, "Come away, come away," which is
similarly indicated by the folio and given in full by Davenant
from The Witch, we may, I think, reasonably suppose, not
that Rowe had taken the trouble to collate Davenant's version
with the folio text, but that he had seen the play acted--or
possibly read it--and chanced to remember the little song
which he inserted. It is perhaps worth mentioning that this
"Black Spirits and White" song remained part of the text of
Macbeth through all the editions from Rowe's to that of Capell, who first threw it out.

There seems therefore to have been little justification for Rowe's claim to have consulted all the available editions of Shakespeare in the preparation of his text. It is in
fact little more--at least with the exception of Hamlet--than
a revision of the Fourth Folio. At the same time it is only fair to admit that it is on the whole a careful and, for
its date and purpose, an intelligent revision. Apart from
the correction of grammatical errors Rowe was a conservative editor and seldom tampered with anything that made
sense, or tried to introduce gratuitous improvements without
a reasonable ground for supposing the extant text to be
wrong, though there is one instance of this sufficiently curious to seem worth a mention. It occurs in Troilus and
Cressida (II. ii. 166-7), where Hector uses the phrase

> Unlike young men, whom Aristotle thought
> Unfit to hear moral philosophy.

Doubtless on the ground that Hector, being in date some 800
years antecedent to Aristotle, could not very well quote him,

Rowe tried to save Shakespeare's reputation for historical
knowledge by substituting for the name "Aristotle" the words
"graver sages." Curiously enough, Theobald later, not
realizing that the reading originated with Rowe, attacked
Pope for having introduced it.

But more important perhaps than Rowe's somewhat
haphazard revision of the text itself was the work which he
did in introducing uniformity into the designation of the characters, in adding lists of Dramatis Personae where these
were wanting in the folios, in correcting the stage directions, especially the entrances and exits, and, in the later
plays, in dividing the text into scenes and adding the localities of each; all of which improvements add greatly to the
convenience of the reader. To read Shakespeare in Rowe's
edition must have been a very different thing from reading
him in the Fourth Folio, and we ought not, I think, to re-
fuse to recognize that in all probability it was to Rowe and
his publisher Tonson that the beginning of the world-wide
recognition of Shakespeare was due.

First, as regards the characters. It is well known
that in the early texts of many of the plays characters appear under different names in different parts of the play.
Thus in the Comedy of Errors the father of the brothers
Antipholus is in the text named Aegeon, but in none of the
stage directions, nor in the speakers' names, does "Aegeon"
appear. Instead he is variously described as "Merchant of
Syracuse," "Merchant," "Merchant Father," and simply
"Father." This does not, I think, imply that the stage directions and speakers' names were added by some "editor"
but merely that the author, to whom Aegeon was clear-cut
and distinct personality, was in each case thinking of the
function which at the moment he performed in the action of
the play, and instinctively, and naturally, gave him the designation which this function called for. To the reader, however, these changes are disconcerting, and we may be thankful to Rowe that in his edition "Aegeon" is "Aegeon" wher-
ever he appears, and that in the same play the person who
is in the folios sometimes "Angelo" and sometimes "Gold-
smith" has become "Angelo" throughout.

Similarly in Love's Labour's Lost, Ferdinand, King
of Navarre, is in the stage directions of the early editions
sometimes "Ferdinand," sometimes "Navarre," and sometimes "King." Rowe calls him "King" throughout. In A
Midsummer Night's Dream, Puck appears in headings and

stage directions sometimes as "Robin" or "Robin Goodfel-
low" and sometimes as 'Puck." Rowe has in all cases
"Puck," and is indeed responsible for the introduction of
Puck as a proper name. Shakespeare would, I think, have
said that his name was 'Robin," or "Robin the Puck,"
"Puck" being really a common noun equivalent to goblin or
sprite. In the text he is referred to as "sweet puck," "my
gentle puck," "gentle puck," "an honest puck," "the puck"
--only the first of these suggesting that "puck" is in any way
a personal name.

It may have been his work in regularizing the names
of the characters that led Rowe to see the need for a list of
Dramatis Personae before each play: indeed he could hardly do the one thing without constructing the other. None of
the early quartos has such a list, and only seven plays in
the folios. Rowe constructed lists for all the other plays
and amplified the existing ones. These have formed the basis of the lists of Dramatis Personae of all later editions,
though they have been to some extent modified.

As regards the stage directions it need only be said
that Rowe seems to have gone through the plays with some
care in order to make sure that the entrances and exits of
the characters were correctly indicated. He did not otherwise add much, though he occasionally varied the wording. 5
It is perhaps to be regretted that Rowe did not do more for
the stage directions, for had he done this we might well
have been able to learn from them something as to the traditional business surviving to his day in those plays that
still held the stage. There are many points on which enlightenment would be welcome.

Whether Shakespeare had in writing his plays any
idea in his mind of a division into five acts is an unsettled
question. Clearly, however, the manuscripts from which
the plays were printed were not by any means all divided.
Thus none of the quartos printed before the folio of 1623 has
any act divisions, with the exception of Othello. None of
these quartos is divided into scenes. 6

In the First Folio six plays are printed without divisions of any kind; one, Hamlet, is divided as far as the
second act, the rest of the play being undivided; eleven plays
are divided into acts alone, the remaining eighteen into acts
and scenes. There is thus every possible variety. As,
moreover, the plays fully divided in the folio include some

which were printed from undivided quartos, it seems reasonable to suppose that the division was in all cases the
work of the compilers of the folio and to attribute the imperfect way in which it is carried out to their carelessness.

Now when Rowe began his work it does not seem to
have occurred to him that this point was of importance, for
he left the Comedies as he found them, with the exception
of the Merchant of Venice which he divided into scenes partially corresponding to those of an adaptation of the play by
George Granville published in 1701 as The Jew of Venice.
In the Histories he merely readjusted the act division in the
first part of Henry VI and divided the third part, previously
undivided, into acts, splitting one act into scenes. When,
however, he came to Troilus and Cressida, the first of the
Tragedies, he began to take the matter more seriously, and
from this point onwards he introduced scene division into all
the plays where this did not already exist, though his divisions are occasionally, as in Coriolanus, somewhat erratic.
In general he divided into fewer scenes than the modern editors, even in one case, King Lear, making fewer divisions
than the folio, eighteen instead of twenty-three: modern editions generally have twenty-six. [7]

Thus although Rowe deserves credit for beginning to
tidy up the text of Shakespeare in the matter of act and
scene division, he did not carry out his task with any com-
pleteness, and the same thing may be said of his other notable addition, that of the localities of the action.

We need not enter into the vexed question of whether
indications of locality are desirable in an edition of Shakespeare, or whether, as some hold, Shakespeare gives us in
the actual dialogue all that we need know, and when no particular locality is mentioned the scene is not intended to be
precisely localized. We are to imagine two or three people
meeting and talking and to concentrate our attention upon
what they say to one another without troubling to inquire
whether they are in the street or in a house or in the open
country or where, which is a matter of not the least consequence. There is, I think, something to be said for this
view, but, be this as it may, it is undoubtedly true that many
readers find it far easier to appreciate dialogue if they can
place the characters somewhere. Without a locality they cannot see them, and if they are not seen their conversation
carries no conviction. It is indeed likely to produce as little
impression and to be as tedious to follow as many of us find

a broadcast of a play which we have not previously seen on
the stage.   No doubt then the addition of localities begun by
Rowe assisted in the popularity of Shakespeare's plays by
making them more generally readable.

There are no indications of locality at all in the
quartos and only two general ones in the folios, where the
scene of The Tempest is said to be "an vn-inhabited Island"
and that of Measure for Measure "Vienna."   Rowe added general localities for other plays and, in a few of the Comedies
and in all the Tragedies, the localities of the particular
scenes.   He did not, however, as modern editors do, indicate the place of action at the head of every scene, but only
where he regarded it as changing.   Thus even at the beginning of an act no locality is given if it is supposed to be the
same as that of the last scene of the previous act--a system
which is a little confusing until one understands it.   Rowe's
indications of locality have been subjected to a good deal of
improvement by later editors, but he did at least show others
what had to be done.

What is generally called the second edition of Rowe's
Shakespeare appeared in 1714 in nine duodecimo volumes.
It is a little difficult to know what to make of this.   On the
one hand it does not, as one would expect a revised edition
to do, carry out in the earlier volumes those improvements
in scene division and localization which Rowe had only begun
to introduce in the later volumes of his first edition.   On
the other hand the text, while not without errors of its own,
corrects many misprints of the former edition, apparently
from the Fourth, or, at least in one case, from an earlier
folio. [8]   It is, I think, doubtful whether Rowe had much to
do with this edition.   It may, indeed, have been entirely the
work of a certain "Mr. Hughes"--presumably John Hughes,
the poet and editor of Spenser--to whom Tonson paid £28
7 s.   0 d in connexion with it.

Rowe's editions are the last in which Shakespeare is
treated as a contemporary, or at any rate recent, writer,
who can be understood without more elucidation than can be
afforded by simply modernizing the spellings.   Although the
next edition, that of Pope, appeared only sixteen years later
than Rowe's first edition or eleven years later than his so-
called second, Shakespeare seems by that time to have become an old author requiring explanation and commentary for
the average educated person.   On 2 August 1721 the Bishop
of Rochester, Francis Atterbury, who could hardly be called

unlearned, wrote to Pope:

> I have found time to read some parts of Shake-
> speare, which I was least acquainted with. I pro-
> test to you in a hundred places I cannot construe
> him: I do not understand him. The hardest part
> of Chaucer is more intelligible to me than some of
> those scenes, not merely through the faults of the
> edition, but the obscurity of the writer, for ob-
> scure he is, and a little (not a little) inclined now
> and then to bombast, whatever apology you may
> have contrived on that head for him. There are
> allusions in him to an hundred things, of which I
> knew nothing and can guess nothing. And yet with-
> out some competent knowledge of those matters
> there is no understanding him. I protest Æschylus
> does not want a comment to me more than he
> does. [9]

It was less than a century since the publication of the
First Folio, but Shakespeare had become unintelligible to a
man who was by no means ignorant of English literature,
and one to whom Milton was a favourite poet. It is rather
remarkable when we remember that a longer period separates
us now from the work of Scott, of Byron, and of Jane Aus-
ten, which, so far as intelligibility is concerned, might also
be contemporary, than separated Atterbury from that of
Shakespeare.

Unfortunately there seems to be little record of the
inception of Pope's edition of Shakespeare, and we may conclude that it arose simply out of a business offer of Tonson's, to whom it might reasonably seem that the foremost
poet and critic of the day was the best possible man to edit
our foremost dramatist. Work on the book seems to have
begun soon after the completion of Pope's translation of the
Iliad, the final volume of which was issued in May 1720,
and by 1723 the text of five out of the six volumes of the
Shakespeare--if not of the whole six--was printed, though the
edition was not actually published until March 1725, owing
apparently to Pope's delay over his Preface.

Before we consider what Pope actually did for the
text of Shakespeare, let us get rid of one or two accessory
matters in which he carried out improvements begun by
Rowe. He kept Rowe's lists of Dramatis Personae almost
unchanged, but he improved greatly upon his indications of

locality, giving these carefully throughout all the plays, instead of only in the later ones as Rowe had done. He also
divided all the plays fully into scenes, following, though not
always very strictly, the Italian and French custom of marking a new scene whenever a character of importance enters
or leaves the stage. Pope's disposition of the scenes was
followed by Hanmer and with certain modifications by Warburton and Johnson. It means, of course, a far larger number of scenes than are found in modern editions. King Lear,
which as we saw had eighteen scenes in Rowe's edition and
twenty-six in most modern ones, has in Pope's no less than
sixty.

Rowe, basing his text upon the Fourth Folio, had followed the order of the plays in that edition, and had included in his last volume, with Anthony and Cleopatra and Cymbeline, Pericles and the six pseudo-Shakespearian plays
which had been first added in the Third Folio. Pope rejected all seven plays as undoubtedly spurious, and for some
reason which he does not explain rearranged the whole in a
new order, grouping them as Comedies; Historical Plays, in
which he includes King Lear; "Tragedies from History," including most of the classical plays and Macbeth; and "Tragedies from Fable," including Troilus and Cressida, Cymbeline, Romeo and Juliet, Hamlet, and Othello. The result
was, it is true, six volumes of fairly equal bulk, but if
there is any other justification for the arrangement, it is not
easy to discover this.

But we must pass to the text itself. Pope evidently
took his work seriously. He had tried to enlist the aid of
Atterbury, and there are indications that he welcomed corrections and suggestions from others. He also did his best
to collect, or at least obtain access to, as many of the early
editions of the plays as possible, especially all quartos prior
to 1616, the year of Shakespeare's death, for he regarded
those published after that date as without authority.[10] At
the end of his edition he gives a list of quartos used by him,
from which we see that he had, or was aware of, at least
one quarto edition of every play of which quartos are known
to exist, except of Much Ado about Nothing, though he had
first quartos of only six, namely, Romeo and Juliet, of which
he had both the first imperfect one and the first good one,
Love's Labour's Lost, The Merchant of Venice, the second
part of Henry IV, Henry V, and Troilus and Cressida (both
issues). He seems to have had a complete set of the 1619
quartos. He had also a copy of the First Folio, and ap-

parently of the Second.

Apart from the introduction of new readings either
from other texts or conjectural emendations of obscure passages, to which I will refer later, the work done by Pope
on the text of Rowe, which he used as the basis of his edition, consists mainly in further modernizing the spelling, in
improving the punctuation, which, in spite of Theobald's
strictures, is in Pope's edition on the whole very careful,
in redividing the lines where the metre requires this, and
in regularizing the printing of the text according as it was
prose or verse.

Such changes as these would be generally accepted as
quite legitimate in a modern-spelling edition. But Pope
went farther in his desire to improve the text of Shakespeare,
and it is these further emendations which have caused him to
be looked on as an injudicious meddler.

He not only went beyond Rowe in his substitutions of
more modern for older usages, printing, for example, "if"
for "and" or "an" in such phrases as "and it were," but
made a number of verbal changes for the sake of greater
metrical regularity. To give a couple of examples, in the
Two Gentlemen of Verona he reads "Lady, good day" for
"Gentlewoman, good day" because the latter phrase is met-
rically awkward at the beginning of a line, and in Hamlet he
replaces "Dared to the combat" by "Dared to the fight" for
a similar reason. But this was not all, for he made a certain number of alterations in the text for which he could not
even plead the exigencies of metre as an excuse. One may
perhaps be permitted to suspect that in making these changes
Pope was not thinking solely of Shakespeare. The author
whom he edited and professed to admire might be permitted
to be at times too bombastic, at others too flat, to mix his
metaphors, or to indulge in other stylistic offences, for he
belonged to a less cultured age; but there seem to have been
certain things which a literary man of Pope's eminence simply could not let him do, such as to refer to "hats" in a
classical play. It seems odd, in view of the many anachron-
isms that Pope allowed to pass, even allowing Caesar to
pluck open his doublet, that he should so much have objected
to Coriolanus waving his hat. But the fact remains that finding "hat" four times in the plays on classical subjects, twice
in Coriolanus, once in Timon of Athens, and once in Julius
Caesar, Pope in the first three cases altered "hat" to "cap."
In the fourth there was a difficulty; the phrase was "Their

hats are pluck'd about their ears," and I suppose that he did
not quite see how one could do this with a cap.   Still "hat"
could not be allowed to stand, so he cut the word out and
substituted a dash.

So much for those of Pope's alterations which must be
regarded rather as attempts to improve Shakespeare than to
recover what he actually wrote.   We come now to the more
important question of his attempts to restore the text by the
use of the earlier editions.   And here we must remember,
that though Rowe had professed to give the true readings
from the several editions and to supply the omissions of the
later texts, his actual performance in this respect was very
slight.   Pope with all his shortcomings was the first editor
of Shakespeare to make a genuine attempt to collect all the
available material and to use it for the construction of what
he regarded as the best possible text, and for this I think we
may be grateful to him.

Unfortunately, however, having got his material together, Pope used it in an entirely wrong fashion, owing to
his failure to appreciate a very elementary point in textual
criticism.   In this he was not alone, for failure to appreciate the point in question seems to have been common to all
Pope's immediate successors, with the single exception of
Johnson; and indeed I am not sure that even now, in spite of
the stress which has been laid upon it in recent years by Dr.
Pollard and others, it is as well understood as it should be.
It is not that there is anything at all abstruse in it; it is just
one of those simple and obvious things that we tend most
easily to overlook because for generations everybody else has
been doing the same.   The matter is so important that I
must be pardoned for a short digression.

All the early editors of Shakespeare, with the exception of Johnson, who though I think he saw the truth did not
altogether follow it, make it perfectly clear either by their
prefaces or by their text, or by both, that they considered
that the way to form a good text of Shakespeare was by comparing as many as possible of the early editions and taking
from them the best readings.   How they were to select the
"best," though a matter, one would think, of some importance, is not usually discussed.   Now the least consideration
of the material available to them for selection would have
shown them that if they aimed, as they evidently did, at re-
constructing as nearly as possible the text as Shakespeare
wrote it, such a method was absurd.   They knew, as well

as we do, that each edition of a book after the first is normally printed from an earlier edition and not from a fresh
manuscript, and that in almost every case it is perfectly
easy to make out the line of descent of any series of printed
texts. If they had thought for a moment, they would have
seen that no reading which appears in a later text, but not
in the one from which that later text was printed, can possibly have any authority except on the extremely unlikely assumption that the text used as copy had, before being so
used, been corrected from a manuscript; a state of affairs
which, if it exists, will almost always show itself unmis-
takably. The truth is, of course, that new readings of authority can never be obtained by comparing texts in the same
line of descent, where the earliest must obviously be the
most authoritative, but only by comparing texts in different
lines of descent.

        The explanation of their failure to appreciate so obvi-
ous a fact is that the eighteenth-century editors of Shakespeare had, of course, received a classical education, and
the textual criticism to which they were accustomed was the
criticism of classical texts. Now in the great majority of
cases the available sources of classical texts are manuscripts each of which represents the end of a line of descent;
only in rare cases does it occur that a manuscript and one
of its direct ancestors have both survived, and when this
does occur the descendant would in practice be ignored.
Now when we have to deal with manuscripts each of which
may represent the end of a separate line of descent, none
being demonstrably the ancestor of any other, and supposing
that, as is frequently the case, we have insufficient evidence
to enable us to work out their relationships with certainty,
we are bound to assume that any particular reading in any
manuscript, even if it differs from the reading of every other manuscript, may be correct, for it may have come down,
through the lost ancestors of the manuscript alone, from the
author's original copy. [11] And this may evidently be the
case even if the manuscript containing the reading under consideration is in general a particularly bad one. The existence, therefore, of several manifest errors in a passage
constitutes no argument that other words in the passage,
which seem to be correct, are wrong. Clearly then if we
are dealing with manuscripts it may be a quite reasonable
and indeed necessary proceeding to collate all that are available and consider the claim of every separate reading to
represent the original words of the author.

It appears to me that it simply never occurred to men like Pope, Theobald, and Capell that the Shakespeare quartos were not in the same position with respect to the author's original text as the classical manuscripts were, in that they did not represent ends of separate lines of descent from it, but in most cases successive members of a single line. If they had reflected they would have seen that if we want Shakespeare's original text the only place where we have any chance of finding it is in a quarto or folio which is at the head of a line of descent, and that if descendants of such a quarto or folio have different readings from their ancestor, those readings must be either accidental corruptions or deliberate alterations by compositors or proof-readers, and can in no case have an authority superior to, or even as great as, the readings of the text from which they differ.

Pope's list of quartos collected by him contains twenty-nine items, excluding the non-Shakespearian Taming of A Shrew, and while it would be hazardous to say that he did actually make use of all of them, it is evident that he used the majority. Of those in which the most important differences exist between the folio and quarto texts, namely, Hamlet, Lear, and Romeo and Juliet, he certainly made very considerable use. In Hamlet, as we have seen, Rowe had restored some 131 lines out of the 231 omitted by the folios: Pope restored a further 36. In Lear, where the folios had omitted about 284, none of which had been inserted by Rowe in his text, Pope restored 142, exactly half. In the case of Romeo and Juliet Pope's use of the first quarto though extensive was somewhat different, for he used it mainly as an excuse for omitting what he calls "a great number of the mean conceits and ribaldries" that are found in the later texts.

It is difficult to make out exactly how Pope used the quartos and the First Folio. Some have written as though he only consulted them when he found Rowe's text unsatisfactory, and made no attempt to collate them throughout, and in certain cases, he seems undoubtedly to have worked in this way. In other cases, however, we find him inserting readings from the earlier editions when there was nothing at all in Rowe's text to suggest that this was wrong. The only possible conclusion is that he had no consistent practice in the matter. Probably he collated those plays, or those passages of plays, which interested him, throughout, and for the rest merely consulted the early texts when it seemed to him that the reading before him was unsatisfactory.

As a kind of substitute for detailed criticism Pope had devised a system of printing in smaller type at the foot of the page those passages which in his view were of doubtful authenticity, and this peculiarity of his edition was one of the features for which it was attacked. As a matter of fact, however, several of the passages which he regarded as inter- polations, notably the vision in the fifth act of Cymbeline, have been rejected by many other critics, and the total amount of matter "degraded," as he calls it, in his edition, some 1,560 lines, about one and half per cent. of the whole number of lines in the plays, is much less than has been re- jected by many more recent writers.

But we must leave Pope's edition. It may be de- scribed as the work of a brilliant amateur, a real lover of Shakespeare as he saw him, but one incapable of the long- continued drudgery which was necessary to the accomplish- ment of the task which he had undertaken, and with no clear- er understanding of the problem before him than had others of his time; and come to the man who in many ways was the true founder of modern Shakespearian scholarship, Lewis Theobald, or "Tebold" or "Tibbald" as the name seems to have been variously pronounced.

Theobald has come down to us with the reputation of a brilliant emender, on the strength of a few really fine con- jectures, of which the best known, Mistress Quickly's words about the dying Falstaff in Henry V "a' babbled of green fields" was, as he fully admits, suggested to him by a mar- ginal correction made by "a gentleman sometime deceased," who in an edition in Theobald's possession, had emended "a Table of greene fields" of the Folios, to "a talked of green fields." The truth is, however, that Theobald's far more important claim to recognition is that of having been the first to point out the value of comparing other passages of Shake- speare with those which it is sought to emend--as he himself puts it--"every author is best expounded and explain'd in One Place, by his own Usage and Manner of Expression in Others." 12 In his Shakespeare Restored and his edition of the plays he constantly supports his emendations by parallel passages, a method which has, of course, been followed by every commentator upon Shakespeare since his day.

Just a year after the publication of Pope's edition of Shakespeare, Theobald issued an attack upon it under the singularly offensive title Shakespeare restored: or, a Speci- men of the Many Errors, as well Committed, as Unamended,

by Mr. Pope in his Late Edition of this Poet. Designed not
only to correct the said Edition, but to restore the True
Reading of Shakespeare in all the Editions ever yet publish'd.
Though the fact does not appear on the title-page, the book
is mainly concerned with Hamlet, to which play 132 out of
its 194 pages are devoted, the remaining 62 containing notes
on the other plays. The "corrections" proposed by Theobald
in the text of Hamlet are about 106, of which 22 are either
corrections of obvious misprints in Pope's edition or improvements in his punctuation. Of the remainder, 51 are
readings from other editions than those followed by Pope,
and it is interesting to notice that 45 of them--all but 6--
have been adopted by such a conservative text as the Aldis
Wright "Cambridge" edition. On the other hand, of 33 con-
jectures of Theobald's not taken from other texts, only three
have been adopted by modern editors, of which only one is
of importance, the famous "sanctified and pious bawds" for
the "bonds" of the quartos and folios. Clearly so far as
Hamlet is concerned the influence of Theobald was far more
in the number of almost certainly correct readings which he
recovered from the earlier editions than in his own conjec-
tureal emendations.

At the date of Shakespeare Restored Theobald had already acquired a few quarto editions of the plays, including
the 1600 quarto of Much Ado, which Pope had not seen, and
he evidently continued with great zeal to collect others, being probably still further stimulated by the contemptuous
treatment accorded to his book in Pope's second edition of
Shakespeare, 1728, where Pope stated that he had taken from
Theobald's work as many of the proposed emendations "as
are judg'd of any the least advantage to the poet; the whole
amounting to about twenty-five words." By the date of his
own edition of 1733 he had obtained, or borrowed, 38 quartos,
against the 29 listed by Pope, [13] the new ones including first
quartos of Merry Wives, Midsummer Night's Dream, Much
Ado, and Richard III, though he had no first quarto of Love's
Labour's Lost and none at all of Troilus and Cressida.

It seems to be customary among editors of English
classics to use as the basis of their own edition that particular earlier one which in their preface they most vehemently
condemn; and Theobald followed the custom by using Pope's.
This, no doubt, rather than intentional copying, accounts for
a good deal of similarity between the two editions in such
minor points as stage directions and indications of locality,
in which Theobald generally follows the wording of Pope,

though he sometimes amplifies it.   He also to a certain extent retained Pope's arrangement of the plays, though not
his grouping.

When we come to the text itself we find a state of affairs which seems to render it doubtful whether Theobald
was really the meticulously careful collator that many have
supposed him to be.   It is true, of course, that if we com-
pare almost any passage of Theobald's text with Pope's or
Rowe's, we find that Theobald has adopted a number of readings from early editions and that the majority of these have
been accepted by later editors.   Thus in a couple of scenes
taken at random from A Midsummer Night's Dream and
Julius Caesar and amounting together to a little more than
500 lines, I find that Theobald introduced no less than fourteen definite improvements of reading which have become
part of the accepted text of Shakespeare. [14]

But on the other hand we find, especially in the plays
generally regarded as less important, a large number of
cases in which Theobald followed Pope in inferior readings
although better ones were available in the editions which he
professed to have collated.   The only possible conclusion
seems to be that he used the early editions much as Pope
had done, consulting them whenever it struck him that there
was anything suspicious in the text before him; but only occasionally, in plays which especially interested him, collat-
ing them throughout.   At the same time he was evidently
more careful or less easily satisfied than Pope, and the total amount of work which he put into his text must have been
far greater, while he obviously had a much better knowledge
of the English of Shakespeare's time.   But it is important to
observe that Theobald's text, in spite of its many improvements upon Pope's, was still a text constructed on what we
now realize to be a fundamentally wrong principle.   It is a
text based ultimately, by way of Pope and Rowe, on the
Fourth Folio, corrected by earlier editions; that is, a text
based on the worst of the pre-Rowe texts and not, as it
should have been, on the best of them.   The result is that
in a host of passages, when the reading of the Fourth Folio,
though differing from earlier editions, gives a possible
sense, it is this that Theobald followed.   It is curious to observe how the modernized texts of Shakespeare have with the
progress of time gradually approached closer and closer to
the readings of the best of the early texts, but always, until
quite recently, by the process of gradually correcting bad
texts by the elimination of a larger and larger proportion of

their errors, and never by what would seem the much simpler and more obvious method of starting with the good ones and basing the text on these.

But more perhaps than the improvement of the text itself, the feature of Theobald's edition which gives it a place of the first importance in the history of Shakespearian scholarship is his footnotes, which may be said to have initiated the critical study of Sahkespeare's language. Pope had for the most part contented himself with merely giving variant readings, without discussion or explanation of any kind. Theobald, on the other hand, comments, sometimes at great length, on the cruxes, giving parallels both from Shakespeare himself and from other authors--he tells us that he had read above 800 English plays for the purpose of his edition: he undoubtedly made much use of his reading and his comments are to the point.

A second edition of Theobald's Shakespeare appeared in 1740, seven years after the first. This is in a smaller size and was intended as a cheap edition. It contains a number of additional emendations in the text, but these are mostly conjectural, and there seems no evidence of the collation of editions not previously used or of the fresh collation of those already collated. The list of quartos printed at the end is identical with that in Theobald's first edition, which is rather strange, as one would have expected so ardent a collector to acquire in those happy days at least one early quarto of Shakespeare in seven years.

Little time need be spent over the next edition of Shakespeare, the one prepared by Sir Thomas Hanmer and issued at Oxford in 1743-4 in six spaciously printed volumes. Hanmer seems to have known little and cared less about such matters as early editions or the language of Shakespeare's time, and attempted to reform the text by the light of nature alone, with the result that though his conjectural emendations are sometimes ingenious and seem at first sight attractive, the work as a whole can hardly be regarded as a serious contribution to Shakespearian scholarship. [15]

Nor need I say much about the edition of William Warburton, afterwards Bishop of Gloucester, which was issued in 1747. Warburton was a man of very wide reading and interests, though apparently no great scholar, and had helped Theobald, and, it would seem, also Hanmer, with notes for their editions. He had later quarrelled with both these schol-

ars and determined to bring out an edition of his own. The
result may be described as a compound of Theobald's text,
from which Warburton's edition was printed, with Pope's
scene-numbering and with notes mainly of Warburton's
own.[16]

In 1745 Samuel Johnson had published certain Miscel-
aneous Observations on the Tragedy of Macbeth, as a specimen of a projected edition of Shakespeare, and in 1765,
twenty years later, the edition appeared. Johnson's Shakespeare is very far from being a satisfactory piece of work;
indeed it is imperfect in almost every possible way, but
even so it represents a great advance on the edition of Hanmer and Warburton. Its preface alone would render it notable, not only because this is a piece of perfectly efficient
writing which expresses with complete clearness and certainty exactly what the writer meant to say, without self-
adulation and without unnecessary depreciation of his predecessors, but even more because in it we find the first hint
of a rational study of Shakespeare's text. Johnson alone of
all the early editors seems to have seen clearly the principles on which textual criticism of printed books must be
based. Thus in reference to Theobald he writes:

> In his enumeration of editions, he mentions the two
> first folios as of high, and the third folio as of
> middle authority; but the truth is, that the first is
> equivalent to all others, and that the rest only devi-
> ate from it by the printer's negligence. Whoever
> has any of the folios has all, excepting those di-
> versities which mere reiteration of editions will
> produce. I collated them all at the beginning, but
> afterwards used only the first.

We should now, perhaps, to the printer's negligence
have added the proof-reader's guesses as a possible cause
of the deviations in the later folios, but in other respects
Johnson exactly expresses the views held to-day. If only
some editors who followed him had pondered over the significance of his words, how much trouble they might have
saved themselves and of how many superfluous footnotes
would editions of Shakespeare have been relieved.

Johnson made use, as he says, of the First Folio,
but he admits that he had been able to procure few of the
quartos--he seems to have had access to about seventeen,
but only two of these belonged to first editions, and I have

found little or no evidence of any minute collation even of those that were known to him. He printed from the text of Warburton, and his edition contains misprints taken over by Warburton from Theobald's second edition. Indeed Johnson's text shows little advance on that of his predecessors, the merit of his edition, apart from the preface, being largely in the illuminating common sense of his notes, and especially of the critical judgements which follow each play.

The last edition to which I propose to refer is that of Edward Capell, which appeared in ten volumes in the year 1768, and I have thought that this edition might conveniently end the series, not because I share the opinion which sees in Capell "the father of all legitimate commentary on Shakespeare," but because it seems to me that his work represents the climax of the selective type of textual criticism. Capell seems to have been greatly impressed by the irresponsibility of Hanmer's treatment of the text in his edition of 1744, and at once began to collect every edition of Shakespeare, new and old, that he could procure, with the result that in a few years he had copies of all the quartos which had been previously recorded except six, and a further twelve which up to that time were unknown. He had thus the largest collection of Shakespeare material that had ever been assembled, and it is a thing for which all Cambridge men and indeed all Shakespearians owe him very lively gratitude that at his death instead of allowing this collection to be dispersed, he left it to Trinity College and thus incidentally much facilitated the work of the Cambridge editors of 1863-6. It may be worth while to note that Capell had, or knew of, fifty-nine quartos (including those of the Contention of York and Lancaster) and that the total now known (of those falling within the period with which he concerned himself) amounts to no more than sixty-nine. Of the ten additional ones three differ merely in the title-pages from those previously known, so that actually only seven new editions of Shakespearian quartos have come to light since his day.[17]

Unfortunately having got together this magnificent collection of material for editing Shakespeare, Capell did not know, any better than his predecessors, how to use it. That he was perfectly capable of working out the relationship of the texts seems obvious from remarks in his preface concerning modern editions. He saw quite clearly that editions tend to degenerate with each reprint, but he seems never to have drawn the inference that Johnson did, that readings in a late text which differed from those of an earli-

er one from which it had itself been printed could not possibly be of any authority. He is very clear on the point that
though one should base a new edition on whatever text seems
to one best, one should look into the other editions and select from thence whatever improves the Author; "that they do
improve him was with the editor an argument in their favour;
and a presumption of genuineness for what is thus selected,
whether additions, or differences of any other nature." Capell's preface is perhaps, in spite of what Johnson called its
"gabble," the clearest exposition of the selective theory of
editing--the idea that if an editor likes a reading, that reading is (a) good, and (b) attributable to Shakespeare.

       Capell's edition suffered greatly by being almost en-
tirely without notes or various readings, and having merely
a general explanation of how he had constructed his text.
He seems to have intended to follow it at once by a series
of volumes of notes in which all would be explained--the
sources of the emendations adopted and his reasons for
adopting them--but it was six years before the first volume
appeared and the whole was not issued until 1783, two years
after his death, a fact which no doubt told strongly against
the acceptance of the edition by his contemporaries.

       In spite, however, of this absence of notes, Capell's
edition has great merits. He was a careful and thorough
collator and seems to have taken infinite pains with his work,
and he seems, unlike every editor before him, to have had
his text set up from a fresh transcript of his own, instead
of from the edition of one of his predecessors, a method
which enabled him to avoid an immense number of accumulated corruptions which had hitherto passed unnoticed. He
took great care also with subsidiary matters, such as stage
directions, in which he is perhaps a little over-elaborate,
the localization of scenes, and scene division. In several
cases his disposition of the scenes has been accepted by all
later editors.

       Capell's is probably the best of the eclectic texts of
Shakespeare, though it was by no means the last. On the
whole, however, Shakespearian study for almost a century
after 1768 concerned itself more largely with explanation
and commentary than with the improvement of the text, and
the attempts at this were, with certain exceptions, somewhat haphazard. Before further progress could be made,
minuter study of the conditions of Shakespeare's time, of
the theatre, and, above all, of the language was necessary.

But the editors at whose work we have been glancing...did, each in his way, something to make Shakespeare more accessible to the reading public.

      To sum up the whole story very briefly. Rowe made the text of Shakespeare more easily readable by a general tidying up of the character-indications, stage directions, and text, and his publisher Tonson assisted by presenting it in a handier form than that of the cumbersome folios. Pope for the first time gave the text serious critical consideration, especially from the point of view of metre, and by attention to the line division, and to the contracted and uncontracted verbal forms, greatly improved the verse in a vast number of passages. He also first made a real attempt to compare the various editions, and freed the text from numerous corruptions. Theobald carried further the use of the early editions, and by readings taken from these and by his own conjectural emendations produced a much better text than that of any previous editor, while by the citation of parallels from Shakespeare himself and from other authors of his time he cleared up many obscurities and brought the idea of textual criticism before the public in a way which none had previously attempted. Of Hanmer and Warburton I need only say that each contributed a few emendations which have been accepted by later critics, and a few useful notes. Johnson realized, as apparently no previous editor had done, the essential difference between the textual criticism of printed texts and that of the classical manuscripts, and in this gave the first suggestion of modern editorial methods. And lastly Capell--I hardly know what to say of Capell, for though he was the most thorough, the most painstaking editor of them all, his edition was somehow a failure, at any rate in its appeal to the public. At the same time, though it was never reprinted, it was greatly used by the editors who came after him, and later texts of Shakespeare owe much to his work. One and all, in their several ways, contributed to the honour of the master to whom they devoted their service, and to all of them we owe our gratitude to-day.

Notes

1.   Apart from the normal modernizations there are in all the folios a certain number of attempts to emend passages which appeared unintelligible, but these were probably mere guesses. There is, further, some evidence that the Second Folio was printed from a

copy of the First which contained manuscript corrections (see especially Richard III, IV. i. 92-4, and the
note of the Cambridge editors), but here again there
is nothing to indicate that the corrector had had access to an independent source, while there is much to
suggest that he was an incompetent meddler with little
knowledge of the language of Shakespeare's time.   It
is of course impossible to assert that all the changes
found in this folio had been made in the copy from
which it was printed, but the character of many is
consistent with a deliberate attempt to substitute what
doubtless appeared at the time easier readings.   This
had the curious result that in the early eighteenth
century the Second Folio was regarded as the best
(cf. Theobald's Shakespeare Restored, p. 70).   Malone later attacked this view and gave a long list of
absurd alterations made in this folio through ignorance of Shakespeare's language.   He maintained indeed that the corrector of the Second Folio (or perhaps he should have said the corrector of the copy of
the First Folio from which it was printed), "whoever
he was, and Mr. Pope, were the two great corrup-
tors of our poet's text" (Preface of 1790; Variorum
1821, i. 208).

2.   In one respect Rowe's text appears to-day more old-
      fashioned than the Fourth Folio, for he, or his printer,
      introduced the practice common in his time of capital-
      izing almost all nouns.   Pope's text on the other hand,
      though printed from Rowe's, has hardly more capi-
      tals than a modern edition.

3.   The Evening Post, May 5, 1722, quoted by Wheatley in
      Transactions of the Bibliographical Society, xiv. 155.

4.   There are, however, one or two doubtful cases, the
      most important of which is perhaps one cited by Dr.
      Greg in his lecture on Principles of Emendation in
      Shakespeare, p. 45, from Henry V, I. ii. 173, where
      the Fourth Folio has "To tame and havock." Rowe in
      his first edition substitutes for "tame" (the reading of
      all the folios) the word "spoil," which is the reading
      of the quartos.   While at first sight it is natural to
      conclude that the reading actually comes from a quarto,
      I feel that this is not altogether certain.   It is, I be-
      lieve, the only case in the play which definitely sug-
      gests that a quarto was used, for the remaining in-

stances of quarto readings found in Rowe's text, such
as at I. ii. 197, 243, III. vi. 118, and IV. i. 120,
may easily have been his own corrections; while on
the other hand there are in the quarto several readings which, if he were aware of them, one would have
expected Rowe to adopt.   The folio reading "To tame
and havock" was clearly wrong, and "spoil" was a
not unlikely guess.   It was, after all, probably a
mere guess in the first quarto.

A similar problem arises with respect to A Midsummer Night's Dream, III. ii. 260, where for the
nonsensical "thou but" of the later folios Rowe reads
"thou burr" in agreement with the quartos and First
Folio.   But here again the emendation is one which,
in the context, demands no great ingenuity, and it
may be merely a happy conjecture.

5.   Thus for the odd-looking direction in 3 Henry VI, II. i,
"Enter one blowing" Rowe has merely "Enter a Messenger," and when, in Titus Andronicus, II. i, we
have in the folios "Enter Chiron and Demetrius braving," i. e. quarrelling, he omits the word "braving."

6.   The text of the first quarto of Romeo and Juliet (1597)
is in the last third of the play divided by lines of
ornament into portion, most, though not all, of which
correspond with the accepted scene divisions.   I believe, however, that in introducing these ornaments
the printer had no intention of marking the scenes,
but that his purpose was merely to fill up space and
thus help to drive out the matter to the length that it
was expected to occupy; the ornaments being naturally inserted at places where there was some interruption in the dialogue.   For some unknown reason the
type selected for this edition was changed for a smaller one after the first four sheets.   A simple calculation shows that the blank lines occurring before and
after the stage directions in the later portion of the
play, together with the before-mentioned ornaments,
occupy almost exactly the amount of space which was
saved by the reduction in the size of type.   The book
is therefore of the same length as it would have been
if the larger type had been continued throughout.

7.   Including one scene which is not in the folios or Rowe's
edition.

8.   As an example of the corrections in the second edition
     of Rowe, I may mention the name of the character in
     Hamlet whom we know as Rosencranz. Rowe's first
     edition had bestowed upon him the curious name of
     "Roseneraus," though the Fourth Folio, which he usu-
     ally followed, had called him "Rosincros." Why Rowe
     chose to substitute, as he does most carefully every-
     where, a form which does not seem to occur in any
     other text whatsoever, and which upsets the scansion
     of almost every line in which it occurs, is somewhat
     of a mystery, unless, possibly, it is explained by the
     defective printing of the list of Dramatis Personae in
     one of the 1676 quartos (that with a five-line imprint),
     where owing to a choked c the name might--at least
     in the B.M. copy--be misread as "Rosinoraus" or
     "Rosineraus." In the second edition the name is al-
     tered throughout, except in the Dramatis Personae,
     to Rosincrosse, the form though not the spelling given
     by the Fourth Folio.
         A reading of Rowe ii in 2 Henry VI, I. iii. 46,
     namely "Fashion in" where F 1, F 2, F 3 have "Fa-
     shions in" and F 4 and Rowe i have "Fashion of"
     (which last reading makes perfectly good sense),
     seems to indicate that for the second edition some
     folio earlier than the fourth was collated.

9.   Works of Alexander Pope, ed. Elwin and Courthope,
     ix. 26-7.

10. Works, v.s., viii. 48.

11. In the comparatively rare cases in which the number
     and character of the surviving manuscripts enable us
     to construct a satisfactory scheme of descent, we may
     be able to show that a particular reading cannot be
     original, e.g. when a manuscript which evidently
     branched off from the line of descent at a point earli-
     er than the manuscript containing the reading in ques-
     tion agrees with others more closely allied to the lat-
     ter in presenting a different reading. In such a case
     the reading under discussion must have arisen at, or
     after, the branching off of the line terminating in the
     manuscript which contains it, but not before.

12. Shakespeare Restored, p. viii; cf. Preface to his edi-
     tion of 1733, p. xliii.

13.   Including in both cases the imperfect quartos of the
      second and third parts of Henry VI known as The
      first part of the Contention of York and Lancaster
      and The true tragedy of Richard Duke of York. Theo-
      bald divided his list of editions into three groups,
      "Editions of Authority" (the first two folios and the
      earlier quartos up to the date of the First Folio),
      "Editions of Middle Authority" (the later folios and
      the quartos after 1623), and "Editions of No Author-
      ity" (the editions of Rowe and Pope); a division which,
      I believe, has had a very bad effect on Shakespearian
      criticism as tending to strengthen the idea that the
      authority of an edition depends upon its date rather
      than upon its origin. Pope's way of treating all be-
      fore his own, including Rowe's, as "the old edition"
      was a better beginning for a bibliographical inquiry,
      though not, of course, of much use without the next
      step of considering the relationship of these editions
      to one another.

14.   A matter which should perhaps be mentioned, as Theo-
      bald evidently took much trouble over it, is the punc-
      tuation of his edition. His Shakespeare Restored
      showed him to have very definite views on the sub-
      ject. He revised Pope's punctuation very thoroughly,
      making it much heavier and in particular greatly in-
      creasing the number of commas. Thus in the two
      scenes mentioned, A Midsummer Night's Dream, I. i,
      and Julius Caesar, III. ii, amounting to 523 lines in
      all, Theobald inserted no less than 80 commas and
      replaced 34 of Pope's commas by semicolons, besides
      substituting a few colons for semicolons and adding
      some full stops to Pope's dashes. By modern stan-
      dards Theobald's punctuation is much too heavy.

15.   As instances of Hanmer's more curious emendations
      may be mentioned his substitution of "Bythinia" for
      "Bohemia" as a locality in The Winter's Tale, on ac-
      count, of course, of the well-known difficulty about
      the sea-coast, and his ingenious but absurd correc-
      tion of Costard's phrase for Moth in Love's Labour's
      Lost, III. i. 136, "my incony Jew" to "my ink-horn,
      adieu!" But it would be quite unfair to judge his edi-
      tion by these two oddities.

16.   Much of Warburton's best work on Shakespeare is con-
      tained in the notes which he contributed to Theobald's

edition. These are for the most part explanatory and
critical, but include a few good emendations such as
"the wolf behowls the moon" in <u>Midsummer Night's
Dream</u>, V. i. 379, an improvement on the "beholds"
of all the early texts which has been universally accepted. The new matter contributed by his own edition is relatively unimportant, though he does seem
to have collated certain quartos afresh.

17. In his list of quartos Capell includes an undated <u>Othello</u>,
which he probably took over from Pope's list, and
which appears to be only a shaved copy of the edition of 1622. I have therefore omitted it from the
count. Of the 59 quartos listed Capell seems to have
possessed 51 and to have seen another 4, leaving only
4 included on the reports of others. Twelve quartos
are marked by him as not previously recorded. It
may, I think, have been disgust at finding that the
list of quartos contributed by Steevens to Johnson's
edition of 1765 contained no less than eight out of
these twelve that decided Capell to ignore Johnson's
edition as completely as he did, though it may have
been quite true that a great part of his own edition
was already printed when Johnson's appeared (Capell's "Introduction," p. 19, note).

CHAPTER 16

BOOK REVIEW*

An Enquiry into the Nature of Certain Nineteenth Century
Pamphlets. By John Carter and Graham Pollard. London:
Constable and Co., Ltd. New York: Charles Scribner's
Sons. 1934. Pp. xii+400. Price 15 s. net.

Few, if any, who read The Library are likely to be
ignorant of the stir in the book-world which has been created by Messrs. Carter and Pollard's brilliant demonstration
of the fraudulent character of a number of pamphlets pur-
porting to be first or separate editions of works by such
famous Victorians as Tennyson, the Brownings, Swinburne,
Ruskin, and others, and no detailed discussion of their argument is needed here. It must suffice to say that if the
facts upon which they rely are as they state them to be, and
no one, so far as I am aware, has challenged them in any
material point, there can be no possible doubt that the great
majority of the 46 pamphlets dealt with, bearing dates from
1842 to 1899, were not produced in the years of their imprints, but at various, generally much later, dates; and further that they are not even genuine piracies, if such a
phrase be permitted, of actual editions intended for use by
the author or for sale to the public, but things specially
manufactured for the rare-book market.

The main points of Messrs. Carter and Pollard's
demonstration are that, in the case of many of the pamph-

---

*The Library, 4th Series, Vol. XV, no. 3, December 1934,
pp. 379-84. Again McKerrow's fairness and objectivity may
be seen in this clear and discerning review of Carter and
Pollard's major work. Reprinted by permission of the Council of The Bibliographical Society.

lets, either the paper upon which they are printed is of a
kind not on the market at the ostensible date, or that the
type used belongs to a fount not then cut; in the case of several, both these proofs of spuriousness being present. Further, although these technical discrepancies cannot be demonstrated in the case of all members of the group, the whole
of the 46 pamphlets are linked together in so many ways,
especially in the manner of their appearance on the market,
that it can hardly be doubted that all have a common source.
If, then, some of the group can be proved to be fraudulent,
while not one can be shown on any convincing ground to be
genuine, the probability of all being fraudulent becomes almost a certainty.

        The strongest point as regards the paper is that while,
according to the authors, esparto was not used in the manufacture of any paper generally available before 1861, this
material is present in ten of the pamphlets dated from 1842
to 1858.   The date of 1861 has indeed been challenged by
Mr. William Talbot, [1] but even if esparto paper was, as he
maintains, on the market five or six years earlier, it was
certainly not available at the dates of five of the pamphlets
which use it, and the argument is therefore not affected.

        As regards the types, the proof depends mainly on
the presence in certain of the early-dated pamphlets of a
somewhat peculiar lower-case f and j, which are not kerned,
the stem of the letters being bent slightly back to allow the
part of the letter which normally projects to come on the
body.   The authors tell us how the kernless f and j were
invented by Richard Clay and how the firm of P. M. Shanks
& Co., typefounders, "cut for him some time after 1880 the
first design for a lower-case f without a kern" (p. 59).   But
though it is perfectly true that the popularity of the kernless
f dates from after 1880 they are surely wrong in suggesting
that no such f existed before that year.   It is unnecessary
to insist on the kernless f which was cut to the design of the
famous third Early Stanhope at the beginning of the century,
and which can be seen in Johnson's Typographia, 1824, vol.
ii, p. 104, and in the diagram of Stanhope's type-case on p.
103, for this never came into general use, but there certainly seem to have been attempts at a similar design before
1880.   For example there is a kernless f with the top half
slightly bent back and an unusually long cross-bar in the
text-type of the edition of Lady Guest's Mabinogion printed
by Wyman & Sons in 1877.   There is also in this book what
appears to be a kernless j of a design very similar to that

shown in Plate 1, fig. g, of the work under discussion. [2]

Though, however, Messrs. Carter and Pollard seem to be too positive in their assertion that books with a kernless f and j cannot date from before 1880, their identification of the type of certain of the pamphlets with a fount used by Messrs. Clay from 1880 onwards, in conjunction with the appearance of a particular form of query mark[3] not properly belonging to the fount but used with it by that firm, seems to place beyond any doubt the printers of the books in question and to show that they cannot possibly have been printed at the dates which they bear.

What will be to many perhaps the most interesting part of the authors' work is the careful and methodical discussion of the separate books, in which many varied lines of argument are brought to bear upon them. In some cases imprints are clearly false, either as containing the names of imaginary printers, or because they are inconsistent with the known style of the firm at the supposed date. Other tracts exhibit readings which can be shown to be corrections introduced into the text at a later date than that at which they purport to have been printed. In others again there are palpable inconsistencies in the explanation given of how the pamphlets came into existence. There seems, indeed, to be hardly any possible line of investigation which Messrs. Carter and Pollard have not followed up.

Perhaps if it could be traced back to its beginning this series of frauds might be found to have originated in a somewhat more innocent way than its continuation might lead one to suppose. When one remembers the Twenty-five Old Ballads and Songs which J. P. Collier printed in 1869 as a gift to the subscribers to the series of Elizabethan reprints which he was then issuing, and which was suggested perhaps by a puckish desire to see how many of his friends would be taken in by the booklet and suppose the ballads to be genuine; and remembers also that the series of these pamphlets began, in all probability, at the time of the Shelley and Browning Societies' reprints, it is impossible not to wonder whether the first pamphlet--perhaps the Sonnets of "1847" [4] --was not in its inception a somewhat similar jest. If something of this sort was really its origin it is easy to imagine circumstances, perhaps a sudden awakening to questions of copyright, which would lead to the pamphlet being discarded. If then the copies came into the hands of some ingenious and unscrupulous person who saw their possibilities, and the possibilities of other pamphlets like them, the one comparatively harmless booklet might have given rise to the whole series of frauds.

It is easy to be wise after the event, but I think that few will read Messrs. Carter and Pollard's book without feeling that what happened shows a singular lack of mental alertness--to say the least of it--among collectors of nine-teenth-century books and the dealers who supplied their wants. A collector, indeed, who possessed only one or two of these pamphlets, and who did not watch the way in which others drifted into the market, might well be pardoned for not hav-ing his suspicions aroused, but any one who owned, or had passing through his hands, any considerable number of them ought surely to have noticed the odd similarity in their meth-od of appearance--all in practically "mint" condition; all coming to light several years after their supposed dates of printing; all presumably printed for presentation to friends, yet all lacking the contemporary inscriptions which they might be expected to bear; most of them turning up as remainders, with a suggestion that they had been accidentally left un-claimed at the printers: and not one or two, nor even a dozen pamphlets, but nearly fifty! It is indeed a curious story and one which reflects little credit on any one con-cerned with it, except on the two bibliographers who have eventually cleared the matter up.

And unfortunately they have not entirely cleared it up, for to do this would require the discovery of the originator of the frauds, and here they have had to confess themselves baffled. In the abstract it is perhaps of no great importance, now that the deception has been so completely exposed, that we should know the name of the villain; but at the same time the position is a very unsatisfactory one, for so long as we do not know for certain whom we should blame, others be-sides the perpetrator will necessarily remain under a cloud of suspicion. One thing may perhaps be said, that if the eminent bibliographer whose name is most frequently men-tioned in the volume under discussion had any more intimate connexion with these pamphlets than that of being deceived by them, he must have acted in a manner strangely inconsistent with the character of his bibliographical work as a whole. Surely no bibliographer of any experience at all, inventing a "first edition" of a well-known piece, would have overlooked the necessity of using the utmost care in the choice of the text to be reprinted, and yet in at least two of the pamphlets we find mistakes of the most elementary kind, namely in

Swinburne's Laus Veneris which is reprinted from the corrected issue of Poems and Ballads,[5] and Tennyson's Ode for
the Opening of the International Exhibition (of 1862), the text
of which follows that of the Works of 1889 as against all the
earlier editions.[6] I do not think that I am wrong in saying
that carelessness of this particular kind points much more
clearly to an enterprising dealer or literary hack than to one
who had already spent years in the practice of the more exact kinds of bibliography.

Notes

1. In the Bookseller, 11 July 1934; see also the issues of
    8 August and 5 September.

2. The authors have not found a kernless f in type-founders'
    specimens before 1883, but this does not prove that it
    was not available before that date. A kernless f and
    j are mixed with kerned ones in F. W. Farrar's
    Early Days of Christianity, 3rd ed., 1882, an indica-
    tion of course that the designs were just coming into
    use. There were types with much reduced kerns a
    few years earlier.

3. I do not understand what is meant by the authors' state-
    ment on p. 63, that this resembles "an italic cast on
    a roman body."

4. The paper wrappers of this pamphlet, which have left
    traces on extant copies, but of which no example is
    now known, may even have borne something which to
    the instructed reader revealed the jest for what it
    was. If so, their disappearance is accounted for.

5. Apart from being free from certain misprints the pamph-
    let follows the corrected issue in two readings which
    are probably author's alterations. I have been unable
    to discover the precise date at which the peculiarities
    of Moxon's first (suppressed) printing of Poems and
    Ballads became known; but as the American (Carleton-
    Moxon) edition of 1866, entitled Laus Veneris, and
    other Poems and Ballads, which was printed from it,
    and which seems to be a fairly common book, repro-
    duces its errors, the original text has always been
    accessible.

6. All the editions, at least, which Messrs. Carter and
    Pollard have seen.   The Ode was also printed in the
    official programme of the Opening, and until a copy
    of this is traced it is of course impossible to say
    that the text there given does not correspond with that
    of the pamphlet.   But in any case it seems most im-
    probable that the edition of 1889 would be corrected
    in details of punctuation from a text of 27 years earli-
    er.

CHAPTER 17

FORM AND MATTER IN
THE PUBLICATION OF RESEARCH*

May I as one who has had occasion both as a publisher and an editor to read a very considerable number of
books and articles embodying the results of research into
English literary history plead for more attention to form in
the presentation of such work?

I do not know whether advancing age has made me
thicker in the head than I used to be or whether I have
merely become more impatient--there is so much that one
still wants to do and constantly less and less time in which
to do it--but it certainly seems to me that there has been
a tendency in recent years for the way in which the results
of research are set out to become progressively less efficient, especially among the younger students, both in England and in America. And when I say "less efficient" I am
not thinking of any high qualities of literary art, but of the
simplest qualities of precision and intelligibility. Indeed, I
have sometimes wondered whether the fate of "English studies" will not eventually be to be smothered in a kind of
woolly and impenetrable fog of wordiness that few or none
will be bothered to penetrate.

It may perhaps surprise some readers of R.E.S. if
I tell them that I have several times been compelled to re-
fuse articles offered to me which seemed, from the evidence
of the footnotes, to have been the product of real research,

*Review of English Studies, Vol. XVI, 1940, pp. 116-21.
Greg states about this last published writing of McKerrow,
"It crystallizes fifteen years' experience of the shortcomings
of contributors with all and more than all his wonted vigor."
Reprinted by permission of The Clarendon Press, Oxford.

for no other reason than that after several readings I have
completely failed to discover the point or points which the
author was trying to make.   In one or two cases this has
perhaps been due to the author's inability to express himself
in English at all, but in others the trouble has seemed to be
rather due to a complete ignorance of the way in which he
should present his material.   Being himself fully cognizant
of the point at issue and with the way in which his research
corrects or supplements views currently held on his subject,
the author has apparently assumed that all would become
clear to his readers by the mere recital of his investiga-
tions without any commentary on the results as they appear
to him.   But such a mere recital of an investigation will only convey what is intended by the author to a person with the
same knowledge and mental outlook as the author himself,
and to anyone else may be almost meaningless.

          Articles of which I have been unable to make out the
point at all I have necessarily rejected, generally after trying them on a friend or two, lest I were at the time more
than usually dense; but I must confess to having printed in
R. E. S. a certain number of articles which I regarded as
definitely bad work.   These were some which contained good
research which I was assured would be useful to those with
knowledge of the subject and willing to spend time and effort
in puzzling out the bearing of the new matter, but of little if
any use to others.   Such articles cannot, of course, be
lightly rejected.   The pity is they could so easily, by a
writer of adequate training in presenting his facts, or with
sufficient imagination to enable him to dispense with such
training, have been made really interesting contributions to
knowledge which would have appealed to a wide circle of
readers, instead of only being absorbed with difficulty and
distaste by the few.

          For it is imagination which is, before all else, nec-
essary in presenting a piece of research.   It is not to be
considered as, so to say, an emanation of the author's
brain which has been allowed to escape into the void, a
mere fragment of knowledge detached from its originator,
but one which is intended to become part of the knowledge
of others, and in order that it may do this it must be so
shaped and adapted that it may fit with ease and certainty
on to the knowledge of others, those others being of course
the likely readers.

          New facts, skilfully prepared for our easy assimilation, for forming part of our existing aggregate of knowledge, are invariably welcomed, even when the subject is not one in which we are normally much interested, when a badly presented bit of what should be our own special subject may completely fail to make any impression on our consciousness.

We ought, I think, at the start to realize that no readers whom we are likely to have will be nearly as much interested in our views or discoveries as we ourselves are. Most of them will be people who are a little tired, a little bored, and who read us rather out of a sense of duty and a wish to keep up with what is being done than because they have any real interest in the subject; and in return for our reader's complaisance it is our duty as well as our interest to put what we have to say before him with as little trouble to him as possible. It is our duty because we ought to be kind to our fellow creature; it is our interest because if the view that we wish to put before him is clearly and competently expressed, so that he understands without trouble what we are trying to say, he will be gratified at the smooth working of his own intelligence and will inevitably think better of our theory and of its author than if he had had to puzzle himself over what we mean and then in the end doubt whether he had really understood us, so raising in himself an uneasy doubt whether his brains are quite what they used to be!

Now I suggest that if we analyse almost any piece of research which seems to us thoroughly workmanlike and satisfactory from all points of view, we shall almost always find that it falls into five parts in the following order.

1. The introduction, in which the author briefly states the present position of research on his subject and the views currently held on it.

2. The proposal, in which he describes in outline what he hopes to prove.

3. The boost, in which he proceeds to magnify the importance of his discovery or argument and to explain what a revolution it will create in the views generally held on the whole period with which he is dealing. This is, as it were, a taste of sauce to stimulate the reader's appetite.

4.   The <u>demonstration,</u> in which he sets forth his dis-
     covery or argument in an orderly fashion.

5.   The <u>conclusion,</u> or <u>crow,</u> in which he summarizes
     what he claims to have shown, and points out how
     complete and unshakeable is his proof.

Of course I am not serious in this! It is not to be
supposed necessary that we should <u>formally</u> divide our research articles in this way, but it <u>is a real</u> and practical
division and there are few research articles which would not
be improved by the adoption of such a framework, at least
under the surface.

The following points might, I believe, be worth much
more serious consideration than seems frequently to be given
to them.

1.   The subject of a research article should always
be a unity. The paper should always deal either with a
single subject or with a well-defined group of subjects of the
same general character. Thus a particular literary work
might be dealt with in all its aspects, or any one aspect
might be dealt with, say, its origin, its date, its popularity,
or what not, or its author's life or any one period or inci-
dent of it. On the other hand it is seldom well to mix two
pieces of research on different scales, an account of a
man's works as a whole and of a particular one of his works
dealt with in much greater detail. Similarly, an article in
which an attempt is made both to give new discoveries in
an author's biography and a correction in the bibliography of
one of his books will almost certainly turn out an unreadable
muddle. These various kinds of discovery may often arise
as the result of a single piece of research, but it is much
better to put them forward in quite independent articles.
Opportunity may always be found to insert a cross-reference
from one to the other in order to ensure that students do
not overlook the author's other discoveries.

2.   Give your book or article a name which tells at
once what it is all about. Facetious and cryptic titles
should be utterly eschewed. At best they annoy, and at
worst they tend to be forgotten and to render the work under
which they are concealed untraceable. Fancy names, pastoral and the like, should never be used, however familiar
they may be to students versed in the literature of a particular period. Thus Katherine Philips may have been well

known to students of her time as the "Matchless Orinda,"
but one who writes about her by the latter name risks his
work being entered in indexes under headings where it will
be missed by scholars searching for her under her family
name.

3.   Remember that though the great majority of your
readers are likely to have a considerable knowledge of English Literature as a whole and an expert knowledge of a certain part of it, only a minority are likely to be experts in
your particular period or field.   In any case very few indeed
can be expected to possess the minute knowledge of it which
you who have just been devoting all your time to the study of
it have or ought to have.   (Indeed, if you do not know <u>much</u>
more than others, why are you writing about it?)   Keep this
in mind in the whole of your writing and adjust what you say
to the knowledge which you may reasonably expect your
readers to have.   This is really the whole secret of exposition, and it is so simple that it seems incredible that writers
of research articles should so often be ignorant of it.   But
they are, they are!   If you have a young brother or sister
of, say, fifteen years old or so, think that you have him or
her before you and that you are trying to explain the point of
your article to them and at the same time to prevent them
from thinking what an ass you are to be wasting their time
and yours about anything so completely futile.   If in your
imagination you see their eyes light up and their faces set
with a desire to protest or argue, you will know that whether
the thesis of your paper is sound or not its presentation is
at least on the right lines!

Naturally the method of presenting an argument must
depend on the persons for whom it is intended.   You need
not in an article in <u>R. E. S.</u> explain who Ben Jonson or John
Dryden or Cynewulf or Lazamon were, but it would be un-
wise to expect all your readers to have precise knowledge as
to their dates or the details of their biography.   If these are
required for your argument it is easy to give them without
the reader being moved to indignation by the feeling that he
is being treated like a child.   In this connection much of-
fence may often be avoided by the insertion of the little
phrases "of course," or "as everyone knows"--e. g. "Stephen
Hawes, who was of course writing in the earliest years of
the sixteenth century, and called Lydgate 'master' " gives information which every reader of <u>R. E. S.</u> must have known at
some time, but of which a few may need to be reminded in
an article concerning the poetical associations of Henry VIII's
court.

In your introduction, then, take your reader meta-
phorically by the hand and lead him gently up to the thresh-
old of your research, reminding him courteously and without
any appearance of dogmatism, not with the gestures of a
teacher but gently as a comrade in study, of what he ought
to know in order to understand what you have to tell him--
the object of your research. He will be far better able to
appreciate your demonstration if he knows what to look for,
and to know what to look for if you tell him at once just
what the current views of the matter are and how your own
differ from them.

4. So far as possible state your facts in chronological order. When a digression is necessary, make quite
clear that it is a digression, and when you reach the end of
it, make quite clear that you are returning to the main
course of the story. And always give plenty of dates, real
dates, not the kind of dates of which many of the historical
people seem to be so fond--"about two years before the conclusion of the events which we have described" or "later in
the same year," which after reading several earlier pages
turns out to be the year in which "the king" attained his majority, necessitating further research to discover what king
and in what year and what part of the year he was born and
what "majority" meant at the time. But enough! We have
all suffered. Keep on remembering that though you are perhaps completely familiar with all aspects of your subject,
your reader may not be.

5. State your facts as simply as possible, even bold-
ly. No one wants flowers of eloquence or literary ornaments
in a research article. On the other hand do not be slangy,
and, especially if you are writing for R.E.S., do not use
American slang. We may be interested in it, but we may
not always understand it. Only a few days ago I had to beg
the author of an excellent article which I was printing to substitute some phrase more intelligible to us over in England
for a statement that certain evidence--"is not quite enough to
convict of actual skulduggery (and the aroma of high-binding
will not down) ..."

6. Never be cryptic nor use literary paraphrases.
Needless mysteries are out of place in research articles.
There are plenty of them there already. If they think that
you are trying to be superior, most readers will stop reading at once.

7. Do not try to be humorous. Humour is well
enough in its place, but nothing more infuriates a man who
is looking for a plain statement of facts than untimely humour, especially if he does not know whether the writer is
really trying to be humorous or not, a point which some
would-be humorists fail to make clear.

8. Do not use ambiguous expressions. The worst of
these are perhaps phrases containing the word "question."
If you say "there is no question that Ben Jonson was in Edinburgh in 1618" most people, perhaps all, will take you to
mean that he was there in that year; and the same if you say
that "there is no question of Jonson having been in Edinburgh
in 1618," most people, though I think not all, will take you
to mean that he was not there in that year. But there is
certainly no question that it would be better to use a phrase
the meaning of which is not open to question.

Avoid also the word "doubtless," which has been defined as "a word used when making a statement for the truth
of which the speaker is unaware of any evidence."

Do not overtask such expressions as "it is generally
admitted that," "there can be no doubt that," "it is well
known that" unless you can shift your responsibility on to at
least one other person by giving a reference.

9. Always be precise and careful in references and
quotations, and never fear the charge of pedantry. After all,
"pedant" is merely the name which one gives to anyone whose
standard of accuracy happens to be a little higher than one's
own!

10. Do not treat the subjects of your research with
levity. Above all avoid that hateful back-slapping "hearti-
ness" which caused certain nineteenth-century Elizabethans
to refer to "Tom Nash," "Bob Green," "Will Shakespeare"
and so on, with its horrible flavour of modern gutter journal-
ism which refers in this way to film stars, long-distance
fliers, and the like. These Elizabethans had certain qualities which have made it seem worth while to keep their mem-
ories green for more than 300 years, and on this account, if
for no other, they should be given the courtesy which is their
due.

11. Above all, whatever inner doubts you may have
as to whether the piece of research upon which you have

been spending your time was really worth while, you must
on no account allow it to appear that you have ever thought
of it otherwise than of supreme importance to the human
race! In the first place, unless you yourself believe in what
you are doing, you will certainly not do good work, and,
secondly, if your reader suspects for a moment that you do
not set the very highest value on your work yourself he will
set no value on it at all. He will on the other hand be full
of fury that you should have induced him to waste his pre-
cious time in reading stuff that you do not believe in yourself, an attitude which will completely prevent him from ap-
preciating any real and evident merit which there may be in
it. After all, one can never be certain of the value of one's
own work. Often in scientific research a discovery which in
itself seemed most trivial has led to results of the utmost
importance, and though sensational occurrences of this kind
may be rarer in literary research than in science, it is
still true that what is merely a side-issue in one research
may give rise, when critically examined, to results of quite
unexpected value.

As a general rule the interest and importance of a
piece of research lies either in the facts disclosed or the
methods by which they have been brought to light--or in both.
To these prior considerations the manner of presentation
may indeed be subordinate. Nevertheless good presentation
may help enormously in the effective value of good research,
while bad presentation may rob it of the recognition which is
its due.

CHAPTER 18

A LIST OF THE WRITINGS OF
RONALD BRUNLEES McKERROW[*]

By F. C. Francis

This list is intended as a tribute to the memory of a
man to whom the Bibliographical Society and the whole world
of bibliography owes a big debt. I have little doubt that he
would himself have rejected the idea of making a "bibliography" of his writings; indeed it is a fact that when the desir-
ability of such a list was suggested to him by the late George
Watson Cole, who had had his own writings listed, McKerrow
received the idea without enthusiasm. Moreover, I do not
myself suppose, nor do I wish to suggest to others, that a
mere list is the measure of his achievement or his influence; such a supposition would be as erroneous in his case
as it is with most scholars. At the same time it is interesting to know what a volume of work he was able to produce
in the midst of a busy life as a publisher and to see at what
periods of his life books and articles were written, and to
trace the development and the underlying unity of his studies.

The "high spots" of his work are undoubtedly his edition of Nashe, his Review of English Studies, the Introduction to Bibliography for Literary Students, and Prolegomena
for the Oxford Sahkespeare, each in its clearness and direct-
ness of aim and exposition typical of his works as a whole.
Dr. Greg in his Memoir speaks of his acuteness in dealing
with bibliographical problems. But it is not only his percep-
tion of a problem, but also the pains he took to master it
and to explain clearly his views on it that students find so
valuable. Those who have corresponded with him will know

*The Library, 4th Series, Vol. XXI, no. 3, 4, December
1940, March 1941, pp. 229-63. Reprinted by permission of
The Council of the Bibliographical Society, with revisions by
the compiler [indicated in brackets].

that his letters were characterized by a similar painstaking
exposition of any point which was likely to cause difficulty.
All students of English literature and of bibliography will regret most sincerely that his death prevented him from applying these qualities to the edition of Shakespeare he had himself looked forward to so eagerly.

The items in this list are arranged chronologically by
years. Within each year books and articles are arranged
alphabetically, but the chronological arrangement is retained
for reviews. I have not thought it necessary to use abbreviations except for the Review of English Studies (RES). Many
of the items, especially after 1925, are reviews, but McKerrow set a high standard for himself as well as for others in
reviewing and those written for RES are far from being "editorial" reviews, in the bad sense of the word.

1895

Joan of Arc. A poem which obtained the Chancellor's Medal
at the Cambridge Commencement MDCCCXCV. By R. B.
McKerrow, Trinity College.
   pp. 8.
   Prolusiones academicae praemiis annuis dignatae et
   in Curia Cantabrigiensi recitatae...A.D. M.DCCC.XCV.
   Cantabrigiae, 1895.

1901

[A Book on English Phonetics, written in collaboration with
H. Katayama, issued only in a Japanese version.]
   In the Prefatory Note McKerrow wrote, with characteristic modesty, "This book is in great part an expansion and rearrangement of notes on English pro-
   nunciation made some time ago for teaching purposes
   during my connection with the Tokyo School of Foreign Languages.
   "It should be clearly understood that it has no pretensions to originality, except in its special adaptation to the needs of Japanese students--chiefly Mr.
   Katayama's work...."

The Use of So-called Classical Metres in Elizabethan Verse.
I.
   Modern Language Quarterly, vol. 4, no. 3, Dec.

1901, pp. 172-80.   Part II appeared in vol. 5, no. 1, Apr. 1902.

Reviews

The Old Dramatists, Conjectural Readings.   By K. Deighton.   London, 1896.
------Second Series.   Calcutta, 1896.
> Modern Language Quarterly, vol. 4, no. 1, May 1901, pp. 13-14.

The Legend of Sir Lancelot du Lac.   By Jessie L. Weston. London, 1901.
> Modern Language Quarterly, vol. 4, no. 3, Dec. 1901, pp. 190-2.

1902

A Note on So-called Classical Metres in Elizabethan Verse.
> Modern Language Quarterly, vol. 5, no. 3, Dec. 1902, pp. 148-9.

The Use of So-called Classical Metres in Elizabethan Verse. II.
> Modern Language Quarterly, vol. 5, no. 1, Apr. 1902, pp. 6-13.

Review

The Wallace and the Bruce Restudied.   By J. T. T. Brown. Bonn, 1900.
Huchown of the Awle Ryale and his Poems examined in the Light of Recent Criticism.   By J. T. T. Brown.   Glasgow, 1902.
> Modern Language Quarterly, vol. 5, no. 2, July 1902, pp. 73-6.

1903

Fairfax Eighth Eclogue.
> Modern Language Quarterly, vol. 6, no. 2, Aug. 1903, pp. 73-4.

"Observations" by R. B. McKerrow, communicated
by W. W. Greg.

A Note on Variations in Certain Copies of the "Returne of
Pasquill. "
    The Library, 2nd Series, vol. 4, no. 16, Oct. 1903,
pp. 384-91.

Reviews

The Three Days' Tournament. By Jessie L. Weston. London, 1902.
    Modern Language Quarterly, vol. 6, no. 1, Apr.
1903, pp. 30-1.

Les Débuts de la critique dramatique en Angleterre jusqu'à
la mort de Shakespeare. Par Harold S. Symmes. Paris,
1903.
    Modern Language Quarterly, vol. 6, no. 2, Aug.
1903, pp. 90-1.

Select Translations from Old English Poetry. Edited by A.
S. Cook and C. B. Tinker. Boston, 1902.
    Modern Language Quarterly, vol. 6, no. 2, Aug.
1903, pp. 93-4.

The Mediaeval Stage. By E. K. Chambers. Oxford, 1903.
    Modern Language Quarterly, vol. 6, no. 3, Dec.
1903, pp. 144-6.

The Life and Repentaunce of Marie Magdalene. By Lewis
Wager. Edited by F. I. Carpenter. Chicago, 1902.
    Modern Language Quarterly, vol. 6, no. 3, Dec.
1903, pp. 146-8

English Metrists. By J. S. Omond. Tunbridge Wells, 1903.
    Modern Language Quarterly, vol. 6, no. 3, Dec.
1903, p. 150.

Etude phonétique de la langue japonaise. Par E. R. Ed-
wards. Leipzig, 1903.
    Modern Language Quarterly, vol. 6, no. 3, Dec.
1903, pp. 151-2.

1904

The Devil's Charter by Barnabe Barnes. Edited from the
quarto of 1607 by R. B. McKerrow. Louvain, A. Uystpruyst;
Leipzig, O. Harrassowitz; London, David Nutt. 1904.
>   pp. xxiii+144.
>   Materialien zur Kunde des älteren englischen Dramas.
>   Bd. 6.
>   From 1904 onwards the general title-page of this se-
>   ries reads as follows:
>   "Materialien zur Kunde des älteren englischen
>   Dramas. Unter Mitwirkung der Herren F. S. Boas-
>   Belfast... R. B. McKerrow-London... begruendet und
>   herausgegeben von W. Bang...."

Euphues and the 'Colloquies' of Erasmus.
>   Modern Language Quarterly, vol. 7, no. 2, Oct.
>   1904, pp. 99-100.

The Gull's Hornbook by Thomas Dekker, edited by R. B.
McKerrow. At the De La More Press, 298 Regent Street,
London, W. , MDCCCIV. [Reprinted, New York: AMS
Press, 1971.]
>   pp. viii+107.
>   The King's Library. De La More Press Quartos. II.
>   50 copies on Japanese vellum and 650 on hand-made
>   paper.

The Works of Thomas Nashe. Edited from the original texts
by Ronald B. McKerrow. Text: Vol. I. A. H. Bullen, 47
Great Russell Street, London, MCMIV.
>   pp. xvi+386.

The Works of Thomas Nashe... Text: Vol. II. A. H.
Bullen.... London. MCMIV.
>   pp. 397.
>   Later vols. : Vol. III, 1905; Vol. IV, 1908; Vol. V,
>   1910. [Reprinted from the Original Edition with Cor-
>   rections and Supplementary Notes, Edited by F. P.
>   Wilson." Oxford: Basil Blackwell, 1958.]

Reviews

The Gentle Craft. By Thomas Deloney. Edited by A. F.
Lange. Berlin, 1903.

Modern Language Quarterly, vol. 7, no. 1, Apr.
1904, pp. 29-30.

Studies and Notes in Philology and Literature.   Vol. VIII.
Boston, 1903.
Studies in the Fairy Mythology of Arthurian Romance.   By
L. A. Paton.   Boston, 1903.
Modern Language Quarterly, vol. 7, no. 2, Oct.
1904, pp. 100-2.

De usu articuli finiti anglici quantum differat in Scripturae
Sacrae translatione A. D. MDCXI edita et in hodierno ser-
mone thesim proponebat...A. Barbeau.   Lut. Par., 1904.
Modern Language Quarterly, vol. 7, no. 2, Oct.
1904, pp. 102-4.

1905

The Enterlude of Youth nebst Fragmenten des Playe of
Lucres und von Nature.   Herausgegeben von W. Bang und
R. B. McKerrow.   Louvain, A. Uystpruyst; Leipzig, O. Har-
rassowitz; London, David Nutt. 1905.   [Reprinted, Vaduz:
Kraus Reprints, 1963.]
     pp. xxiv+108.
     Materialien zur Kunde des älteren englischen Dramas.
     Bd. 12.

The Gull's Hornbook by Thomas Dekker, edited by R. B.
McKerrow.   Alexander Moring Ltd., The De La More Press,
32 George Street, Hanover Square, London, W., 1905.
     pp. xiv+126.
     The King's Classics.
     Pref., p. xiii: '...the present edition, which is, in
     the main, a reprint of that issued last year in "The
     King's Library"....'

Hand-Lists of English Printers, 1501-1556.   Part III.   T.
Berthelet...R. Grafton...By E. Gordon Duff.   W. W. Greg.
R. B. McKerrow.   A. W. Pollard.   London: Printed by
Blades, East & Blades, for the Bibliographical Society,
November, 1905.
     Richard Grafton, by R. B. McKerrow.   On the com-
     pletion of this work in 1913, a general title-page was
     issued reading, "Hand-Lists of Books printed by Lon-
     don Printers, 1501-1556. By E. G. Duff, W. W.
     Greg, R. B. McKerrow, H. R. Plomer, A. W. Pol-

lard, R. Proctor. London: Printed by Blades,
East & Blades, for the Bibliographical Society, September, 1913. "

The Spanish Curate.   Edited by R. B. McKerrow.
   The Works of Francis Beaumont and John Fletcher.
   Variorum edition. George Bell & Sons & A. H. Bul-
   len: London, 1904-12. Vol. ii, pp. 101-227.

Wit Without Money.   Edited by R. B. McKerrow.
   The Works of Francis Beaumont and John Fletcher.
   Variorum edition. George Bell & Sons & A. H. Bul-
   len: London, 1904-12. Vol. ii, pp. 229-337.

The Works of Thomas Nashe.... Text: Vol. III. A. H.
Bullen.... London.   MCMV.
   pp. 416.

Review

Ernst Rühl, Grobianus in England. Berlin, 1904.
   Englische Studien, Bd. 35, Heft 2, Juli 1905, pp.
   305-9.

1906

The Gentleman's Magazine.   New series, vol. ccc. (February to June 1906.) London.
_____   _____   vol. ccci.   (July to December 1906.)
   The Gentleman's Magazine was acquired in 1906 by
   Lord Northcliffe and a new series was started on 16
   Feb. under the editorship of A. H. Bullen with Mc-
   Kerrow as assistant.   Bullen edited only the volumes
   for 1906, though it was continued during 1907 and
   "copyright registration copies, consisting of the
   wrappers only, continued to be sent to the British
   Museum until 1922.   In a letter to The Times Literary Supplement of 18 June 1931, where he implies
   that The Gentleman's came to an end in 1906, Mc-
   Kerrow named some of the contributors to these volumes, but his own copy contains attributions for most
   of the articles.   His own were as follows:
   Vol. ccc. Feb.-June 1906.
      February, pp. 53-62.   Retrospective Review:
      "Wilson's Discourse of Usury (1572). "

68-71. Correspondence: "Early Editions of
Greene's Quip for an Upstart Courtier (1592)."
Signed: R. B. McK.
88-9. Review: The Itinerary in Wales of John
Leland in or about the years 1536-1539. Edited
by Lucy Toulmin Smith. (London, 1906.)
97-100. Learned Societies. [Containing notices
of publications of The Hakluyt Society, The Bibliographical Society and The London Topographi-
cal Society.]
March, p. 220. Short Notice: The Modern Language Review. Edited by John G. Robertson.
No. 2. (Cambridge, January 1906.)
220-1. Short Notice: The New Zealand Official
Year-Book, 1905.
April, pp. 277-84. Retrospective Review: "Richard Robinson's Eupolemia, Archippus, and Pan-
oplia (1603)."
317-20. Learned Societies. [Containing notices
of publications of The Roman Antiquities Committee for Yorkshire, The Royal Historical Society, The Yorkshire Dialect Society and The
Graphical Society.]
320-1. Short Notice: Oldcastle-Falstaff in der
englischen Literatur bis zu Shakespeare. Von
Wilhelm Beaske. (Berlin, 1905.)
321. Short Notice: Sicily. By the late Augus-
tus J. C. Hare and St. Clair Baddeley. (London, 1905.)
May, pp. 379-89. Article: "Some English Earth-
quakes."
390-403. Retrospective Review: "W. Fulwood's
Enemy of Idleness."
425-7. Learned Societies. [Containing notices of
publications of The Catholic Record Society, The
Hakluyt Society, The Navy Records Society and
The Selden Society.] "Mostly R. B. McK."
428. Short Notice: The Modern Language Review. Edited by John G. Robertson. No. 3.
(Cambridge, April 1906.)
428-9. Short Notice: Northern Notes and Queries; a quarterly magazine. Nos. 1 and 2.
(Newcastle-upon-Tyne, Jan. and April 1906.)
429. Short Notice: Peeps into the Past; or, By-
gone City Life, Traditions, Customs and Festi-
vals. By F. E. Tyler. London.
June, pp. 526-7. Correspondence: "An Untamed

Shrew." Signed: D. S. W.

Vol. ccci. July-Dec. 1906.
July, pp. 58-64. Retrospective Review: "The
Golden Booke of the Leaden Goddes...By Stephen
Batman...1577."
August, pp. 173-9. Retrospective Review: "The
Golden-groue...Made by W. Vaughan...Second
edition...1608."
205-6. Learned Societies. [Containing notices of
publications of The Royal Historical Society and
the Gesellschaft für Typenkunde des XV. Jahrhunderts.]
208-9. Short Notice: Northern Notes and Queries. No. 3. (July 1906.)
September, pp. 280-7. Retrospective Review:
"The Institucion of a gentleman. Anno Domini
M. D. L. V."
304-8. Sylvanus Urban's Notebook. [Sections by
R. B. McKerrow.]
319-20. Short Notice: The Legend of Sir Perce-
val. By Jessie L. Weston. Vol. I (David Nutt,
1906.)
320-1. Short Notice: Cornish Notes and Queries.
(First series). Edited by Peter Penn. (Elliot
Stock, 1906.)
321. Short Notice: Northamptonshire Notes and
Queries. Edited by Christopher A. Markham.
(Northampton, June 1906.)
October, pp. 392-9. Retrospective Review: "W.
Alley's Poor Man's Library."
November, pp. 511-21. Retrospective Review:
"T. Lupton's Thousand Notable Things."

[Notes on The Devil's Charter by Barnabe Barnes.]
Modern Language Review, vol. I, no. 2, Jan. 1906,
pp. 126-7.
Appended to an article by A. E. H. Swaen & G. C.
Moore Smith, with the above title, having reference
to the edition by R. B. McKerrow of The Devil's
Charter in Bang's Materialien zur Kunde des älteren
englischen Dramas, Bd. 6.

Review

A History of English Prosody. By G. Saintsbury. Vol. I.
London, 1906.

Modern Language Review, vol. 2, no. 1, Oct. 1906,
pp. 65-70.

1907

The History of Orlando Furioso 1594.   The Malone Society
Reprints 1907.   Printed for the Malone Society by Horace
Hart M.A., at the Oxford University Press.
     "This reprint of the 1594 edition of Orlando Furioso
     has been prepared by the General Editor and checked
     by Robert B. McKerrow. W. W. Greg."
     A cancel leaf was subsequently issued in which Dr.
     McKerrow's name was given correctly.

1908

The Story of Asseneth.   London, Sidgwick & Jackson, Ltd.
     A "Christmas-card booklet." The French text from
     Moland and d'Héricault, Nouvelles françoises du
     XIVe siècle, with an English version by R. B. Mc-
     Kerrow.

The Tragedy of Locrine 1595.   The Malone Society Reprints
1908.   Printed for the Malone Society by Horace Hart M. A.,
at the Oxford University Press.
     "This reprint of the Tragedy of Locrine has been pre-
     pared by Ronald B. McKerrow and checked by the
     General Editor. W. W. Greg."

The Works of Thomas Nashe...Notes . A. H. Bullen...
London.   MCMVIII.
     pp. 484.

1909

The Play of Patient Grissell by John Phillip.   The Malone
Society Reprints 1909.   Printed for the Malone Society by
Charles Whittingham & Co. at the Chiswick Press.
     "This reprint of John Phillip's play of Patient Gris-
     sell has been prepared by Ronald B. McKerrow and
     the General Editor jointly. W. W. Greg."

The Virtuous Octavia 1598.   The Malone Society Reprints
1909.   Printed for the Malone Society by Horace Hart M.A.,
at the Oxford University Press.

"This reprint of Brandon's Virtuous Octavia has been prepared by Ronald B. McKerrow and checked by the General Editor. W. W. Greg."

1910

A Dictionary of Printers and Booksellers in England, Scotland and Ireland, and of Foreign Printers of English Books 1557-1640. By H. G. Aldis; Robert Bowes; E. R. McC. Dix; E. Gordon Duff; Strickland Gibson; G. J. Gray; R. B. McKerrow; Falconer Madan, and H. R. Plomer. General Editor: R. B. McKerrow. London: Printed for the Bibliographical Society, by Blades, East & Blades, 1910. [Reprint, London: Bibliographical Society, 1968.]
pp. xxiii+346.

Some Notes on the Letters i, j, u and v in Sixteenth Century Printing.
The Library, 3rd Series, vol. I, no. 3, July 1910, pp. 239-59.

The Supposed Calling-in of Drayton's "Harmony of the Church," 1591.
The Library, 3rd Series, vol. I, no. 4, Oct. 1910, pp. 348-50.

The Works of Thomas Nashe... Introduction and Index. Sidgwick & Jackson Ltd., 3 Adam Street, Adelphi, London.
pp. ix+382. Without date.

1911

Apius and Virginia 1575. The Malone Society Reprints 1911. Printed for the Malone Society by Charles Whittingham & Co. at the Chiswick Press.
"This reprint of Apius and Virginia has been prepared by Ronald B. McKerrow with the assistance of the General Editor. W. W. Greg."

B. R. --R. B. Greenes Newes both from Heauen and Hell 1593 and Greenes Funeralls 1594. Reprinted from the original editions with Notes, &c., by R. B. McKerrow. Published for the Editor by Sidgwick & Jackson, Ltd., 3 Adam Street, Adelphi, London. 1911.
pp. xii+96.

"The tracts are reproduced page for page and line
for line." (Introductory note, p. v.)

John Weever. Epigrammes in the Oldest Cut and Newest
Fashion 1599. Reprinted from the original edition with
Notes, &c., by R. B. McKerrow. Published for the Editor
by Sidgwick & Jackson, Ltd., 3 Adam Street, Adelphi, London. 1911.
pp. xiii+129.

A Newe Interlude of Impacyente Pouerte from the quarto of
1560. Edited by R. B. McKerrow. Louvain, A. Uystpruyst;
Leipzig, O. Harrassowitz; London, David Nutt. 1911. [Re-
print, Vaduz: Kraus Reprints, 1963.]
pp. xix+70.
Materialien zur Kunde des älteren englischen Dramas.
Bd. 33.

The Red Printing in the 1611 Bible.
The Library, 3rd Series, vol. 2, no. 7, July 1911,
pp. 323-7.

1912

Did Sir Roger Williams write the Marprelate Tracts?
The Library, 3rd Series, vol. 3, no. 12, Oct. 1912,
pp. 364-74.
The second of two articles under this title, the first
being by William Pierce, having reference to an article by J. Dover Wilson in The Library for April
and July 1912.

Review

William Rowley, his All's Lost by Lust, and A Shoemaker
a Gentleman. With an introduction on Rowley's place in
the drama. By C. W. Stork. Philadelphia, 1910.
Modern Language Review, vol. 7, no. 4, Oct. 1912,
pp. 548-50.

1913

Printers' & Publishers' Devices in England & Scotland 1485-
1640. By Ronald B. McKerrow. London, Printed for the

Bibliographical Society at the Chiswick Press, 1913.
  pp. liv+216+facs.
  Bibliographical Society, Illustrated Monographs, No.
  13.
  [See Joseph A. Lavin, "Additions to McKerrow's Devices," The Library, 5th Series, Vol. XXIII, no. 3,
  September 1968, pp. 191-205.   Lavin's article is also published separately by the Bibliographical Society,
  1968.]

1914

The Marks or Devices used by English Printers and Publishers to the close of the year 1640.
  Transactions of the Bibliographical Society, vol. 12,
  Oct. 1911-Apr. 1913, pp. 13, 14.
  Summary of a paper read 18 March 1912 before the
  Bibliographical Society.   The full text appeared as
  the introduction to Printers' & Publishers' Devices
  (1913).   A leaflet illustrating the paper was distributed
  at the meeting.

Notes on Bibliographical Evidence for Literary Students and
Editors of English Works of the Sixteenth and Seventeenth
Centuries.   By Ronald B. McKerrow.
  Transactions of the Bibliographical Society, vol. 12,
  Oct. 1911-Apr. 193, pp. 211-318.
  A number of copies of this were printed separately.
  This work formed the basis of An Introduction to Bib-
  liography for Literary Students (1927), q.v.

1916

Booksellers, Printers, and the Stationers' Trade.
  Shakespeare's England.   An account of the life &
  manners of his age.   Oxford, 1916.   Vol. 2, pp. 212-
  39.

Review

Robert Greene.   By J. C. Jordan.   New York, 1915.
  Modern Language Review, Vol. II, no. 2, Apr. 1916,
  pp. 233-5.

1920

Reviews

Philip Massinger.   By A. H. Cruickshank.   Oxford, 1920.
New Statesman, 7 Aug. 1920, p. 507.

The Lollard Bible and other Medieval Biblical Versions.   By
Margaret Deanesley.   Cambridge, 1920.
New Statesman, 25 Sept. 1920, pp. 682-4.

A Study in the New Metamorphoses, written by J. M. , Gent. ,
1600.   New York, 1919.
New Statesman, 9 Oct. 1920, p. 26.

1921

A Note on the Teaching of "English Language and Literature, " with some suggestions.   By R. B. McKerrow... June,
1921.
pp. 32.
The English Association.   Pamphlet No. 49.

The Use of the Galley in Elizabethan Printing.
The Library, 4th Series, vol. 2, no. 2, Sept. 1921,
pp. 97-108.

Review

The Yale Shakespeare.   (1) The First Part of King Henry
the Sixth.   Edited by Tucker Brooke.   (2) The Tragedy of
Othello the Moor of Venice.   Edited by Laurence Mason.
New Haven, 1918.
The Australasian Shakespeare.   Shakespeare's Life of Henry
the Fifth.   Edited by L. Le Gay Brereton.   Melbourne &
Sydney, 1918.
Modern Language Review, vol. 16, no. 2, Apr. 1921,
pp. 177-8.

1922

A Dictionary of the Printers and Booksellers who were at
work in England, Scotland and Ireland from 1668 to 1725.

By Henry R. Plomer. With the help of H. G. Aldis, E. R.
McC. Dix, G. J. Gray, and R. B. McKerrow. Edited by
Arundell Esdaile. Printed for the Bibliographical Society,
at the Oxford University Press. 1922.
> pp. xii+342.

English Grammar and Grammars.
> Essays and Studies by Members of the English Asso-
> ciation, vol. viii, pp. 148-67.

Review

German Literature.
> The Library, 4th Series, vol. 3, no. 2, Sept. 1922,
> p. 142.
> A review of Systematische Bibliographie der wissen-
> schaftlichen Literatur Deutschlands der Jahre 1914-
> 1921. Bd. 1. Berlin, 1922.

1923

Greene and Gabriel Harvey.
> Letter in The Times Literary Supplement, 8 Mar.
> 1923, p. 160.

Contribution to the discussion on a paper by R. W. Chapman:
"Notes on Eighteenth Century Bookbuilding."
> The Library, 4th Series, vol. 4, no. 3, Dec. 1923,
> pp. 177-80.

Reviews

Robert Greene, Notable Discovery of Coosnage, 1591; The
Second Part of Conny-Catching, 1592; Gabriel Harvey, Foure
Letters and certeine Sonnets, 1592. Edited by G. B. Harri-
son. London.
> Modern Language Review, vol. 18, no. 4, Oct. 1923,
> p. 504.

Shakespeare's Hand in the Play of "Sir Thomas More."
Cambridge, 1923.
> The Library, 4th Series, vol. 4, no. 3, Dec. 1923,
> pp. 238-42.

1924

Border-Pieces used by English Printers before 1641.
    The Library, 4th Series, vol. 5, no. 1, June 1924,
    pp. 1-37.
    Paper read before the Bibliographical Society 21 Jan-
    uary 1924. A leaflet illustrating the paper was dis-
    tributed at the meeting.

"The Divils Charter."
    Letter in The Times, 26 Jan. 1924, p. 6.
    A reply to a letter by M. H. Spielmann in The Times,
    24 Jan. 1924.

"The Divils Charter."
    Letter in The Times, 2 Feb. 1924, p. 6.
    Further reply to M. H. Spielmann.

The Nonesuch Congreve.
    Letter in The London Mercury, vol. 9, no. 53, Mar.
    1924, p. 526.

Reviews

The Elizabethan Stage.   By E. K. Chambers.   Oxford, 1923.
    English Historical Review, vol. 155, July 1924, pp.
    430-4.

An Enquiry on a Psychological Basis into the Use of the Progressive Form in Late Modern English.   Door Jacobus van
der Laan.   Gorinchem, 1922.
    Modern Language Review, vol. 19, no. 4, Oct. 1924,
    pp. 487-8.

1925

Bibliographical Terms.
    Letter in The Times Literary Supplement, 29 Oct.
    1925, p. 719.
    This letter was reprinted in The Publishers' Circular,
    7 Nov. 1925.

Elizabethan Printers and the Composition of Reprints.
    The Library, 4th Series, vol. 5, no. 4, Mar. 1925,
    pp. 357-64.

<u>English Literary Autographs 1550-1650</u>. Selected for repro-
duction and edited by W. W. Greg in collaboration with J. P.
Gilson, Hilary Jenkinson, R. B. McKerrow, A. W. Pollard.
Part I--Dramatists. Printed at the Oxford University Press,
1925. [Reprinted in one volume, Nendeln, Liechtenstein:
Kraus Reprint, 1968.]
   Part II--Poets, 1928; Part III--Prose Writers & Ap-
   pendix, 1932.
   On the completion of the work a general title-page
   was issued bearing the date 1932.

Greene and Dekker.
   Letter in <u>The Times Literary Supplement,</u> 18 June
   1925, p. 416.

A Note on English Printing of To-day.
   <u>Gutenberg-Festschrift</u>, Mainz, 1925, pp. 33-7.

<u>The Review of English Studies</u>. A quarterly journal of Eng-
lish literature and the English language. Edited by R. B.
McKerrow. London, Sidgwick & Jackson, Ltd....
   vol. 1, no. 1-vol. 15, no. 60. January 1925-
   October 1939.
   In an introductory article in vol. 1, no. 1, the
   Editor wrote as follows:
   "In the preliminary announcement of the Review
   it was stated that its chief attention would be devoted to research in all departments of its subject
   .... In matters of literary history 'research' is not
   quite the same thing as in the natural sciences.
   We have less to do with that which has never previously been known, and more with that which has
   never been rightly interpreted.... Much of our work
   must necessarily be rediscovery, but it is no less
   important on that account and no less worthy of the
   name of research.... It is our task as researchers
   to discover not only the facts, the dry minutiae,
   but the relations between them, their reactions upon one another, those slower changes and developments to which the most clear-sighted of contemporaries must ever be blind...."
   McKerrow continued to edit the Review until his
   death in January 1940, when Professor J. R. Sutherland was appointed to succeed him. Just before Mc-
   Kerrow's death arrangements had been made for the
   transference of the Review from Sidgwick & Jackson
   to the Oxford University Press. The title-page of the

latest volume reads "The Review of English Studies
...Edited by R. B. McKerrow...and James R. Sutherland...Oxford University Press London...."

Inside the wrappers of the first eight numbers Mc-
Kerrow printed miscellaneous information of interest
to students, including a "perpetual" calendar for the
period 1558-1623, devised by himself. The whole of
this information was printed as a pamphlet in 1927
with the title Information for Students.

Dr. McKerrow naturally wrote many reviews for
The Review. These have all been listed below under
their appropriate years. It is possible that he also
wrote most of the unsigned "Short Notices," which appeared from time to time, but I have included these
only when I have found definite evidence of his authorship.

Reviews

Elizabethans. By A. H. Bullen. London, 1924.
        RES. vol. 1, no. 1, Jan. 1925, pp. 118-20.

Gotik und Ruine in der englischen Dichtung des achtzehnten
Jahrhunderts, von Dr. Reinhard Haferkorn. Leipzig, 1924.
        RES. vol. 1, no. 1, Jan. 1925, p. 123.

John Davies of Hereford (1565?-1618) und sein Bild von
Shakespeare's Umgebung. Von Hans Heidrich. Leipzig,
1924.
        RES. vol. 1, no. 2, Apr. 1925, pp. 242-4.

The Year's Work in English Studies. Vol. IV. 1923. London, 1924.
        RES. vol. 1, no. 2, Apr. 1925, pp. 245-6.

The Fable of the Bees: or Private Vices, Publick Benefits.
By Bernard Mandeville. With a commentary by F. B. Kaye.
Oxford, 1924.
        The Library, 4th Series, vol. 6, no. 1, June 1925,
        pp. 109-11.

Bodley Head Quartos, vols. 9, 10: King James's Daemon-
ologie, 1597, Newes from Scotland declaring the Damnable
Life and Death of Doctor Fian, 1591; Robert Greene, Black-
Bookes Messenger, 1592, with 'Cuthbert Conny-Catcher's'
Defence of Conny-Catching, 1592. London, 1924.

Modern Language Review, vol. 20, no. 3, July 1925,
p. 371.

Sidelights on Elizabethan Drama.   By H. Dugdale Sykes.
London, 1924.
　　RES. vol. 1, no. 3, July 1925, pp. 361-3.

Foure Birds of Noahs Arke.   By Thomas Dekker.   Edited by
F. P. Wilson.   Oxford, 1924.
　　RES. vol. 1, no. 3, July 1925, pp. 375-6.

The Bodley Head Quartos.   Edited by G. B. Harrison.
　　RES. vol. 1, no. 3, July 1925, p. 376.

Studies in the First Folio, written for the Shakespeare Association in celebration of the First Folio Tercentenary.   London, 1924.
　　RES. vol. 1, no. 4, Oct. 1925, pp. 492-4.

A Midsummer Night's Dream ("The New Shakespeare.")
Cambridge, 1924.
　　RES. vol. 1, no. 4, Oct. 1925, pp. 495-7

Early Tudor Composers.   By William H. Grattan Flood.
London, 1925.
　　RES. vol. 1, no. 4, Oct. 1925, p. 498.

G. B. Bodoni's Preface to the Manuale Tipografico of 1818.
Now first translated into English with an introduction by H.
V. Marrot.   London, 1925.
　　The Library, 4th Series, vol. 6, no. 3, Dec. 1925,
　　pp. 290-2.

1926

Reply to a letter of R. W. Chapman answering criticisms
contained in R. B. McKerrow's review of The Oxford Book
of English Prose.
　　RES. vol. 2, no. 7, July 1926, p. 349.

Reviews

The Elizabethan Home discovered in 2 Dialogues by Claudius
Hollyband and Peter Erondell.   Edited by M. St. Clare
Byrne.   London, 1925.
　　RES. vol. 2, no. 5, Jan. 1926, pp. 111-13.

S. P. E. Tract No. XIX.   Medium Aevum and the Middle Age.
By George Gordon.   Oxford, 1925.
    RES. vol. 2, no. 5, Jan. 1926, p. 115.

S. P. E. Tract No. XXI.   The Society's Work.   By Robert
Bridges.   Oxford, 1925.
    RES. vol. 2, no. 5, Jan. 1926, pp. 115-18.

Martial and the English Epigram from Sir Thomas Wyatt to
Ben Jonson.   By T. K. Whipple.   Berkeley, California,
1925.
    RES. vol. 2, no. 5, Jan. 1926, p. 120.

Ben Jonson.   Edited by C. H. Herford and Percy Simpson.
Volumes I and II.   Oxford, 1925.
    RES. vol. 2, no. 6, Apr. 1926, pp. 227-30.

The Oxford Book of English Prose.   Chosen and edited by
Sir Arthur Quiller-Couch.   Oxford, 1925.
    RES. vol. 2, no. 6, Apr. 1926, pp. 235-9

England's Helicon.   Reprinted from the edition of 1600.
London, 1925.
    RES. vol. 2, no. 6, Apr. 1926, pp. 245-6.

"Other Books and Pamphlets Received."
    RES. vol. 2, no. 6, Apr. 1926, pp. 246-8.

Mulcaster's Elementarie.   Edited, with an introduction, by
E. T. Campagnac.   Oxford, 1925.
    RES. vol. 2, no. 7, July 1926, pp. 365-7.

Speculum.   A journal of mediaeval studies.   Mediaeval Academy of America.
    RES. vol. 2, no. 7, July 1926, p. 375.

The Year's Work in English Studies.   Vol. V. 1924. London,
1926.
    RES. vol. 2, no. 7, July 1926, p. 376.

Specimens of Books Printed at Oxford with the Types given
to the University by John Fell.   Oxford, 1925.
    The Library, 4th Series, vol. 7, no. 2, Sept. 1926,
    pp. 225-7.

Jahrbuch der Deutschen Shakespeare-Gesellschaft.   Neue
Folge.   I. Band.   Jena, 1924.

Shakespeare Jahrbuch. Band 61. Leipzig, 1925.
    RES. vol. 2, no. 8, Oct. 1926, pp. 493-5.

"Other Books and Pamphlets Received."
    RES. vol. 2, no. 8, Oct. 1926, p. 497.

1927

The Capital Letters in Elizabethan Handwriting.
    RES. vol. 3, no. 9, Jan. 1927, pp. 28-36.

Information for Students.
    Reprinted from notes printed on the wrappers of the
    first eight numbers of The Review of English Studies
    (1925), q. v.

An Introduction to Bibliography for Literary Students. By
Ronald B. McKerrow. Oxford, at the Clarendon Press,
1927. [Many lithographic reprintings from the second impression, i. e. 1948, 1949, 1951, 1959, 1960, 1962, 1964,
1965, 1967.]
    pp. xv+359.
    Preface, pp. v, vi: "In the autumn of 1913 I put to-
    gether certain 'Notes on Bibliographical Evidence for
    Literary Students and Editors of English Works of the
    Sixteenth and Seventeenth Centuries,' and these were
    printed as part of the twelfth volume of the Transac-
    tions of the Bibliographical Society.... That paper has,
    if I may judge from the friendly letters which I have
    received concerning it... proved of real use to many
    .... I have... been repeatedly asked to reissue the
    pamphlet (now out of print) in a more comprehensive
    form, and at a cost, I fear, of somewhat damaging
    the original unity of the scheme, I have rewritten and
    much enlarged it so that in some measure it deals
    with English book-production in general up to about
    1800, though it is still... centred, so to speak, in the
    Shakespearian period."
    Second impression with corrections, 1928.

Types for Phonetic Transcription: a suggestion.
    RES. vol. 3, no. 9, Jan. 1927, wrappers.

Reviews

Fulgens and Lucres. A fifteenth-century secular play. By
Henry Medwall. Edited by F. S. Boas and A. W. Reed.
Oxford, 1926.
      RES. vol. 3, no. 9, Jan. 1927, pp. 83-5.

A Hundreth Sundrie Flowres. London, 1926.
      RES. vol. 3, no. 9, Jan. 1927, pp. 111-14.

A Gorgeous Gallery of Gallant Inventions (1578). Edited by
Hyder E. Rollins. Cambridge, Mass., 1926.
      RES. vol. 3, no. 10, Apr. 1927, pp. 242-3.

The British Museum Quarterly. No. 1-3. London, 1926.
      RES. vol. 3, no. 10, Apr. 1927, pp. 246-7.

Gutenberg to Plantin: an outline of the early history of printing. By George Parker Winship. Cambridge, Mass., 1926.
      RES. vol. 3, no. 10, Apr. 1927, pp. 247-8.

The Lyfe of Saynt Radegunde. Edited by F. Brittain. Cambridge, 1926.
      RES. vol. 3, no. 11, July 1927, p. 372.

The Oxford Book of Eighteenth Century Verse. Chosen by
David Nichol Smith. Oxford, 1926.
      RES. vol. 3, no. 12, Oct. 1927, pp. 478-8.

Tennyson as seen by his Parodists. By Dr. J. Postma.
Amsterdam, 1926.
      RES. vol. 3, no. 12, Oct. 1927, p. 490.

The Year's Work in English Studies. Vol. VI. 1925. London, 1927.
      RES. vol. 3, no. 12, Oct. 1927, pp. 493-4.

A Short-Title Catalogue of Books printed in England, Scotland
and Ireland, and of English Books printed abroad, 1475-1640.
Compiled by A. W. Pollard and G. R. Redgrave. London,
1926.
      RES. vol. 3, no. 12, Oct. 1927, pp. 494-6.

"Other Books and Pamphlets Received."
      RES. vol. 3, no. 12, Oct. 1927, pp. 496-8.

1928

Bibliography.
>   Letter in The Times Literary Supplement, 26 Jan.
>   1928, p. 62.
>   Reply to a letter by J. E. Springarn (T. L. S. , 19 Jan.
>   1928).

Bibliography.
>   Letter in The Times Literary Supplement, 22 Mar.
>   1928, p. 221.
>   Reply to a letter by J. E. Springarn (T. L. S. , 1 Mar.
>   1928).

English Literary Autographs 1550-1650... Part II--Poets...
1928.
>   Part I, 1925.

The Relationship of English Printed Books to Authors' Manuscripts in the Sixteenth and Seventeenth Centuries.
>   The Sandars Lectures, Cambridge University.
>   Typescript in Cambridge University Library.

Reviews

A Register of Bibliographies of the English Language and
Literature.   By Clark Sutherland Northup with contributions
by Joseph Quincy Adams and Andrew Keogh.   New Haven,
Conn. , 1925.
>   Modern Language Review, vol. 23, no. 1, Jan. 1928,
>   pp. 64-5.

The Plague in Shakespeare's London.   By F. 'P. Wilson.
Oxford, 1927.
>   RES. vol. 4, no. 13, Jan. 1928, pp. 109-11.

The Elements of Book-Collecting.   By Iolo A. Williams.
London, 1927.
>   The Library, 4th Series, vol. 8, no. 4, Mar. 1928,
>   pp. 488-91.

The Wandering Scholars.   By Helen Waddell.   London, 1927.
>   RES. vol. 4, no. 14, Apr. 1928, pp. 224-7.

"The Booke of Sir Thomas Moore. "   (A bibliotic study.)

By Samuel A. Tannenbaum.   New York, 1927.
    RES. vol. 4, no. 14, Apr. 1928, pp. 237-41.

The Dialogue concerning Tyndale by Sir Thomas More.   Reproduced in black letter facsimile.   Edited by W. E. Campbell.   London, 1927.
    RES. vol. 4, no. 15, July 1928, pp. 352-4.

The Cambridge History of English Literature.   Vol. XV.
General Index.   Cambridge, 1927.
    RES. vol. 4, no. 15, July 1928, p. 372

The Paradise of Dainty Devices (1576-1606).   Edited by
Hyder Edward Rollins.   Cambridge, Mass., 1927.
    RES. vol. 4, no. 16, Oct. 1928, pp. 480-2.

The Pack of Autolycus or Strange and Terrible News as told
in Broadside Ballads of the years 1624-1693.   Edited by
Hyder Edward Rollins.   Cambridge, Mass., 1927.
    RES. vol. 4, no. 16, Oct. 1928, pp. 482-3.

                              1929

Edward Allde as a Typical Trade Printer.
    The Library, 4th Series, vol. 10, no. 2, Sept. 1929,
    pp. 121-62.
    Paper read before the Bibliographical Society 18 Feb.
    1929.

Opinion in an article by I. A. Williams ("Some Poetical Mis-
cellanies of the Early Eighteenth Century").
    The Library, 4th Series, vol. 10, no. 3, Dec. 1929,
    p. 236.

Reviews

A Bibliography of Writings on the English Language, from
the beginning of printing to the end of 1922.   By Arthur G.
Kennedy.   Cambridge & New Haven, 1927.
    RES. vol. 5, no. 17, Jan. 1929, pp. 120-1.

The History of Rasselas, Prince of Abissinia, a tale.   By
Samuel Johnson, edited by R. W. Chapman.   Oxford, 1927.
    RES. vol. 5, no. 19, July 1929, pp. 363-4.

The Sources of English Literature. A guide for students, by
Arundell Esdaile. Cambridge, 1928.
> RES. vol. 5, no. 19, July 1929, pp. 374-5.

"Other Books and Pamphlets Received."
> RES. vol. 5, no. 19, July 1929, pp. 375-6.

Short notice of Machiavelli and the Elizabethans, the Annual
Italian Lecture of the British Academy for 1928. (London,
1928) by Mario Praz.
> English Historical Review, vol. 44, no. 176, Oct.
> 1929, pp. 680-1.

The Man of Feeling. By Henry Mackenzie, edited by Ham-
ish Miles. London, 1928.
> RES. vol. 5, no. 20, Oct. 1929, pp. 485-6.

Bibliography, Practical, Enumerative, Historical. An introductory manual. By Henry Bartlett van Hoesen, with the
collaboration of Frank Keller Walter. New York, London,
1928.
> RES. vol. 5, no. 20, Oct. 1929, pp. 493-6.

The Year's Work in English Studies. Vol. VIII. 1927. London, 1929.
> RES. vol. 5, no. 20, Oct. 1929, p. 497.

1930

Richard Robinson's Eupolemia and the Licensers.
> The Library, 4th Series, vol. 11, no. 2, Sept. 1930,
> pp. 173-8.

Sir Israel Gollancz.
> RES. vol. 6, no. 24, Oct. 1930, pp. 453-5.

Reviews

A Bibliography of the Writings of William Harvey, M.D.,
Discoverer of the Circulation of the Blood. By Geoffrey
Keynes. Cambridge, 1928.
> RES. vol. 6, no. 21, Jan. 1930, pp. 120-1.

Short notice of G. B. Harrison's Elizabethan Journal (London,
1928).

English Historical Review, vol. 45, no. 177, Jan.
1930, p. 155.

Bibliographia Aberdonensis. By James Fowler Kellas John-
stone, LL.D., and Alexander Webster Robertson. 1472-
1640. Aberdeen, 1929.
RES. vol. 6, no. 22, Apr. 1930, pp. 246-7.

Shakespeare-Jahrbuch. Bd. 65. Leipzig, 1929.
RES. vol. 6, no. 24, Oct. 1930, pp. 470-1.

A Short Catalogue of Books printed in England and English
Books printed abroad before 1641 in the Library of Wadham
College, Oxford. Compiled by H. A. Wheeler. 1918. Lon-
don, 1929.
RES. vol. 6, no. 24, Oct. 1930, pp. 488-9.

Reference Books. A classified and annotated guide to the
principal works of reference. Compiled by John Minto.
London, 1929.
RES. vol. 6, no. 24, Oct. 1930, pp. 491-2.

1931

"Edition" and "Impression."
    Letter in The Times Literary Supplement, 1 Oct.
    1931, p. 760.

The Elizabethan Printer and Dramatic Manuscripts.
    The Library, 4th Series, vol. 12, no. 3, Dec. 1931,
    pp. 253-75.
    Paper read before the Bibliographical Society 19 Oct.
    1931.

Friends of the National Libraries.
    RES. vol. 7, no. 27, July 1931, p. 342.

The Gentleman's Magazine.
    Letter in The Times Literary Supplement, 18 June
    1931, p. 487.

Reviews

An Elegy written in a Country Churchyard. By Thomas Gray.
The text of the first quarto. By Francis Griffin Stokes. Oxford, 1929.

RES. vol. 7, no. 25, Jan. 1931, pp. 107-8.

The Year's Work in English Studies. Vol. IX. 1928. London, 1930.
RES. vol. 7, no. 25, Jan. 1931, p. 118.

The Dunciad Variorum with the Prolegomena of Scriblerus, by Alexander Pope. Reproduced in facsimile with an introductory essay by Robert Kilburn Root. Princeton University Press, 1929.
RES. vol. 7, no. 25, Jan. 1931, p. 121.

The British Museum Quarterly. London. Vol. IV, nos. 1-4.
RES. vol. 7, no. 25, Jan. 1931, p. 121.

Shakspere Forgeries in the Revels Accounts. By Samuel A. Tannenbaum. New York, 1928.
Modern Language Notes, vol. 46, no. 2, Feb. 1931, pp. 120-4.

Fourth Supplement to a Manual of the Writings in Middle English, 1050-1400. By John Edwin Wells. New Haven, Conn., 1929.
RES. vol. 7, no. 26, Apr. 1931, p. 246.

Johnson, Boswell and Mrs. Piozzi: a suppressed passage restored. London, 1929.
RES. vol. 7, no. 26, Apr. 1931, p. 247.

Winter: A poem. By James Thomson, A. M. 1726. Oxford, 1929.
RES. vol. 7, no. 26, Apr. 1931, p. 247.

Evelina or the History of a Young Lady's Entrance into the World. By Frances Burney. Edited by Sir Frank D. Mackinnon. Oxford, 1930.
RES. vol. 7, no. 27, July 1931, pp. 360-1.

Cancels. By R. W. Chapman. London; New York, 1930.
RES. vol. 7, no. 27, July 1931, pp. 373-4.

Shakespeare-Jahrbuch. Bd. 66. Leipzig, 1930.
RES. vol. 7, no. 28, Oct. 1931, pp. 469-70.

Shakespeare Studies Biographical and Literary. By Edgar I. Fripp. London, 1930.
RES. vol. 7, no. 28, Oct. 1931, p. 499.

1932

English Literary Autographs 1550-1650...Part III--Prose
Writers & Appendix...1932.
  Part I, 1925; Part II, 1928.

A Publishing Agreement of the Late Seventeenth Century.
  The Library, 4th Series, vol. 13, no. 2, Sept. 1932,
  pp. 184-7

Title-page Borders used in England & Scotland 1485-1640.
By R. B. McKerrow & F. S. Ferguson. London, Printed for
the Bibliographical Society at the Oxford University Press,
1932 (for 1931).
  pp. xlvii+234+facs.
  Bibliographical Society, Illustrated Monographs, no.
  xxi.

Reviews

The Wizard, a play by Simon Baylie. Edited by Henry de
Vocht. Louvain, 1930.
  RES. vol. 8, no. 31, July 1932, pp. 337-9.

The Year's Work in English Studies. Vol. X. 1929. London, 1931.
  RES. vol. 8, no. 31, July 1932, pp. 368-9.

Shakespeare's Hamlet. The First Quarto, 1603. Repro-
duced in facsimile from the copy in the Henry E. Huntington
Library. Cambridge, Mass., 1931.
  RES. vol. 8, no. 31, July 1932, pp. 369-70.

Plutarch's Quyete of Mynde, translated by Thomas Wyat.
Reproduced in facsimile, with an introduction by Charles
Read Baskervill. Cambridge, Mass., 1931.
  RES. vol. 8, no. 31, July 1932, p. 370.

Collected Essays, Papers, etc., of Robert Bridges, V:
George Darley. London, 1930.
  RES. vol. 8, no. 31, July 1932, p. 371.

The Huntington Library Bulletin. Cambridge, Mass. No. 1,
May 1931. No. 2, November 1931.
  RES. vol. 8, no. 31, July 1932, p. 371.

Medium Ævum. Oxford. Vol. 1, No. 1, May 1932.
    RES. vol. 8, no. 32, Oct. 1932, p. 499.

1933

A Note on Henry VI, Part II, and The Contention of York and Lancaster.
    RES. vol. 9, no. 34, Apr. 1933, pp. 157-69.

2 Henry VI and The Contention--A Correction.
    RES. vol. 9, no. 35, July 1933, pp. 315-16.

The Treatment of Shakespeare's Text by his Earlier Editors, 1709-1768 by Ronald B. McKerrow. Annual Shakespeare Lecture of the British Academy 1933. London: Humphrey Milford, Amen House, E. C.
    pp. 35.
    Proceedings of the British Academy, vol. 19. [Reprints, Folcroft, Pa.: Folcroft Press, 1969. Freeport, N. Y.: Books for Libraries Press, 1970.]

Reviews

Ichabod Dawks and his "News-Letter." By Stanley Morison. Cambridge, 1931.
The English Newspaper. By Stanley Morison. Cambridge, 1932.
    RES. vol. 9, no. 34, Apr. 1933, pp. 234-6.

John Dryden: Epilogue spoken to the King, March the Nineteenth, 1681. Oxford University Press. 1932.
    RES. vol. 9, no. 35, July 1933, p. 373.

Erläuterungen und Textverbesserungen zu vierzehn Dramen Shakespeares. Von Leon Kellner. Leipzig, 1931.
    RES. vol. 9, no. 36, Oct. 1933, pp. 474-6.

1934

A Note on Titus Andronicus.
    The Library, 4th Series, vol. 15, no. 1, June 1934, pp. 49-53.

Rowe's Shakespeare, "1709."
>   Letter in The Times Literary Supplement, 8 Mar.
>   1934, p. 168.

[Postscript to article by C. F. Bühler.]
>   The Library, 4th Series, vol. 15, no. 3, Dec. 1934,
>   pp. 326-9.

Reviews

Annual Bibliography of English Language and Literature.
Vol. XII. 1931. Cambridge, 1932.
The Year's Work in English Studies. Vol. XI. 1930. London, 1932.
>   RES. vol. 10, no. 37, Jan. 1934, pp. 116-17.

Seven Letters from Charles Lamb to Charles Ryle of the
East India House, 1828-1832. London, 1931.
>   RES. vol. 10, no. 38, Apr. 1934, p. 246.

A Description of the Hand-Press in the Department of English, at University College, London. By A. H. Smith. Privately printed in the Department of English at University College, London, 1934.
>   The Library, 4th Series, vol. 15, no. 1, June 1934,
>   pp. 126-8.

Report on the British Gift of Books to the Tokyo Imperial
University Library, 1923-1933. London, 1934.
>   The Library, 4th Series, vol. 15, no. 1, June 1934,
>   p. 128.

The Oxford Companion to English Literature. Compiled and
edited by Sir Paul Harvey. Oxford, 1932.
>   RES. vol. 10, no. 39, July 1934, pp. 367-9.

An Enquiry into the Nature of Certain Nineteenth Century
Pamphlets. By John Carter and Graham Pollard. London;
New York, 1934.
>   The Library, 4th Series, vol. 15, no. 3, Dec. 1934,
>   pp. 379-84.

1935

A Suggestion regarding Shakespeare's Manuscripts.

RES. vol. 11, no. 44, Oct. 1935, pp. 459-65.

Transactions of the Bibliographical Society. Second Series.
Volume XV(-XVI). The Library. A quarterly review of bib-
liography. Edited by Ronald B. McKerrow. Fourth series.
Volume XV(-XVI). Printed for the Bibliographical Society
at the Oxford University Press. Published by Humphrey
Milford London...1935(-6).

> R. B. McKerrow succeeded A. W. Pollard as editor of
> The Library in June 1935. He edited it alone until
> 1936, when the present writer was called in to assist
> him. The title-page of Vol. XVII reads, "Edited by
> R. B. McKerrow and F. C. Francis." After one
> year of collaboration Dr. McKerrow gave up the edi-
> torship in order to be able to devote more time to
> his work on the Oxford Shakespeare.

Reviews

Points in Eighteenth Century Verse. By Iolo A. Williams.
London; New York, 1934.
> RES. vol. 11, no. 41, Jan. 1935, pp. 118-20.

National Libraries of the World: their history, administration and public services. By Arundell Esdaile. London,
1934.
> The Library, 4th Series, vol. 16, no. 1, June 1935,
> pp. 119-20.

Ratseis Ghost, or the Second Part of his Madde Prankes and
Robberies [1605]. Reproduced in facsimile with an introduction by H. B. Charlton. Manchester, 1932.
> RES. vol. 11, no. 43, July 1935, p. 373.

Proof-reading in the Sixteenth, Seventeenth and Eighteenth
Centuries. By Percy Simpson. London, 1935.
> The Library, 4th Series, vol. 16, no. 3, Dec. 1935,
> pp. 347-52.

A List of Books printed in Cambridge at the University
Press, 1521-1800. Cambridge, 1935.
> The Library, 4th Series, vol. 16, no. 3, Dec. 1935,
> pp. 353-4.

1936

The Printing of "Romeo and Juliet."
        Letter in The Times Literary Supplement, 4 July
        1936, p. 564.

Reviews

Devices of the Early Printers 1457-1560: their history and
development. By Hugh William Davies. London, 1935.
        The Library, 4th Series, vol. 16, no. 4, Mar. 1936,
        pp. 466-9.

Shakespeare 1700-1740. A collation of the editions and separate plays with some account of T. Johnson and R. Walker.
By H. L. Ford. Oxford, 1935.
        The Library, 4th Series, vol. 17, no. 1, June 136,
        pp. 117-20.

The Book-Trade in Shropshire. By Llewelyn C. Lloyd. (Reprinted from the Transactions of the Shropshire Archaeologi-
cal and Natural History Society, vol. 48 (1935-6).)
        The Library, 4th Series, vol. 17, no. 1, June 136,
        p. 122-3.

Catalogue of a Collection of Works on Publishing and Bookselling in the British Library of Political and Economic Science. London School of Economics and Political Science,
London, 1936.
        The Library, 4th Series, vol. 17, no. 3, Dec. 1936,
        p. 368.

1937

A Note on the "Bad Quartos" of 2 and 3 Henry VI and the
Folio Text.
        RES. vol. 13, no. 49, Jan. 1937, pp. 64-72.

Review

Edmund Garratt Gardner, 12 May, 1869--27 July, 1935. A
bibliography of his publications, with appreciations by C. J.
Sisson and C. Foligno. London, 1936.

RES. vol. 13, no. 51, July 1937, p. 377.

1938

Reviews

Shakespeare's Titus Andronicus: the First Quarto, 1594.
Reproduced in facsimile with an introduction by Joseph Quincy Adams. New York & London, 1936.
    RES. vol. 14, no. 53, Jan. 1938, pp. 86-8.

Francis Meres's Treatise "Poetrie": a critical edition by
Don Cameron Allen. Urbana, 1933.
    RES. vol. 14, no. 53, Jan. 1938, pp. 88-91.

A History of Modern Colloquial English. By Henry Cecil
Wyld. Third edition, with additions. Oxford, 1936.
    RES. vol. 14, no. 53, Jan. 1938, p. 120.

A New Variorum Edition of Shakespeare. Henry the Fourth,
Part I. Edited by Samuel Burdett Hemingway. Philadelphia & London, 1936.
    Modern Language Notes, vol. 53, no. 3, Mar. 1938,
    pp. 207-11.

The Huntington Library Bulletin. Cambridge, Mass. No. 4,
Oct. 1933.
    RES. vol. 14, no. 54, Apr. 1938, p. 247.

An A. B. C. of English Usage. By H. A. Treble and G. H.
Vallins. Oxford, 1936.
    RES. vol. 14, no. 55, July 1938, pp. 375-6.

Two Pamphlets of Nicholas Breton. Grimellos Fortunes
(1604). An Olde Mans Lesson (1605). Edited by E. G.
Morice. Bristol, 1936.
    RES. vol. 14, no. 56, Oct. 1938, pp. 469-71.

1939

Line Division in "Julius Caesar."
    Letter in The Times Literary Supplement, 19 Aug.
    1939, p. 492.

Note to article by Robert M. Smith, "Why a First Folio

Shakespeare remained in England."
    RES. vol. 15, no. 59, July 1939, p. 264.

Prolegomena for the Oxford Shakespeare. A study in editorial method. By Ronald B. McKerrow. Oxford, at the Clarendon Press. 1939. [Reprint Folcroft, Pa.: Folcroft
Press, 1973]
        pp. xiv+110+two specimen pages from the Oxford
        Shakespeare.

Reviews

Shakespeare's Hamlet, the Second Quarto, 1604, reproduced
in facsimile. With an introduction by Oscar James Campbell. San Marino, California, 1938.
        RES. vol. 15, no. 57, Jan. 1939, pp. 96-7.

The Pilgrim's Progress from this World to that which is to
Come. By John Bunyan. Bedford, 1938. (The Bedford
Edition. Edited by Frank Mott Harrison.)
Borough of Bedford Public Library. Catalogue of the John
Bunyan Library (Frank Mott Harrison Collection). Bedford,
1938.
        The Library, 4th Series, vol. 19, no. 4, Mar. 1939,
        pp. 496-7.

The Pierpont Morgan Library: review of the activities and
acquisitions of the Library from 1930 through 1935. New
York.
        The Library, 4th Series, vol. 19, no. 4, Mar. 1939,
        pp. 497-9.

Seventh Supplement to a Manual of the Writings in Middle
English, 1050-1400. By John Edwin Wells. New Haven,
Conn., 1938.
        RES. vol. 15, no. 59, July 1939, p. 371.

1940

Form and Matter in the Publication of Research.
        RES. vol. 16, no. 61, Jan. 1940, pp. 116-21.

Reviews

The Mirror for Magistrates, edited by Lily B. Campbell.
Cambridge, 1938.
    RES. vol. 16, no. 61, Jan. 1940, pp. 78-81.

Elizabethan England.   Museum Extension Publication.   Illus-
trative Set, vol. 1.   Museum of Fine Arts, Boston.
    RES. vol. 16, no. 61, Jan. 1940, pp. 87-9.

Rossetti's "Sister Helen." Edited by Janet Camp Troxell.
New Haven, Conn., 1939.
    RES. vol. 16, no. 61, Jan. 1940, pp. 108-9.

Work in Progress 1939 in the Modern Humanities.   Edited by
James M. Osborn and Robert G. Sawyer.   Modern Humanities Research Association.
    RES. vol. 16, no. 61, Jan. 1940, p. 114.

1941

Review

The First Magazine.   A history of "The Gentleman's Magazine." By C. Lennart Carlson.   Providence, R.I., 1938.
    RES. vol. 17, no. 65, Jan. 1941, pp. 107-9.

The Bibliographical Society.   News Sheet.
    In a note in the final number (Jan. 1920) A. W. Pol-
    lard wrote: "The editor believes that one number
    was written for him by Mr. Proctor and another by
    Mr. McKerrow." There is, however, no means of
    telling which were the two numbers out of the 140
    published which did not proceed from the pen of A.
    W. Pollard.

Obituary Notices and Memoirs

Obituary in The Times, 22 January 1940.

Obituary in The Times Literary Supplement, 27 Jan. 1940.

Ronald Brunlees McKerrow, 12 December 1872--20 January
1940.   By Harold Williams.
        The Library, 4th Series, vol. 20, no. 4, Mar. 1940,
        pp. 346-9.
        With a portrait.

Ronald Brunlees McKerrow.   By G. B. Harrison.
        RES. vol. 16, no. 63, July 1940, pp. 257-61.

Memoir by W. W. Greg.
        Proceedings of the British Academy, vol. 26.   [1940,
        pp. 488-515, entitled: "Ronald Brunlees McKerrow,
        1872-1940"]

INDEX